REVIEW
of
PERSONALITY
and
SOCIAL
PSYCHOLOGY

——————2——————

Edited by
LADD WHEELER

*Published in cooperation with the SOCIETY FOR PERSONALITY AND
SOCIAL PSYCHOLOGY (Division 8, American Psychological Association)*

SAGE PUBLICATIONS   Beverly Hills   London

For information address:

SAGE PUBLICATIONS, INC.
275 South Beverly Drive
Beverly Hills, California 90212

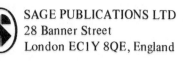

SAGE PUBLICATIONS LTD
28 Banner Street
London EC1Y 8QE, England

Printed in the United States of America

International Standard Book Number 0-8039-1667-1 (hardcover)
0-8039-1668-X (softcover)

International Standard Serial Number 0270-1987

FIRST PRINTING

REVIEW of PERSONALITY
and SOCIAL PSYCHOLOGY: 2

REVIEW OF
PERSONALITY AND SOCIAL PSYCHOLOGY

Editor: LADD WHEELER, *University of Rochester*

Associate Editors:

Henry Alker, *Humanistic Psychology Institute, San Francisco*
Clyde Hendrick, *University of Miami*
Brendan Gail Rule, *University of Alberta*
Lawrence S. Wrightsman, *University of Kansas*

Editorial Board

CONTENTS

Editor's Introduction

A year ago the *Review of Personality and Social Psychology* was an exciting but untried idea. We were attempting to find and publish original pieces on the frontier of theory and method in the hope that it would bring the worlds of the personality researcher and social psychologist closer together and add an international dimension to the work in both fields. The idea became a reality with the publication of Volume 1 last year. Though the process of review in academic journals is a slow one, so that there is no "official" published validation of the worth of our work, the informal responses received in my office and the flow of orders to Sage have convinced me that this series has already begun to serve as a major source of interdisciplinary communication in our fields.

This achievement should be enhanced by Volume 2 of the *Review*—for the quality of articles matches or exceeds that of last year's. The wide range of subjects addressed is further testimony to the vitality of the fields which the REVIEW serves.

In their chapter on sex and gender, Wallston and O'Leary review the literature on physical attractiveness and competence and on attributions for the cause of competence. One of their interesting discoveries is that responses to levels of male competence and female attractiveness are particularly variable, depending upon the context. Continuing (loosely) this sexual theme, Silverman and Fishel describe absolutely fascinating laboratory studies on the Oedipus Complex, using subliminal perception and hypnosis in separate sets of studies. The Oedipus Complex appears to be alive and well! Adding another dimension of the sexual theme, but certainly not limited himself to that, Cunningham explores the heuristic value of sociobiology for social psychology in the areas of altruism, attraction, sexual behavior, child care, sibling relations, agression, and conformity. The chapter suggests a number of hypotheses which should interest researchers.

Carver and Scheier propose using cybernetic principles as a meta-theory for behavioral self-regulation. Noting that such attempts are not totally new, they suggest that social learning theorists have now moved in the direction of feedback models and that there is a more adequate empirical literature for testing cybernetic hypotheses. A nice rapprochement between personality and social is suggested by Goldberg, who argues that the "big five" personality factors, perhaps universally coded in natural languages and certainly emerging repeatedly in English, all focus on persons' transactions with one another. This chapter promises to be a major contribution to the literature. Alker attempts another kind of bridging in his chapter on political creativity by superimposing psychological concepts (especially Machiavellianism) upon the typologies offered by political scientists. Scheier and Carver present a simple yet powerful model of self information-processing supported by the results of a large number of ingenious experiments, most of which have not been published. It should be of equal interest to personality and social psychologists.

Moving into more methodological-strategic concerns, Simonton discusses the use of archival data and gives numerous examples of different types of data and problems. Anderson takes a closer look at a smaller part of the archival data set in describing his experiences in doing a psychobiographical study of William James. I loved it. Finally, Kiesler suggests that mental health policy is a ripe research area for social psychologists. Given current and projected funding in the social sciences, his suggestions are timely. I welcome suggestions from our readers for articles to be published in future *Review* volumes. In considering whether to send your article here or to some other outlet, potential authors should remember that the *Review* is an official publication of the Society for Personality and Social Psychology. As such, the Society receives all royalties on sales—a benefit passed on to members in the form of discount prices on books in the series and lower membership dues.

In addition to members of the Editorial Board and the Associate Editors, I thank John Atkinson, Emory Cowen, Linda Keil, T. A. Ryan, Neill Watson, Joel Raynor, and Dan Wegner for their thoughtful reviews.

—Ladd Wheeler
Rochester, New York

1

Sex Makes a Difference:
DIFFERENTIAL PERCEPTIONS OF WOMEN AND MEN

BARBARA STRUDLER WALLSTON

VIRGINIA E. O'LEARY

Barbara Strudler Wallston is Associate Professor of Psychology at George Peabody College of Vanderbilt University. In addition to research on sex and gender, her work focuses on health behavior, including the study of health locus of control and actual control in health care settings. She is coediting (with Virginia E. O'Leary and Rhoda K. Unger) *Women, Gender, and Social Psychology* (Erlbaum, in press).

Virginia E. O'Leary is Administrative Officer for Social and Ethical Responsibility for Psychology and the Executive Officer's Liaison for Publications and Communications at the American Psychological Association. She has conducted extensive research on women and achievement and on sex-determined attributions. She is the author of *Toward Understanding Women*.

Research evidence accumulated during the last decade suggests clearly that the behavioral similarities between women and men are substantially greater than the differences in a variety of domains, such as achievement, influenceability, and sexual responsiveness (cf. Deaux, 1976; Eagly, 1978;

AUTHOR'S NOTE: This was a joint effort and order of authorship was determined randomly. This review was prepared while the first author was on leave. She appreciates the facilities, services, and colleagueship provided by the Department of

Maccoby & Jacklin, 1974; O'Leary, 1977; Unger, 1979). Nevertheless, the belief in sex differences persists. Perceivers (both men and women) attribute differential behavioral characteristics, traits, and even causes for identical performances by women or men.

We have examined representative literature relevant to differential perceptions of women and men in terms of (1) stereotyped attributions of behavioral characteristics or traits, (2) physical attractiveness and competence (the former traditionally reserved for women and the latter for men), and (3) attributions for cause of women's and men's performances. These research literatures are sufficiently separated that cross-references are infrequent.

In the section on perception of characteristics, psychologists' bias toward accepting certain variables as masculine and feminine is evident in the literature on attractiveness (where women's attractiveness is focal and affective ratings are typical) and on competence (where men's performance is modal and cognitive ratings are typical).

Since perception of persons involves attitudes toward them, in the course of our literature reviews we note the use of cognitive, affective, or behavioral measures as dependent variables (the traditional components of attitude). These distinctions do not parallel the distinction between paper and pencil versus behavior observation sometimes made in personality-social psychology. Instead, we viewed any measure as "cognitive" when it reflected the cognitive domain, that is, ideas, impressions, memories, evaluations, and so on. Affective measures reflect liking or emotional responses to the person. Finally, behavioral measures include both actions in response to the person and "behavioroid" responses such as decisions about the person and intentions to act.

The literature reviewed was limited to adults' perceptions of adults and to research comparing perceptions of men and women (sex). Gender, as considered in this review, refers to information regarding psychological

Psychology, University of Maryland and the Department of Medical Psychology, Uniformed Services University of the Health Sciences, Bethesda, Maryland.

We are indebted to Arlene C. Stephens, without whose assistance this manuscript could not have been completed.

We also gratefully acknowledge the valuable comments of Richard Ashmore, Ruth Czirr, John Harvey, Carolyn W. Sherif, and an anonymous reviewer on an earlier draft of the manuscript.

characteristics of women and men (i.e., femininity and masculinity). Since white college students have been the primary subject samples and analogue studies the most frequent research vehicle, we have been particularly attentive to research where race, age, or experience was varied or other adult populations sampled. Perhaps the most significant distinction made in organizing the reviews is that between context-free or out-of-context responses to men and women and those in which social or task contexts are specified or varied.

As will be evident, our reviews led to the conclusion that our knowledge of social perception of women and men is limited to the degree that we lack information on cognitive, affective, or behavioral measures, on gender as well as sex, and on variations by social context.

PERCEPTIONS OF BEHAVIORAL CHARACTERISTICS

Literature on differential perceptions of men and women is typically conceptualized under the rubric of stereotyping. Within the sex stereotype literature, there has been particular interest in stereotyping by mental health professionals. Due to the number of extant reviews in this area and to their specificity, we will not consider this literature here except to note that until recently it has been predominantely atheoretical (Sherman, 1980; Zeldow, 1978). The lack of agreement on definitions and conceptualizations has often resulted in a divergence of opinion regarding the conclusions to be drawn from a review of this literature (e.g., Sherman, 1980, in contrast to Abramowitz & Dokecki, 1977; Davidson & Abramowitz, 1980; Whitley, 1979). Recent social psychological theory and research on stereotyping (e.g., Ashmore, in press; Brewer, 1979; Hamilton, in press; McCaulay, Stitt, & Segal, 1980; Taylor, in press) provide useful theoretical perspectives which will be brought to bear where appropriate.

There is clear evidence that sex is an important mediator of cognitive person perception (cf. Taylor, in press). Although men are perceived as more instrumental and women as more expressive (e.g., Bem, 1974; Broverman, Vogel, Broverman, Clarkson, & Rosenkrantz, 1972; Brooks-Gunn & Fisch, 1980; Rosenkrantz, Vogel, Bee, Broverman, & Broverman, 1968; Taylor, Fiske, Etcoff, & Ruderman, 1978), the differences are frequently small in magnitude, on the same side of the neutral point, and may represent quantitative rather than qualitative differences (cf. Stricker, 1977; Whitley, 1979). Only on ratings of masculinity-femininity or summary factors reflecting this dimension do we find nonoverlapping distributions (e.g., Del Boca & Ashmore, 1980; Lippa, 1978; Wallston, DeVellis, & Wallston, in press). While main effects are frequently found in studies using only social category information, interactions with sex are more common where additional information is provided.

Strong manipulations can overcome perceptions of individuals in stereo-typic terms. For example, Locksley, Borgida, Brekke, and Hepburn (1980) found effects of passive versus assertive behavior which did not interact with sex of target. However, behaviors are viewed within the context of the stimulus person's sex. For example, Del Boca and Ashmore (1980) found an interaction of sex, social desirability (operationalized as warm-cold), and intellectual desirability (operationalized as intelligent-unin-telligent) on judgments of masculinity-femininity. The cold intelligent male was seen as the most masculine male stimulus and the cold unintelligent male was the least masculine; the warm intelligent female was the most feminine and the cold unintelligent female the least feminine.

Gender of stimulus person (the stereotypic or nonstereotypic nature of the information provided) frequently interacts with sex of stimulus per-son. For example, Costrich, Feinstein, Kidder, Marecek, and Pascale (1975) found that the aggressive woman was rated as even more dominant than the aggressive man even with identical scripts. Moreover, sex-role violators were more unpopular than their counterparts when rated by male subjects. Studies of this interaction which further delineate the context, the nature of the deviance, and the nature of the subject population as these influence person perception are an important research direction.

The context for judgments is a particularly important variable which has received insufficient attention. For example, Taylor et al. (1978) found that subjects who listened to a group discussion with three men and three women made more within-sex than cross-sex errors in attributing comments to speakers. In a second study, male and female group members were seen as more assertive and made a stronger impression, the fewer other members of the same sex were present in the group, consistent with a distinctiveness hypothesis.

Bayesian formulations with stereotypic beliefs defining the prior prob-abilities (cf. Locksley et al., 1980; McCauley et al., 1980), implicit personality theory (cf. Ashmore & Del Boca, 1979), categorization (cf.

Taylor, in press), and other constructs from cognitive psychology (cf. Hamilton, 1979, in press) provide useful theoretical perspectives on which to base further research. But when borrowing from other a.reas, it must be remembered that persons are not the same as objects and a theory of person perception must take the social interactions into account.

Stereotype research has given insufficient attention to affective and behavioral dependent variables. There is clear evidence that men are viewed in more socially desirable terms than women (e.g., Rosenkrantz et al., 1968; Wallston et al., in press; Wolff & Taylor, 1979). However, studies rarely find differential liking for men and women (e.g., Costrich et al., 1975). Recent research conducted in the context of polarization of out-group members has provided weak evidence that opposite-sex persons (e.g., Goldman Olczak, & Tripp, 1980; Linville & Jones, 1980) or the solo individual (Taylor, Fiske, Close, Anderson, & Ruderman, Note 1, described in Taylor, in press) may be evaluated more extremely.

Behavioral responses to men and women are inconsistent. Sex and gender interactions are frequent, but some studies show behavioral preferences for nontraditional persons (e.g., O'Leary & Donoghue, 1978; Shapiro, 1977) while others show judgments of deviance and less willingness to interact with nontraditional persons (e.g., Appleton & Gurwitz, 1976; Costrich et al., 1975; Tilbey & Kalin, 1980). The relationship between affective, cognitive, and behavioral dependent measures is an important area for further study.

The influence of individual difference factors in sex stereotyping is also worthy of further inquiry. Data are insufficient to draw conclusions at this time, but research on androgyny and attitudes toward men (cf. Taylor, in press) is promising.

Some of the best recent research on sex stereotyping investigates parallels with race stereotyping (e.g., Linville & Jones, 1980; Taylor, in press) and stereotyping of other social categories. Our theory of person perception must delineate what social categories have in common and where sex as a category is distinctive. Sex and race are probably the most central categories in person perception (e.g., Grady, 1977) and, as such, they are likely to have some distinctive processes involved.

Sex stereotyping is a ripe area for future research. If conducted within appropriate theoretical perspectives, such research will elucidate our knowledge of sex as a stimulus variable in particular and our understanding of person perception more generally.

PERCEPTION OF PHYSICAL ATTRACTIVENESS AND COMPETENCE

While many characteristics have been studied in the psychological literature, we have selected physical attractiveness and competence as our focus because they are traditionally central characteristics for females and males, respectively. Each area represents a relatively large body of psychological literature; there is reason to believe that these traits differentially affect the perceptions of women and men; there are interesting parallels and disparities in these literatures, and some research investigates the joint influence of these traits on perception. Physical attractiveness will be discussed first followed by competence. Our conclusion will discuss the parallels and disparities.

Physical Attractiveness

While Aronson (1970) noted the neglect of the systematic study of physical beauty and Berscheid and Walster's (1974) review of the physical attractiveness literature begins with a discussion of why this variable had been ignored by social psychologists, building a case for its importance, Bar-Tal and Saxe (1976b) begin their review noting the increased attention social psychologists have given to this variable. In fact, Huston and Levinger (1978) located more than 40 studies between 1972 and 1976 and Cash (Note 2) has compiled an annotated bibliography with over 400 references. Even with this burgeoning literature, there are gaping holes which are apparent when one reads it from the perspective of an increased understanding of the perception of women and men.

Our focus will be on studies utilizing both males and females as stimuli. However, this fails to reflect accurately the literature where many studies use only female stimuli and male subjects (cf. comments by Bar-Tal & Saxe, 1976b: 127; Unger, 1979: 248). Psychologists have shared society's bias that physical attractiveness in women is more important and conclusions from this literature may reflect this bias in what we study as much as person's perceptions and behavior. In fact, it is extremely rare that studies vary only male attractiveness (Brundage, Derlega, & Cash, 1977; Cash & Selzbach, 1978; Maddux & Rogers, 1980). The unwitting bias is most evident from the number of single-sex studies where the sex of subjects and/or targets go unmentioned in the abstract (e.g., Kerr, 1978; Maddux & Rogers, 1980; Maruyama & Miller, 1980; Solomon & Schopler, 1978) although recent literature is somewhat more likely to include subject and target sex in the abstract (e.g., Cash, Kehr, Polyson, & Freeman, 1977b; Gross & Crofton, 1977; Jacobson & Koch, 1978; Snyder, Tanke, & Berscheid, 1977).

Methodological problems beyond the general ones discussed in the introduction plague the physical attractiveness literature. There are major questions regarding external validity when most studies manipulate physical attractiveness using photos. However, some field studies (e.g., Byrne, Ervin, & Lamberth, 1970) provide evidence of continuity with laboratory findings. A difficult problem in relation to comparison across studies is the nature of the physical attractiveness manipulation. Some studies purposely use extremes (e.g., Benson, Karabenick, & Lerner, 1976; Maddux & Rogers, 1980; Maruyama & Miller, 1980), while others eliminate the extremely attractive (e.g., Bar-Tal & Saxe, 1976a; Dion, Berscheid, & Walster, 1972). Studies of live interaction sometimes physically alter the same person to appear attractive or unattractive (e.g., Cash, Begley, McCown, & Weise, 1975; Kleck & Rubenstein, 1975; Scherwitz & Helmreich, 1973; Sigall, Page, & Brown, 1971), while others use confederates differently rated as attractive (e.g., Dabbs & Stokes, 1975; Kleinke, Staneski, & Berger, 1975a; Sroufe, Chaiken, Cook, & Freeman, 1977) and still others use actual subjects rated on attractiveness (e.g., Berscheid, Dion, Walster, & Walster, 1971; Chaiken, 1979; Goldman & Lewis, 1977; Walster, Aronson, Abrahams, & Rottman, 1966).

Equating male and female attractiveness is also a major problem. For example, Benson et al.(1976) used the two most extremely rated photos in seven of their eight conditions but noting that three attractive white females' photos received higher ratings than any of the other pictures, they selected two white female pictures closest to the mean of the other six attractive pictures. Kaplan (1978) noted that variance of the ratings of male photos was 30% higher than for female photos, and Unger, Hilderbrand, and Madar (Note 3) did separate analyses for male and female stimulus persons, since the average rating for female photos was higher than for male photos.

Recognizing the limitations to our conclusions and generalizations, based on these methodological problems and biases in the physical attractiveness research literature, we will review responses to men and women differing in physical attractiveness. The context of these responses is an important aspect of the literature. Heterosexual attraction provides the context for a large portion of the literature, with a small literature on same-sex friendship (cf. Morin, 1977, for a discussion of heterosexist bias in research). These studies can be subsumed as social interactions. Task-oriented interactions form the other major context, including research on job applicants, jury decision making, and a variety of other specific situations. Some studies, particularly those asking subjects to provide accurate judgments regarding the individuals depicted, do not fall clearly into either of these categories. These person perception studies which provide evidence ragarding the nature of the physical attractiveness stereo-type will be reviewed first.

Person perception studies. Although evidence from a number of studies provides support for the physical attractiveness stereotype which has been termed "What is beautiful is good" (Berscheid & Walster, 1974; Brigham, 1980; Dion et al., 1972), there are indications of limits to this notion which vary by sex.

For example, unattractive females were rated as more honest (Adams & Huston, 1975) and unattractive males were rated as more intelligent (Byrne, London, & Reeves, 1968). Although ratings of male and female stimuli are generally in the same direction, studies have found evidence that the physical attractiveness stereotype is stronger for females (e.g., Adams & Huston, 1975; Bar-Tal & Saxe, 1976a; Miller, 1970; Morse, Gruzen, & Reis, 1976).

While we focus on physical attractiveness as an independent variable, creative research has shown that other characteristics affect perceptions of physical attractiveness (e.g., Gross & Crofton, 1977; Morse et al., 1976; Owens & Ford, 1978; Unger et al., Note 3). Person perception is an interactional process and the choice of independent and dependent variables may be arbitrary (cf. Wallston, in press). Data indicate that beauty is, to a certain extent, in the eye of the beholder, and our unidirectional focus must not cause us to lose sight of this process.

Studies in a social context. Studies in this area have emphasized affective and behavioral rather than cognitive variables. Physical attractiveness stereotypes are present in the context of opposite-sex interaction (e.g., Kleinke, Staneski, & Pipp, 1975b; Snyder et al., 1977). There is evidence that individual differences affect such perceptions (e.g., Kleinke & Kahn, 1980; Touhey, 1979), as does the interaction context (e.g., Byrne et al.,

1968; Mathes, 1975; Stroebe, Insko, Thompson, & Layton, 1971; Touhey, 1979; Walster et al., 1966). Sex of subject or stimulus differences are rare within this area. While males are more likely to report the importance of physical attractiveness than are females (e.g., Byrne et al., 1968; Morse et al., 1976), only Murstein and Christy (1970) found empirical evidence that women's affective responses were less affected by male physical attractiveness. In a rare study investigating same-sex friendship, Krebs and Adinolfi (1975) found that the physically unattractive were ignored but the rejected were highly attractive.

There is evidence from correlational studies of actual couples supporting the "matching hypothesis" (cf. Goffman, 1952; Berscheid & Walster, 1974)—that people will seek out partners at similar levels of attractiveness (e.g., Cavior & Boblett, 1972; Hill, Rubin, & Peplau, 1976; Murstein, 1972; Murstein & Christy, 1976; Silverman, 1971). Experimental research is more likely to show main effects of physical attractiveness with dating intent or behavior as the dependent variable (e.g., Brislin & Lewis, 1968; Byrne et al., 1970; Tesser & Brodies, 1971; Walster et al., 1966). However, Berscheid et al. (1971) found evidence for matching in two computer dance experiments.

There is evidence that physical attractiveness is more important in women's but not men's dating and popularity (e.g., Berscheid et al., 1971; Krebs & Adinolfi, 1975; Reis, Nezlek, & Wheeler, 1980; Walster et al., 1966). However, extreme attractiveness can be a source of power which keeps others away (Dabbs & Stokes, 1975).

In an extremely important study, Snyder et al., (1977) demonstrated that perceptions of physical attractiveness can affect the nature of social interactions. Men, in a telephone interaction, who believed they were talking to an attractive woman, were judged as manifesting more sociability on a number of dimensions.

More research is needed on physical attractiveness as it mediates same-sex interaction including friendship and romance. The anecdotal notion of the importance of physical attractiveness in the gay male culture makes this a particularly interesting area for inquiry.

There is evidence that the impact of physical attractiveness extends beyond the formation of first impressions (e.g., Hill et al., 1976; Kleck & Rubenstein, 1975; Mathes, 1975). More research investigating on-going interactions in natural settings, in conjunction with continued controlled experimental research, is called for.

Studies in a task context. Main effects of physical attractiveness using cognitive measures are rare in a task context (e.g., Cash, Gillen, & Burns, 1977a; Chaiken, 1979; Dipboye, Arvey, & Terpstra, 1977). However, studies of counseling have shown the importance of client and therapist physical attractiveness to perceptions, prognosis, and outcome for male and female stimulus persons (e.g., Barocas & Vance, 1974; Cash et al., 1975, 1977b; Cash & Kehr, 1978; Shapiro, Struening, Shapiro, & Barton, 1976). Moreover, there is evidence that attractive communicators are more persuasive (Chaiken, 1979) and attractive targets receive more help (Benson et al., 1976).

More frequently attractiveness interacts with stimulus person sex in influencing perceptions (e.g., Kaplan, 1978), and the relationship is moderated by gender. For example, Cash and Trimer (Note 4) found that physical attractiveness of authors was less beneficial for essays on traditionally masculine topics written by female stimulus persons. Some studies actually find that unattractive women are viewed as more qualified for traditionally masculine positions (e.g., Cash et al., 1977a; Dipboye et al., 1977), termed "beauty is beastly" by Heilman and Saruwatari (1979).

Some studies have identified limits to the assertion that "What is beautiful is good." Physical attractiveness can inhibit help seeking of female subjects by females when the helper is a peer (Stokes & Bickman, 1974) or when future interaction is expected (Nadler, 1980). Sigall and Aronson (1969) found that an attractive female providing negative evaluations to male subjects was liked least. Although attractive defendants may be viewed as less guilty and receive less punishment (Efran, 1974), Sigall and Ostrove (1975) found such differences only when the crime was not attractiveness related (burglary). There were no differences in sentences between attractive and unattractive female swindlers. Further delineating the boundaries of people's positive responses to attractive individuals is an important research direction. Theories which specify such delineating conditions are needed.

Additional delineation of contexts and how they mediate perceptions and responses to the physically attractive and unattractive is needed. More research needs to address directly gender as a moderator variable. For example, Heilman and Saruwatari (1979) found that analysis of covariance with feminity-masculinity as the covariate eliminated the Sex X Physical Attractiveness interaction on rated qualifications, hiring and suggested salary for a managerial position. More studies of this kind will further our understanding of perceptions of the physically attractive and unattractive.

Competence

Unlike physical attractiveness, competence has received much attention in the social psychological literature (cf. White, 1959). This reflects American society's pervasive concern with achievement and success in the marketplace, a concern generally believed to be greater among men than women (cf. Atkinson, 1958; O'Leary, 1977). Indeed, early competence studies used male stimuli and male subjects exclusively. However, the Federal Pay Act of 1963 and Title VII of the Federal Civil Rights Act of 1964 provided the impetus for studies of perceptions of competence as a function of sex.

Variability of manipulations in the literature relevant to perceived competence present methodological problems, although they are less serious than those in the physical attractiveness literature. The majority of studies rely on written materials to vary credentials, experience, and qualifications, independent of face-to-face interactions, raising external validity issues. The strong association of success with maleness (cf. Feldman-Summers & Keisler, 1974) makes competency difficult to hold constant. Competency manipulations often contrast success and failure, rather than moderate departures from average or adequate performances. In addition, status or prestige of occupation or task is often confounded with the quality of the performance (cf. Touhey, 1974a, 1974b).

It is important to note that although a number of studies have not found real differences in the level of competence exhibited by women and men in specific positions (see Brown, 1979, for an extensive review of leadership), differences are perceived to exist. One explanation for this evaluative bias (Berger, Cohen, & Zelditch, 1972; Lockheed & Hall, 1976; Unger, 1976) is the effect of sex as a status characteristic. Since the male sex is more highly valued, men's behavior is frequently valued more, even when compared to equally effective behavior performed by women.

Competent persons are generally rated more favorably than incompetent ones, but when women and men are asked to rate male and female stimulus persons along the competency dimension, they typically agree that men are more competent than women (cf. Deaux, 1972; Dipboye, Fromkin, & Wibeck, 1975; Dipboye et al., 1977). In the landmark study of competency bias favoring men (Goldberg, 1968), college women rated professional articles for value, persuasiveness, profundity, writing style, and competence. Higher ratings were given to identical papers when the author of the article was portrayed as male rather than female. In 1970 Bem and Bem replicated these findings with male college students. Similar results have been obtained in studies where women and men evaluated the artistic merit of paintings (Pheterson, Keisler, & Goldberg, 1971), the qualifications of student applicants for a study abroad program (Deaux & Taynor, 1973), and the qualifications of applicants for employment (Henemann, 1977; Haefner, 1977; Rosen & Jerdee, 1974a, 1978; Zickmund, Hick, & Dickens, 1978). But although this finding is generally considered to be well-established, it has not always been replicated (cf. Bigoness, 1976; Etaugh & Rose, 1975; Hamner, Kim, Baird, & Bigoness, 1974; Levinson, Burford, Bonno, & Davis, 1975; Muchinsky & Harris, 1977). Further, main effects for sex on perceived competence are not always obtained (Frank & Drucker, 1977; Linsenmeir & Wortman, 1979; Peck, 1978; Renwick & Tosi, 1978).

Several attempts have been made to establish the conditions under which a woman's achievement may be regarded as at least as meritorious as a man's. The results indicate that women are likely to be evaluated as being as competent as men when their performance is deemed exceptional, either because it is judged on explicit criteria (Abramson, Goldberg, Greenberg, and Abramson, 1977; Jacobson & Effertz, 1974) or its worth is acknowledged by an authoritative source (Kaschak, cited in Basow, 1980; Pheterson et al., 1971; Taynor & Deaux, 1973).

Another situation in which women may be viewed as competent is suggested by Abramson et al. (1977), who found that when women were depicted as achieving unexpected success (in traditionally male occupations), their achievement was magnified. Jacobson and Effertz (1974) also obtained results illustrating the "talking platypus phenomenon." According to Abramson et al., "It matters little what the platypus says, the wonder is it can say anything at all" (1977: 123). However, other researchers (Cash et al., 1977; Nilson, 1976) have found that unexpected success in sex-atypical occupations results in lower (not higher) competence ratings. Based on these findings, Nieva and Gutek (1980) have suggested that the promale bias reflects reactions to sex-role incongruence.

Indeed, competence biases favoring men are more pronounced when women engage in tasts or seek jobs typically reserved for men (Cohen & Bunker, 1975; Feather, 1975; Feather & Simon, 1975; Rosen & Jerdee, 1974b). Gruber and Gaebelin (1979) found that when a knowledgeable man and woman say the same thing, more attention is paid to the man. Levinson (1975) had students respond to newspaper employment ads, most of which were sex-typed jobs requiring little skill or education.

Applicants who applied for sex-incongruent jobs were more likely to be turned away. Sharp and Post (1980) found that although personnel officers did not systematically discriminate against applicants for sex-incongruent positions, those with conventional sex-role stereotypes were more likely to discriminate. The effect was stronger for women applying for an out-of-role position than men. On the other hand, Shinar (1978) found that college students rated men as less well-adjusted than women in sex-incongruent occupations.

In a naturalistic study of the joint effect of sex-role congruence and competence, a knowledgeable (competent) or ignorant (incompetent) man or woman obtained price quotes from used-car dealers (Larrance, Pavelich, Storer, Polezzi, Baron, Soland, Jordan, and Reis, 1979). Although competent women did not benefit more than men for displaying knowledge of a masculine task, incompetent women received smaller price quotes than incompetent men. Evidence of similar derogation of incompetent men was also obtained by Deaux and Taynor (1973). Larrance et al. (1979) suggest that social desirability mediates the effects of sex-incongruent behavior. Interestingly, no experimental evidence indicates that men who are competent at feminine tasks are advantaged over women who are. Additional research is needed before we can accept the validity of the many asymmetrical findings obtained to date with confidence.

When applicant sex and qualifications are varied, qualifications account for a substantial proportion of the variance, and the predicted interactions between sex and qualifications are not consistently obtained (Avery, 1979). But to manipulate qualifications many studies give raters detailed evaluative information, and evaluators are more likely to respond on the basis of stereotypes when given only minimal information than when given sufficient details for individuation to occur.

As Nieva and Gutek (1980) suggest, the detrimental effects of sex-role incongruence may be stronger in selection decisions (access) than in evaluations of job incumbents (treatment; Terborg, 1977). In many studies where access discrimination cannot be demonstrated, treatment discrimination is clear.

Few studies have assessed the affective responses to individuals who behave competently or incompetently. But where liking is measured, a main effect for competence is invariably obtained. Thus, men like competent men better than incompetent ones (Aronson, Willerman, & Floyd, 1966; Helmreich, Aronson, and Le Fan, 1970), although in the Aronson et al. study competent men who committed pratfalls were liked better than those who did not. Deaux (1972) demonstrated that women also like competent men better than incompetent ones and that this competency effect extends to female stimulus persons. Other researchers have replicated this finding (Spence & Helmreich, 1972, 1973).

In an exploration of the effects of sex congruence and competence on likability of women and men, Spence, Helmreich, and Stapp (1975) obtained main effects for competence and sex role. Competent persons were liked better than incompetent ones and the masculine stimulus person was liked better than the feminine one. But when a projective technique (rather than a rating scale) was used to assess liking, complex interactions were obtained: Almost all subjects found the feminine/competent female somewhat more likable than the masculine/competent female. Shaffer and Wegley (1974) obtained similar results. Shaffer and Johnson (1980) found that both competent males and competent females were better liked when their gender preferences were sex-role consistent.

Two studies have assessed the effects of competence on liking when subjects actually interacted with the target woman or man. In a simulated business setting, Arnett, Higgins, and Preim (1980) explored the impact of sex-role expectations upon male and female managers' leadership behavior and liking by subordinates. Competence was held constant, although leadership style (accommodative versus directive) was varied. Females were liked as well as males, consistent with the findings of Barter (1959), Maier (1970), and Merkel (1963). However, a Sex × Style interaction was obtained. Directive female managers were better liked than directive males. Hagen and Kahn (1975) also found that type of interaction influenced reactions to both competent and incompetent others. Male subjects liked other men most when competing with them and least when observing them. The reverse was true of their affective reactions to women. When required to interact with women, men liked incompetent ones best. At the same time, when asked to select women as leaders, men did prefer competent women to incompetent ones. Under certain conditions men seem willing to credit competent women despite the fact they dislike them.

As in studies of physical attractiveness, context is important. Studies of competence should be extended outside the occupational arena. The high competence which benefits women at work may disadvantage them socially (Hagen and Kahn, 1975) and few studies have considered this. An important research task is to delineate contexts and how they mediate perceptions of incompetence. Gender appears to moderate sex in particular contexts and the two should be studied concurrently.

Research suggests that the impact of competence is greatest in ambiguous situations in which initial impressions are formed and diminishes as familiarity with others increases, but further research is required to specify what information contributes to this effect. Field studies are urgently needed; and they must consider subtle behavioral forms of discrimination against women. For example, Sanders and Schmidt (1980) found that both men and women sorted more cards when a male set their production quota than when a female did. The quota setter's competence was not deliberately manipulated, but subjects (particularly men) may not have been convinced that the engineering student calculated the quota correctly before "she" established it.

PERCEPTIONS OF CAUSE

People's naive causal explanations for why they believe other people behave as they do have potential value for understanding the persistence of the belief in sex differences. This approach is grounded in attributional research. It argues that people's causal explanations for events enhance understanding and prediction of how they will react to such events (Green & Mitchell, 1979). Weiner's two-dimensional taxonomy for the perceived determinants of achievement behavior has provided the framework for much research on the effects of sex on causal attributions (Weiner, 1974, 1979; Weiner, Freize, Kukla, Reed, Rest, & Rosenbaum, 1971). More recently, researchers have studied these effects from the perspective of the well-elaborated attribution models of Jones (Jones & Davis, 1965; Jones & McGillis, 1976) and Kelley (Kelley, 1967, 1972; Orvis Cunningham & Kelley, 1975) and a model proposed by Hansen (1980). Each attributional perspective offers mechanisms whereby perceivers might arrive at different causal explanations for the identical behaviors of women and men.

Four causes of success and failure have been studied extensively from an attributional perspective: ability, effort, luck, and task difficulty (Weiner et al., 1971). Each of these causes has two dimensions: the source controlling the outcome (internal versus external) and the temporal stability of the factor influencing outcomes (stable versus temporary). Within Weiner's scheme, ability is described as internal and stable, effort as internal and unstable. Although the heuristic value of this model is clear, it should be noted that attempts to match these theoretical dimensions with the taxonomy used by perceivers have had mixed results (cf. Elig & Frieze, 1979; Falbo & Beck, 1979; Meyer, 1980; Ostrove, 1978).

According to attribution theory, people have well-established patterns of making causal attributions. Data on perceived sex differences in causal attributions for performance using the Weiner taxonomy suggest that the explanations offered for the success or failure of women and men differ markedly (Cash et al., 1977; Deaux & Emswiller, 1974; Etaugh & Brown, 1975; Feather & Simon, 1975; Feldman-Summers & Keisler, 1974; Haccoun & Stacy, 1980; Taynor & Deaux, 1972, 1975; Yarkin, Towne, & Wallston, in press). A man's successful performance on a task is generally attributed to skill, whereas a woman's identical performance is attributed to effort or luck. On the other hand, men's failure is attributed to (bad) luck, women's to (low) ability.

Two of the most frequently cited studies that explored the effects of sex on causal attributions for success and failure were conducted by Deaux and Emswiller (1974) and Feldman-Summers and Keisler (1974). In the first, male and female subjects evaluated a man or woman on a male- or female-oriented task. Performance by a male on a masculine task was attributed to his skill, while an equivalent performance by a female on the same task was attributed to her luck; but there were no differences in attributions regarding the performance of males and females on the feminine task. Feldman-Summers and Kiesler (1974) asked male and female subjects to attribute cause for the identical performance of women and men on logical and mathematical problems and as physicians specializing in either pediatrics or surgery. In the first of their two studies, subjects of both sexes attributed greater motivation to women than men regardless of their level of success. Greater motivation was also attributed to women physicians than to men and an interaction between sex of stimulus person and sex of subject was obtained. Male subjects attributed greater ability to the male than female physician and viewed the female's success as caused by greater motivation or an easier task than the success of the male. Female subjects perceived the male as having an easier task, the female as more motivated.

The tendency of perceivers to view men's success as caused by ability and women's success by effort or luck has been replicated in a number of studies (Feather & Simon, 1975; Haccoun & Stacy, 1980; Yarkin et al., in press). This effect is most consistent and pronounced when the task is one on which males are expected to excel, but it is still not uniform. For example, Cash et al. (1977) found no significant differences in attributions to effort, even when a female succeeded on a masculine task. The fact that Cash et al. employed low-status occupations suggests that the effects of sex on causal attributions may be limited to high-status occupations, paralleling the findings on perceived competence.

Most studies look at the perception of cause for success only, but Cash et al. (1977) assessed responses to the failure of women and men. Female's failure was more likely to be attributed to lack of ability on masculine jobs than feminine or neutral ones. Male's failure on feminine jobs was more likely to be attributed to lack of ability than their failure on masculine jobs. Women's failure was more likely to be attributed to task difficulty than men's failure. Subjects of both sexes attributed men's failure on masculine jobs more to bad luck than women's failure on feminine jobs. Haccoun and Stacy (1980) found that lack of ability was seen as a more important cause of failure on feminine jobs while lack of effort was viewed as a more important cause of failure on masculine jobs.

Only one study using Weiner's taxonomy has varied the gender or mode (masculine or feminine) of the stimulus person's behavior (Deaux & Taynor, 1975). Behaving in a masculine mode (assertive and dominant) was seen as a better performance and more deserving of reward than behaving in a feminine (sensitive and intuitive) mode across tasks and actors. Additionally, performance on a masculine task was seen as more deserving of reward, more socially desirable, and was evaluated more positively than performance on a feminine task. A woman performing well on a masculine task was seen as more deserving of reward than a man, paralleling the "talking platypus" effect obtained on competence. A man performing well on a feminine task was not seen as more deserving of reward than a woman.

It seems reasonable to expect that sex differences in the perceived cause of success will produce different reactions to that success. For example, most organizational rewards are designed to recognize personal accomplishments. To be judged deserving of a reward, one must be perceived as having played a role in the (successful) outcome. Heilman and Guzzo (1978) asked male and female Masters of Business Administration students to judge the appropriateness of various personnel actions taken on successful employees of both sexes. Four different causes for the employees' successes were described. The causal factors typically used to explain women's success (effort and luck) reduced the degree to which organizational rewards were viewed as appropriate; and when a reward was deemed fitting, its scope and magnitude were diminished. Even male employees were disadvantaged when their success was attributed to luck or effort.

Although most of the research assessing the effects of sex on causal attributions has utilized Weiner's taxonomy, several attempts have been made to explore sex-determined attributions from a more global perspective (Jones & McGillis, 1965; Kelley, 1967, 1972). Perceivers' inferences about the prior probabilities associated with women's and men's behavior form a basis for understanding the different attributions made for women's and men's achievements (cf. Deaux, 1976; Frieze, Fisher, Hanusa, McHugh, & Valle, 1978). In a series of experiments (Hansen & O'Leary, in press) perceivers' naive expectations regarding the cause of a behavior differs as a function of the sex of the performer. Perceivers of both sexes tended to explain women's behavior with personal attributions (dispositions) and men's identical behavior with attributions to environmental stimuli (entities). The behavior of performers acting in ways believed to have low prior probabilities for a person of their sex was more likely to be attributed to dispositions than entities. Thus, the strongest personal attributions were made for a woman performing a male-linked behavior (placing a risky bet or refusing to comply) and the strongest environmental attributions were made for a man performing the same behavior. Similar findings have been obtained by other researchers (Block, cited in Denmark, 1980; Cowan & Koziej, 1977; Galper & Luck, 1980).

In the Hansen and O'Leary study the impact of behavioral expectancies based on category membership was demonstrated. When presented with causal quandries such as "twelve different women (men) completed twelve different tasks or played twelve games (accomplishments)" and asked to solve for variance, perceivers of both sexes ascribed the variance in women's behavior less to the environmental stimuli in the presence of which these behaviors were performed (entities) and more to the differences among the women (dispositions). The reverse was true for perceivers of men. In order to explore the effect of beliefs about prior probabilities for behavior based on the performer's membership in a sex category on causal attributions, O'Leary and Hansen (Note 5) used a behavioral outcome independent of any expectations based on sex, consumer product ratings. The traditional paradigm used to explore the effects of sex on the attribution process has relied on the manipulation of sex-linked traits or dispositions (cf. Borgida, Locksley, & Brekke, in press; Deaux & Emswiller, 1974; Locksley et al., 1980; Taynor & Deaux, 1975) to produce prior probability estimates of behavior assumed more characteristic of one sex or the other. In contrast, O'Leary and Hansen's approach relied on manipulation of entities with which women and men were shown to be differentially familiar—disposable diapers and shaving cream. Subjects viewed a videotape of six people (either women or men) rating six different brands of the same product (disposable diapers or shaving creams) and were asked to indicate the extent to which differences among people's ratings of products was due to "differences among products" or "differences among raters." The tendency to explain variance in men's behavior more in terms of differences among the products (entities) to which they were responding rather than differences among the men (persons) was clear when men rated shaving creams; this trend disappeared when men rated diapers. The tendency to explain women's behavior in terms of differences among women was evident when women rated shaving creams; when they rated diapers the effect diminished.

To date, there has been only one attempt to explore the relationship between the causal explanations for the performance of women and men described by Weiner's taxonomy and category-based expectations regarding performance outcomes and behaviors (O'Leary & Hansen, Note 6). In that study, success was attributed more to ability than effort, but less to task difficulty than was failure for both men and women. Contrary to predictions, men's outcomes were no more likely to be perceived as caused by ability than women's, but men's outcomes were perceived as caused by effort diagnostic of, rather than compensatory for, ability. Consistent with earlier research (Hansen & O'Leary, in press), women's behavior was attributed more to personal and men's behavior more to environmental causes. There was no relationship between the several attributional measures used: locus of control, stability, dispositions, and entities. Further research is required to establish the theoretical and practical correspondence between the Weiner and Kelley models.

Clearly, observers of both sexes tend to attribute the behavior of women to different factors than the behavior of men, regardless of the attribution model employed. However, when obtained, such attributional differences are frequently qualified by interactions involving sex-typing of task or occupation and/or gender of behavior.

Perhaps, unfortunately, the applied implications of the frequently quoted findings that a man's successful performance on a task is likely to be attributed to skill and a woman's to effort or luck appear so straightforward and compelling that they have been too readily accepted as gospel. Because causal attributions appear to influence rewards directly, further research is required to specify the conditions under which they may affect women differently than men.

CONCLUSIONS AND IMPLICATIONS

The literatures we have reviewed are often parallel rather than interacting and the occasional cross-literature citations are relatively out of date. We believe the newest work and ideas about social cognition and sex-role stereotyping need to be considered and used by researchers of competency, physical attractiveness, and causal attributions. Stereotyping research provides a framework for all these areas. Feedback in the other direction is also important. Neisser's "On social knowing" reiterates many points made here. He stresses the importance of context, the need to explore "the phenomena as they actually occur," (1980: 603) and the danger of social psychology's accepting a passive model of perceiver and knower from cognitive psychology. It is ironic that a cognitive psychologist finds it necessary to remind social psychologists of the importance of social context.

Parallels between the literatures on competence and physical attractiveness are particularly interesting. Responses to male competence/incompetence have more variability as do responses to female physical attractiveness/unattractiveness. Our very language has many more words to describe female than male attractiveness (lovely, stunning, cute, pretty, beautiful versus handsome, good-looking). The reverse may hold for descriptions of competence. For example, letters of reference describe women's hard work and reliability more than their brilliance and make fewer projections of future contributions.

The interaction between competence and physical attractiveness is dramatically illustrated when the findings relating to these variables are juxtaposed. Not only are men more likely than women to be perceived as competent but also they are less likely to be perceived as unattractive. What is competent is beautiful and it is a male.

Gender appears to be an important moderator of responses to perceptions of competence and attractiveness. However, the significance of such perceptions of masculinity-femininity is not fully understood, because they are rarely measured. Heilman and Saruwatari (1979) did find that perceptions of masculinity and feminity accounted for much of their findings. More research investigating moderating effects of these perceptions is important.

To a startling degree, the attributional analyses appear to clarify earlier reported findings of women in nontraditional activities and, especially, occupations. Attributions may provide a link between cognitions about and differential behavior toward women and men. To the extent that identical behaviors are perceived as due to different causes as a function of the sex of the performer, differential responses are to be anticipated. For example, when a successful performance is attributed to ability (men), rather than effort (women), the perceiver is more likely to be confident of the individual's future success and, thus, more likely to hire or promote the performer. Many attribution researchers concentrated on attributional cognitions without sufficient attention to affective or behavioral consequences (cf. Weary, Swanson, Harvey, & Yarkin, 1980; Yarkin, Harvey, & Bloxom, in press). Zajonc (1980) has noted the importance of affect independent of cognition as a source of effects in information processing.

The interrelationship of cognition, affect, and behavior clearly needs more attention in the person perception literature in general and in the literature on perception of women and men in particular. Our current conclusions are limited because studies rarely utilize all three dimensions in a single design. Responses across these dimensions may not be parallel. For example, competent women may be preferred over incompetent ones as work partners but they are less well-liked. Physically attractive women may be preferred to unattractive ones, but they are less likely to be hired for a traditionally masculine position. Only by investigating affect, cognition, and behavior within a single study can we understand more fully consistencies and inconsistencies across dimensions.

Perceptions of women and men vary with the ambiguity of the information provided about them. Social category information is most significant when little other than sex is known. Clear and frequent differences in perceptions based on sex are found in the literatures relevant to stereotypes, competency, and causal attributions. Individuating information, clarity of criteria, and/or authoritative sources reduce the effects of sex on perception. Research specifically designed to investigate the effects of information is needed.

It is clear from the literature we have reviewed that sex and gender are central constructs in person perception. It is just as clear that most findings are more complex than mere sex-of-stimulus-person main effects. Even when main effects are found, their magnitude is small and distributions frequently overlap. Sex interacts with social context. For example, nontraditional occupational contexts appear to sharpen the contrasts between the sexes. Physical attractiveness, particularly women's, may be more important in interpersonal than occupational contexts. Unfortunately, researchers seldom look at more than one social context within a single study. Moreover, the range of social contexts investigated has been narrow. Occupational competence has been investigated often, but studies of social competence are rare. Achievement contexts are usually restricted to those with direct economic consequences. Studies of achievement in child-rearing, homemaking, or civic activities have not been conducted. Until these omissions have been rectified, we cannot assess the impact of social context on perceptions of women and men accurately.

REFERENCE NOTES

1. Taylor, S. E., Fiske, S. T., Close, M., Anderson, C., & Ruderman, A. *Solo status as a psychological variable: The power of being distinctive.* Unpublished manuscript, Harvard University, 1975.

2. Cash, T. F. Personal communication. Old Dominion University, January 1981.

3. Unger, R. K., Hilderbrand, M., & Madar, T. *Physical attractiveness and assumptions about social deviance: Some sex by sex comparisons.* Manuscript submitted for publication, 1981.

4. Cash, T. F. & Timer, C. A. *Sexism and beautyism in women's evaluations of peer performance.* Manuscript submitted for publication. Old Dominion University, 1980.

5. O'Leary, V. E. & Hansen, R. D. *Experience makes a difference: The impact of sex on attributions.* Unpublished manuscript, American Psychological Association, 1980.

6. O'Leary, V. E. & Hansen, R. D. *Sex affects causal accounting for achievement.* Unpublished manuscript, Oakland University, Rochester, Michigan, 1980.

REFERENCES

Abramowitz, C. V. & Dokecki, P. R. The politics of clinical judgment: Early empirical returns. *Psychological Bulletin,* 1977, *84,* 460-476.

Abramson, P. R., Goldberg, P. A., Greenberg, J. H., & Abramson, L. M. The talking platypus phenomenon: Competency ratings as a function of sex and professional status. *Psychology of Women Quarterly,* 1977, *2* (2), 114-124.

Adams, G. R. & Huston, T. L. Social perception of middle-aged persons varying in physical attractiveness. *Developmental Psychology,* 1975, *11,* 657-658.

Appleton, H. L. & Gurwitz, S. B. Willingness to help as determined by the sex-role appropriateness of the help-seeker's career goals. *Sex Roles,* 1976, *2,* 321-329.

Arnett, M. D., Higgins, R. B., & Priem, A. P. Sex and least preferred co-worker score effects in leadership behavior. *Sex Roles,* 1980, *6,* 139-152.

Aronson, E. Some antecedents of interpersonal attraction. In W. J. Arnold & D. Levine (eds.), *Nebraska symposium on motivation,* 1969. Lincoln: University of Nebraska Press, 1970, 143-177.

Aronson, E., Willerman, B., & Floyd, J. The effect of a pratfall on increasing personal attractiveness. *Psychonomic Science,* 1966, *4,* 227-228.

Ashmore, R. D. Sex stereotypes and implicit personality theory. In D. L. Hamilton (ed.), *Cognitive processes in stereotyping and intergroup behavior.* Hillsdale, N.J.: Erlbaum, in press.

Ashmore, R. D. & Del Boca, F. K. Sex stereotypes and implicit personality theory: Toward a cognitive-social psychological conceptualization. *Sex Roles,* 1979, *5,* 219-248.

Atkinson, J. W. (ed,), *Motives in fantasy, action and society.* Princeton, N.J.: Van Nostrand, 1958.

Avery, R. D. Unfair discrimination in the employment interview: Legal and psychological aspects. *Psychological Bulletin,* 1979, *86,* 736-765.

Barocas, R. & Vance, F. L. Physical appearance and personal adjustment counseling. *Journal of Counseling Psychology,* 1974, *21,* 96-100.

Bar-Tal, D. & Saxe, L. Perceptions of similarly and dissimilarly attractive couples and individuals. *Journal of Personality and Social Psychology,* 1976, *33,* 772-781. (a)

Bar-Tal, D. & Saxe, L. Physical attractiveness and its relationship to sex role stereotyping. *Sex Roles,* 1976, *2,* 123-133. (b)

Barter, A. The status of women in school administration. *Educational Horizon,* 1959, *37,* 72-75.

Basow, S. A. *Sex-role stereotypes: Traditions and alternatives.* Monterey, Calif.: Brooks/Cole, 1980.

Bem, S. L. The measurement of psychological androgyny. *Journal of Clinical and Consulting Psychology,* 1974, *42,* 155-162.

Bem, S. L. & Bem, D. J. Case study of a non-conscious ideology: Training the woman to know her place. In D. J. Bems (ed.), *Beliefs, attitudes and human affairs.* Monterey, Calif.: Brooks/Cole, 1970.

Benson, P. L., Karabenick, S. A., & Lerner, R. M. Pretty pleases: The effects of physical attractiveness, race, and sex on receiving help. *Journal of Experimental Social Psychology*, 1976, *12*, 409-415.

Berscheid, E., Dion, K., Walster, E., & Walster, G. W. Physical attractiveness and dating choice: A test of the matching hypothesis. *Journal of Experimental Social Psychology*, 1971, *7*, 173-189.

Berscheid, E. & Walster, E. Physical attractiveness. In L. Berkowitz (ed.), *Advances in experimental social psychology (Vol. 7)*. New York: Academic Press, 1974.

Bigoness, W. J. Effect of applicant's sex, race, and performance on employer's performance ratings: Some additional findings. *Journal of Applied Psychology*, 1976, *61*, 80-84.

Borgida, E., Locksley, A., & Brekke, N. Social stereotypes and social judgment. In N. Cantor and J. Kihlstrom (eds.), *Cognition, social interaction and personality*. Hillsdale, N.J.: Erlbaum, in press.

Brewer, M. B. In-group bias in the minimal intergroup situation: A cognitive-motivational analysis? *Psychological Bulletin*, 1979, *86*, 307-324.

Brigham, J. C. Limiting conditions of the "physical attractiveness stereotype": Attributions about divorce. *Journal of Research in Personality*, 1980, *14*, 365-375.

Brislin, R. W. & Lewis, S. A. Dating and physical attractiveness: Replication. *Psychological Reports*, 1968, *22*, 976.

Brooks-Gunn, J. & Fisch, M. Psychological androgyny and college students' judgements of mental health. *Sex Roles*, 1980, *6*, 575-580.

Broverman, I., Vogel, S. R., Broverman, D., Clarkson, F. E., & Rosenkrantz, P. S. Sex role stereotypes: A current appraisal. *Journal of Social Issues*, 1972, *28*, 59-78.

Brown, S. H. Male versus female leaders: A comparison of empirical studies. *Sex Roles*, 1979, *5*, 595-612.

Brundage, L. V., Derlega, V. J., & Cash, T. F. The effect of physical attractiveness and need for approval on self-disclosure. *Personality and Social Psychology Bulletin*, 1977, *3*, 63-66.

Byrne, D., Ervin, C. R., & Lamberth, J. Continuity between the experimental study of attraction and real-life computer dating. *Journal of Personality and Social Psychology*, 1970, *16*, 157-165.

Byrne, D., London, L. & Reeves, K. The effects of physical attractiveness, sex, and attitude similarity on interpersonal attraction. *Journal of Personality*, 1968, *36*, 259-271.

Cash, T. F. & Kehr, J. Influence of nonprofessional counselors' physical attractiveness and sex on perceptions of counselor behavior. *Journal of Counseling Psychology*, 1978, *25*, 336-342.

Cash, T. F. & Salzbach, R. F. The beauty of counseling: Effects of counselor physical attractiveness and self-disclosures on perceptions of counselor behavior. *Journal of Counseling Psychology*, 1978, *25*, 283-291.

Cash, T. F., Begley, P. J., McCown, D. A., & Weise, B. C. When counselors are heard but not seen: Initial impact of physical attractiveness. *Journal of Counseling Psychology*, 1975, *22*, 273-279.

Cash, T. F., Gillen, B., & Burns, D. S. Sexism and "beautyism" in personnel consultant decision-making. *Journal of Applied Psychology*, 1977, *62*, 301-310. (a)

Cash, T. F., Kehr, J. A., Polyson, J., & Freeman, V. Role of physical attractiveness in peer attribution of psychological disturbance. *Journal of Consulting and Clinical Psychology*, 1977, *45*, 987-993. (b)

Cavior, N. & Boblett, P. J. Physical attractiveness of dating versus married couples. *Proceedings of the 80th Annual Convention of the American Psychological Association*, 1972, *1*, 175-176.

Chaiken, S. Communicator physical attractiveness and persuasion. *Journal of Personality and Social Psychology*, 1979, *37*, 1387-1397.

Cohen, S. L. & Bunker, K. A. Subtle effects of sex role stereotypes on recruiter's hiring decisions. *Journal of Applied Psychology*, 1975, *60*, 566-572.

Costrich, N., Feinstein, J., Kidder, L., Marecek, J., & Pascale, L. When stereotypes hurt: Studies of penalties for role reversals. *Journal of Experimental Social Psychology*, 1975, *11*, 520-530.

Cowan, G. & Koziej, J. The perception of sex-inconsistent behavior. *Sex Roles*, 1979, *5*, 1-10.

Dabbs, J. M., Jr. & Stokes, N. A., III Beauty is power: The uses of space on the sidewalk. *Sociometry*, 1975, *38*, 551-557.

Davidson, C. V. & Abramowitz, S. I. Sex bias in clinical judgement: Later empirical returns. *Psychology of Women Quarterly*, 1980, *4*, 377-395.

Deaux, K. Sex and the attribution process. In J. H. Harvey, W. J. Ickes, & R. F. Kidd (eds.), *New directions in attribution research, (Vol. 1)*. New York: Wiley, 1976.

Deaux, K. To err is humanizing: But sex makes a difference. *Representative Research in Social Psychology*, 1972, *3*, 20-28.

Deaux, K. & Emswiller, T. Explanations of successful performance on sex-linked tasks: What is skill for the male is luck for the female. *Journal of Personality and Social Psychology*, 1974, *29*, 80-85.

Deaux, K. & Taynor, J. Evaluation of male and female ability: Bias works two ways. *Psychological Reports*, 1973, *32*, 261-262.

Del Boca, F. K. & Ashmore, R. D. Sex stereotypes through the life cycle. In L. Wheeler (ed.), *Review of personality and social psychology* (Vol 1). Beverly Hills, Calif.: Sage, 1980.

Denmark, F. L. Psyche: From rocking the cradle to rocking the boat. *American Psychologist*, 1980, *35*, 1057-1065.

Dion, K., Berscheid, E., & Walster, E. What is beautiful is good. *Journal of Personality and Social Psychology*, 1972, *24*, 285-290.

Dipboye, R. L., Arvey, R. D., & Terpstra, D. E. Sex and physical attractiveness of raters and applicants as determinants of resume evaluations. *Journal of Applied Psychology*, 1977, *62*, 228-294.

Dipboye, R. L., Fromkin, H. L., & Wiback, K. Relative importance of applicant sex, attractiveness and scholastic standing in evaluations of job applicant resumes. *Journal of Applied Psychology*, 1975, *60*, 39-43.

Eagly, A. H. Sex differences in influenceability. *Psychological Bulletin*, 1978, *85*, 86-116.

Efran, M. G. The effect of physical appearance on the attraction and severity of recommended punishment in a simulated jury task. *Journal of Research in Personality*, 1974, *8*, 45-54.

Elig, T. W. & Frieze, I. H. Measuring causal attributions for success and failure. *Journal of Personality and Social Psychology*, 1977, *37*, 621-634.

Etaugh, C. & Brown, B. Perceiving the causes of success and failure of male and female performers. *Developmental Psychology*, 1975, *11*, 103.

Etaugh, C. & Rose, S. Adolescent's sex bias in the evaluation of performance. *Developmental Psychology*, 1975, *11*, 663-664.

Falbo, T. & Beck, R. C. Naive psychology and the attributional model of achievement. *Journal of Personality*, 1979, *47*, 185-195.

Feather, N. T. Attribution of responsibility and valence of success and failure in relation to initial confidence and perceived locus of control. *Journal of Personality and Social Psychology*, 1969, *13*,129-144.

Feather, N. T. & Simon, J. G. Reactions to male and female success and failure in sex-linked occupations: Impressions of personality, causal attribution and perceived likelihood of differential consequences. *Journal of Personality and Social Psychology*, 1975, *31*, 20-31.

Feldman-Summers, S. & Kiesler, S. B. Those who are number two try harder: The effect of sex on attributions of causality. *Journal of Personality and Social Psychology*, 1974, *30*, 846-855.

Frank, F. D. & Drucker, J. The influence of evaluatee's sex on evaluation of a response of a managerial selection instrument. *Sex Roles*, 1977, *3*, 59-64.

Frieze, I. H., Fisher, J. R., Hanusa, B. H., McHugh, M. C., & Valle, V. A. Attributions of the causes of success and failure as internal and external barriers to achievement. In J. Sherman and F. L. Denmark (eds.), *The psychology of women: Future directions of research.* New York: Psychological Dimensions, 1978.

Galper, R. E. & Luck, D. Gender, evaluation, and causal attribution: The double standard is alive and well. *Sex Roles*, 1980, *6*, 278-283.

Goffman, E. On cooling the mark out: Some aspects of adaptation to failure. *Psychiatry*, 1952, *15*, 451-463.

Goldberg, P. A. Are women prejudiced against women? *Transaction*, 1968, *5*, 28-30.

Goldman, J. A., Olczak, P. V., & Tripp, M. H. Sex-role ideology as a moderator of the polarization effect in person perception. *Journal of Research in Personality*, 1980, *14*, 321-328.

Goldman, W. & Lewis, P. Beautiful is good: Evidence that the physically attractive are more socially skillful. *Journal of Experimental Social Psychology*, 1977, *13*, 125-130.

Grady, K. E. Sex as a social label: The illusion of sex differences. Unpublished doctoral dissertation, Graduate Center, City University of New York, 1977.

Green, S. G. & Mitchell, T. R. Attributional processes of leaders in leader-member interactions. *Organizational Behavior and Human Performance*, 1979, *23*, 429-458.

Gross, A. E. & Crofton, C. What is good is beautiful. *Sociometry*, 1977, *40*, 85-90.

Gruber, K. J. & Gaebelein, J. Sex differences in listening comprehension. *Sex Roles*, 1979, *5*, 299-310.

Haccoun D. M. & Stacy, S. Perceptions of male and female success or failure in relation to spouse encouragement and sex-association of occupation. *Sex Roles*, 1980, *6*. 819-831.

Haefner, J. E. Sources of discrimination among employees: A survey investigation. *Journal of Applied Psychology*, 1977, *62*, 265-270.

Hagen, R. L. & Kahn, A. Discrimination against competent women. *Journal of Applied Social Psychology*, 1975, *5*, 362-376.

Hamilton, D. L. A cognitive-attributional analysis of stereotyping. In L. Berkowitz (ed.) *Advances in experimental social psychology (Vol. 12)*. New York: Academic Press, 1979.

Hamilton, D. L. *Cognitive processes in stereotyping and intergroup behavior*. Hillsdale, N. J.: Erlbaum, in press.

Hamner, W. C., Kim, J. S., Baird, L., & Bigoness, W. J. Race and sex as determinants of ratings by potential employers in a simulated work sampling task. *Journal of Applied Psychology*, 1974, *59*, 705-711.

Hansen, R. D. Common sense attribution. *Journal of Personality and Social Psychology*, 1980, *39*, 996-1009.

Hansen, R. D. & O'Leary, V. E. Actresses and actors: the effects of sex on causal attributions. *Basic and Applied Social Psycholoty*, in press.

Heilman, M. E. & Guzzo, R. A. The perceived cause of work success as a mediator of sex discrimination in organizations. *Organizational Behavior and Human Performance*, 1978, *21*, 346-357,

Heilman, M. E. & Saruwatari, L. R. When beauty is beastly: The effects of appearance and sex on evaluations of job applicants for managerial and non-managerial jobs. *Organizational Behavior and Human Performance*, 1979, *23*, 360-372.

Helmreich, R., Aronson, E. & LeFan, J. To err is humanizing—sometimes: Effects of self-esteem, competence and a pratfall on interpersonal attraction. *Journal of Personality and Social Psychology*, 1970, *16*, 259-264.

Heneman, H. G. Impact of test information and applicant sex on applicant evaluations in a selection simulation. *Journal of Applied Psychology*, 1977, *62*, 524-526.

Hill, C. T., Rubins, F., & Peplau, L. A. Breakups before marriage: The end of 103 affairs. *Journal of Social Issues*, 1976, *32*, 147-168.

Huston, T. L. & Levinger, G. Interpersonal attraction and relationships. In M. R. Rosenzweig & L. W. Porter (eds.), *Annual Review of Psychology*, 1978, *29*, 115-156.

Jacobson, M. B. & Effertz, J. Sex roles and leadership: Perception of the leaders and the led. *Organizational Behavior and Human Performance*, 1974, *12*, 383-396.

Jacobson, M. B. & Koch, W. Attributed reasons for support of the feminist movement as a function of attractiveness. *Sex Roles*, 1978, *4*, 169-174.

Jones, E. E. & Davis, K. E. From acts to dispositions: The attribution process in person perception. In L. Berkowitz (ed.), *Advances in experimental social psychology* (Vol. 2). New York: Academic Press, 1965.

Jones, E. E. & McGillis, D. Correspondent inferences and the attribution cube: A comparative reappraisal. In J. H. Jarvey, W. J. Ickes, & R. F. Kidd (eds.), *New directions in attribution research (Vol. 1)*. Hillsdale, N. J.: Erlbaum, 1976.

Kaplan, R. M. Is beauty talent? Sex interaction in the attractiveness halo effect. *Sex Roles*, 1978, *4*, 195-204.

Kaschak, E. Another look at sex bias in students' evaluations of professors: Do winners get the recognition they have been given? *Psychology of Women Quarterly*, in press.

Kelley, H. H. Attribution theory in social psychology. In D. Levine (ed.), *Nebraska symposium on motivation*. Lincoln: Unversity of Nebraska Press, 1967.

Kelley, H. H. *Causal schemata and the attribution process*. Morristown, N. J.: General Learning Press, 1972.

Kerr, N. L. Beautiful and blameless: Effects of victim attractiveness and responsibility on mock jurors' verdicts. *Personality and Social Psychology Bulletin*, 1978, *4*, 479-482.

Kleck, R. E. & Rubenstein, C. Physical attractiveness, perceived attitude similarity, and interpersonal attraction in an opposite-sex encounter. *Journal of Personality and Social Psychology*, 1975, *31*, 107-114.

Kleinke, C. L. & Kahn, M. L. Perceptions of self-disclosures: Effects of sex and physical attractiveness. *Journal of Personality*, 1980, *48*, 190-205.

Kleinke, C. L., Staneski, R. A., & Berger, D. E. Evaluation of an interviewer as a function of interviewer gaze, reinforcement of subject gaze, and interviewer attractiveness. *Journal of Personality and Social Psychology*, 1975, *31*, 115-122. (a)

Kleinke, C., Staneski, R. A., & Pipp, S. L. Effects of gaze, distance and attractiveness on males' first impressions of females. *Representative Research in Social Psychology*, 1975, *6*, 7-12. (b)

Krebs, D. & Adinolfi, A. A. Physical attractiveness, social relations and personality style. *Journal of Personality and Social Psychology*, 1975, *31*, 245-253.

Larrance, D., Pavelich, S., Storer, P., Polizzi, M., Baron, B., Sloan, S., Jordan, P., & Reis, H. T. Competence and incompetence: Asymmetric responses to women and men in a sex-linked task. *Personality and Social Psychology Bulletin*, 1979, *5*, 363-366.

Levenson, H., Burford, B., Bonn, B., & Davis, L. Are women still prejudiced against women? Replication and extension of Goldberg's study. *Journal of Psychology*, 1975, *89*, 67-71.

Levinson, R. M. Sex discrimination and employment practices: An experiment with unconventional job inquiries. *Social Problems*, 1975, *22*, 533-543.

Lewin, K. *Field theory in social science*. New York: Harper & Row, 1951.

Linsenmeier, J.A.W. & Wortman, C. B. Attitudes toward workers and toward their work: More evidence that sex makes a difference. *Journal of Applied Social Psychology*, 1979, *4*, 326-334.

Linville, P. W. & Jones, E. P. Polarized appraisals of out-group members. *Journal of Personality and Social Psychology*, 1980, *38*, 689-703.

Lippa, R. The naive perception of masculinity-femininity on the basis of expressive cues. *Journal of Research in Personality*, 1978, *12*, 1-14.

Locksley, A., Borgida, E., Brekke, N., & Hepburn, C. Sex stereotypes and social judgment. *Journal of Personality and Social Psychology*, 1980, *39*, 821-831.

McCauley, C., Stitt, C. L., & Segal, M. Stereotyping: From prejudice to prediction. *Psychological Bulletin*, 1980, *87*, 195-208.

Maccoby, E. E. & Jacklin, C. N. *The psychology of sex differences.* Stanford, Calif.: Stanford University Press, 1974.

Maddux, J. E. & Rogers, R. W. Effects of source expertness, physical attractiveness, and supporting arguments on persuasion: A case of brains over beauty. *Journal of Personality and Social Psychology,* 1980, *39,* 235-244.

Maier, N.R.F. Male versus female discussion leaders. *Personnel Psychology,* 1970, *23,* 455-461.

Maruyama, G. & Miller, N. Physical attractiveness, race, and essay evaluation. *Personality and Social Psychology Bulletin,* 1980, *6,* 384-390.

Mathes, E. W. The effects of physical attractiveness and anxiety on heterosexual attraction over a series of five encounters. *Journal of Marriage and the Family,* 1975, *37,* 769-773.

Merkel, M. E. Profile of the professional personnel woman. *Personnel Journal,* 1963, *42,* 121-124.

Meyer, J. P. Causal attributions for success and failure: A multivariate investigation of dimensionality, formation and consequences. *Journal of Personality and Social Psychology,* 1980, *38,* 704-718.

Miller, A. G. Role of physical attractiveness in impression formation. *Psychonomic Science,* 1970, *19,* 241-243.

Morin, S. G. Heterosexual bias in psychological research on lesbianism and male homosexuality. *American Psychologist,* 1977, *32,* 624-638.

Morse, S. E., Gruzen, J., & Reis, H. The "eye of the beholder": A neglected variable in the study of physical attractiveness? *Journal of Personality,* 1976, *44,* 209-225.

Muchinsky, P. M. & Harris, S. L. The effect of applicant sex and scholastic standing on the evaluation of job applicant resumes in sex-typed occupations. *Journal of Vocational Behavior,* 1977, *11,* 95-108.

Murstein, B. I. Physical attractiveness and marital choice. *Journal of Personality and Social Psychology,* 1972, *22,* 8-12.

Murstein, B. I. & Christy, P. Physical attractiveness and marital adjustment in middle-aged couples. *Journal of Personality and Social Psychology,* 1976, *39,* 537-542.

Nadler, A. "Good looks do not help": Effects of helper's physical attractiveness and expectations for future interaction on help-seeking behavior. *Personality and Social Psychology Bulletin,* 1980, *6,* 378-383.

Neisser, U. On "social knowing." *Personality and Social Psychology Bulletin,* 1980, *6,* 601-605.

Nieva, V. & Gutek, B. Sex effects on evaluation. *Academy of Management Review,* 1980, *5,* 267-276.

Nilson, L. B. The occupational and sex-related components of social standing. *Sociology and Social Research,* 1976, *60,* 328-336.

O'Leary, V. E. *Toward understanding women.* Calif.: Brooks/Cole, 1977.

O'Leary, V. E. Barriers to professional advancement among female managers. Paper presented at the ninth International Congress of Applied Psychology. Munich, Germany, August 1978.

O'Leary, V. E. & Donoghue, J. M. Latitudes of masculinity: Reactions to sex role deviance in men. *Journal of Social Issues,* 1978, *34,* 17-28.

Orvis, D., Cunningham, J. E., & Kelley, H. H. A closer examination of causal inference: The role of consensus, distinctiveness and consistency information. *Journal of Personality and Social Psychology,* 1975, *32,* 605-616.

Ostrove, N. Expectations for success on effort-determined tasks as a function of incentive and performance feedback. *Journal of Personality and Social Psychology,* 1978, *36,* 909-916.

Owens, G. & Ford, J. G. Further consideration of the "what is good is beautiful" finding. *Social Psychology,* 1978, *41,* 73-75.

Peck, T. When women evaluate women, nothing succeeds like success: The differential effects of status upon evaluations of male and female professional ability. *Sex Roles,* 1978, *4,* 205-213.

Pheterson, G. I., Kiesler, S. B., & Goldberg, P. A. Evaluation of the performance of women as a function of their sex, achievement, and personal history. *Journal of Personality and Social Psychology,* 1971, *19,* 114-118.

Reis, H. T., Nezlek, A., & Wheeler, L. Physical attractiveness in social interaction. *Journal of Personality and Social Psychology,* 1980, *38,* 604-617.

Renwick, P. A. & Tosi, T. The effects of sex, marital status, and educational background on selection decisions. *Academy of Management Journal,* 1978, *21,* 93-103.

Rosen, B. & Jerdee, T. H. Influence of sex-role stereotypes on personnel decisions. *Journal of Applied Psychology,* 1974, *59,* 9-14. (a)

Rosen, B. & Jerdee, T. H. Effects of applicant's sex and difficulty of job on evaluations of candidates for managerial positions. *Journal of Applied Psychology,* 1974, *59,* 511-512. (b)

Rosen, B. & Jerdee, T. Perceived sex differences in managerially relevant characteristics. *Sex Roles,* 1978, *4,* 837-844.

Rosenkrantz, P. L., Vogel, S. R., Bee, H., Broverman, I. K., & Broverman, D. M. Sex-role stereotypes and self-concepts in college students. *Journal of Consulting and Clinical Psychology,* 1968, *32,* 287-295.

Sanders, G. S. & Schmidt, T. Behavioral discrimination against women. *Personality and Social Psychology Bulletin,* 1980, *6,* 484-488.

Scherwitz, L. & Helmreich, R. Interactive effects of eye contact and verbal content on interpersonal attraction in dyads. *Journal of Personality and Social Psychology,* 1973, *25,* 6-14.

Shaffer, D. R. & Johnson, R. D. Effects of occupational choice and sex-role preferences on the attractiveness of competent men and women. *Journal of Personality,* 1980, *48,* 505-519.

Shaffer, D. R. & Wegley, C. Success orientation and sex-role congruence as determinants of the attractiveness of competent women. *Journal of Personality,* 1974, *42,* 586-600.

Shapiro, A. K., Struening, E., Shapiro, E., & Barten, H. Prognostic correlates of psychotherapy in psychiatric outpatients. *American Journal of Psychiatry,* 1976, *133,* 802-808.

Shapiro, J. Socialization of sex roles in the counseling setting: Responses to typical and atypical female sex roles. *Sex Roles,* 1977, *3,* 173-184.

Sharp, C. & Post, R. Evaluation of male and female applicants for sex-congruent and sex-incongruent jobs. *Sex Roles,* 1980, *6,* 391-402.

Sherman, J. A. Therapist attitudes and sex-role stereotyping. In A. M. Brodsky & R. T. Hare-Mustin (eds.), *Women and psychotherapy: An assessment of research and practice.* New York: Guilford, 1980.

Shinar, E. H. Person perception as a function of occupation and sex. *Sex Roles,* 1978, *4,* 679-693.

Sigall, H. & Aronson, E. Liking for an evaluator as a function of her physical attractiveness and nature of the evaluations. *Journal of Experimental Social Psychology,* 1969, *5,* 93-100.

Sigall, H. & Ostrove, N. Beautiful but dangerous: Effects of offender attractiveness and nature of the crime on jurors' judgment. *Journal of Personality and Social Psychology,* 1975, *31,* 410-414.

Sigall, H., Page, R., & Brown, A. C. Effort expenditure as a function of evaluation and evaluator attractiveness. *Representative Research in Social Psychology* 1971, *2,* 19-25.

Silverman, I. Physical attractiveness and courtship. *Sexual Behavior,* 1971, (September), 22-25.

Snyder, M., Tanke, E. D. & Berscheid, E. Social perception and interpersonal behavior: On the self-fulfilling nature of social stereotypes. *Journal of Personality and Social Psychology,* 1977, *35,* 656-666.

Solomon, M. R. & Schopler, J. The relationship of physical attractiveness and punitiveness: Is the linearity assumption out of line? *Personality and Social Psychology Bulletin,* 1978, *4,* 483-486.

Spence, J. T. & Helmreich, R. Who likes competent women: Sex-role congruence of interests and subject's attitudes toward women as determinants of interpersonal attraction. *Journal of Applied Social Psychology,* 1972, *2,* 197-213.

Spence, J. T., Helmreich, R., & Stapp, J. Likability, sex-role congruence of interest, and competence: It all depends on how you ask. *Journal of Applied Social Psychology,* 1975, *5,* 93-109.

Sroufe, R., Chaiken, A., Cook, R., & Freeman, V. The effects of physical attractiveness on honesty: A socially desirable response. *Personality and Social Psychology Bulletin,* 1977, *3,* 59-62.

Stokes, S. J. & Bickman, L. The effect of the physical attractiveness and role of the helper on help-seeking. *Journal of Applied Social Psychology,* 1974, *4,* 286-294.

Stricker, G. Implications of research for psychotherapeutic treatment of women. *American Psychologist,* 1977, *32,* 14-22.

Stroebe, W., Insko, C. A., Thompson, V. D., & Layton, B. D. Effects of physical attractiveness, attitude similarity and sex on various aspects of interpersonal attraction. *Journal of Personality and Social Psychology,* 1971, *18,* 79-91.

Taylor, S. E. A categorization approach to stereotyping. In D. L. Hamilton (ed.), *Cognitive processes in stereotyping and intergroup behavior.* Hillsdale, N. J.: Erlbaum, in press.

Taylor, S. E., Fiske, S. T., Etcoff, N., & Ruderman, A. The categorical and contextual bases of person memory and stereotyping. *Journal of Personality and Social Psychology,* 1978, *36,* 788-793.

Taynor, J., & Deaux, K. Equity and perceived sex differences: Role behavior as defined by the task, the mode and the actor. *Journal of Personality and Social Psychology,* 1975, *32,* 381-390.

Taynor, J. & Deaux, K. When women are more deserving than men: Equity, attribution and perceived sex differences. *Journal of Personality and Social Psychology,* 1973, *28,* 360-367.

Terborg, J. R. Women in management: A research review. *Journal of Applied Psychology,* 1977, *62,* 647-664.

Tesser, A. & Brodie, M. A. A note on the evaluation of a "computer date." *Psychonomic Science,* 1971, *23,* 300.

Tilby, P. J. & Kalin, R. Effects of sex-role deviant lifestyles in otherwise normal persons on the perception of maladjustment. *Sex Roles,* 1980, *6,* 581-592.

Touhey, J. C. Effect of additional women professionals on ratings of occupational prestige and desirability. *Journal of Personality and Social Psychology,* 1974, *29,* 86-89. (a)

Touhey, J. C. Effects of additional men on prestige and desirability of occupations typically performed by women. *Journal of Applied Psychology,* 1974, *4,* 330-335. (b)

Touhey, J. C. Sex-role stereotyping and individual differences in liking for the physically attractive. *Social Psychology Quarterly,* 1979, *42,* 285-289.

Unger, R. K. *Female and male.* New York: Harper & Row, 1979.

Unger, R. K. Male is greater than female: The socialization of status and equity. *Counseling Psychologist,* 1976, *6,* 2-9.

Wallston, B. S. What are the questions in psychology of women? A feminist approach to research. *Psychology of Women Quarterly,* 1981, *5*(3).

Wallston, B. S., DeVellis, B. M., & Wallston, K. A. Licensed practical nurses' sex role stereotypes. *Psychology of Women Quarterly,* in press.

Walster, E., Aronson, V., Abrahams, D., & Rothman, L. Importance of physical behavior. *Journal of Personality and Social Psychology,* 1966, *4,* 508-516.

Weary, G., Swanson, H., Harvey, J. H., & Yarkin, K. L. A molar approach to social knowing. *Personality and Social Psychology Bulletin,* 1980, *6,* 574-581.

Weiner, B. A theory of motivation for some classroom experiences. *Journal of Educational Psychology,* 1979, *71,* 3-25.

Weiner, B. *Achievement motivation and attribution theory.* Morristown, N. J.: General Learning Press, 1974.

Weiner, B., Frieze, I. H., Kukla, A., Reed, L., Rest, S., & Rosenbaum, R. M. *Perceiving the cause of success and failure.* Morristown, N. J.: General Learning Press, 1971.

White, R. Motivation reconsidered: The concept of competence. *Psychological Review,* 1959, *66,* 297-334.

Whitley, B. E. Sex roles and psychotherapy: A current appraisal. *Psychological Bulletin,* 1979, *86,* 1309-1321.

Wolff, L. & Taylor, S. E. Sex, sex-role identification and awareness of sex-role stereotypes. *Journal of Personality,* 1979, *47,* 177-184.

Yarkin, K. L., Harvey, J. H., & Bloxom, B. M. Cognitive sets, attribution and overt behavior. *Journal of Personality and Social Psychology,* in press.

Yarkin, K. L., Towne, J. P., & Wallston, B. S. Attributions of causality based on race and sex of stimulus persons: Blacks and women must try harder. *Personality and Social Psychology Bulletin,* in press.

Zajonc, R. B. Feeling and thinking. Preferences need no inferences. *American Psychologist,* 1980, *35,* 151-175.

Zickmund, W. G., Hitt, M. A., & Pickens, B. A. Influence of sex and scholastic performance on reactions to job applicant resumes. *Journal of Applied Psychology,* 1978, *63,* 252-255.

2

The Oedipus Complex:
STUDIES IN ADULT MALE BEHAVIOR

LLOYD H. SILVERMAN

ANNE K. FISHEL

Lloyd H. Silverman is Research Psychologist at the New York Veterans Administration Regional Office and Adjunct Professor of Psychology at New York University. His main interest is in psychoanalytic research in general and the development of the subliminal psychodynamic activation method in particular. He is the coauthor of *The Search for Oneness* (with Frank Lachmann and Robert Milich), to be published by International Universities Press.

Anne K. Fishel received her B.A. from Harvard University in 1977 and is currently a doctoral student in clinical psychology at the University of North Carolina at Chapel Hill. She has published articles on women's issues in *Ms. Magazine*.

This article is intended as a contribution to a topic about which there has been much debate among psychologists, psychiatrists, psychoanalysts, and philosophers: the validity of psychoanalytic theory (see, for example, Hook, 1959; Jahoda, 1980; Stern, Horowitz, & Lyness, 1977). More

AUTHORS' NOTE: We are grateful to Robert R. Holt, Amy Schneider, Doris K. Silverman, and David Wolitzky for their helpful comments, criticisms, and suggestions.

specifically, the article has two aims: (1) to review the research literature on studies testing a bedrock postulate of psychoanalytic theory—that the oedipus complex is a motivator of adult behavior—and (2) to focus on two methodological problems that have to be resolved for the adequate experimental testing of this and similar psychoanalytic propositions.

We will begin by describing the oedipus complex as conceptualized by Freud and subsequently developed by later psychoanalytic theorists. For two reasons we will limit this discussion to the oedipus complex in males: (1) almost all studies that have addressed this concept have used male subjects and (2) it is only the understanding of the oedipus complex in males for which there is a reasonable consensus among psychoanalytic clinicians.[1]

According to psychoanalytic understanding, the development of the oedipus complex in males comes about in the following way. As psychosexual development during infancy proceeds, there is a progressive shift from the "pregenital zones" (mouth and anus) to the penis as a locus of sensual pleasure. Whereas the pregenital zones never lose their potential for providing this pleasure and whereas there is considerable individual variation in the degree to which the above-described change takes place, psychoanalysts consider this intrapsychic shift important enough to view it as ushering in a new phase of psychosexual development, namely, the phallic phase. Occurring at the same time as this shift in zonal pleasure, there is also a development in the boy's relationship with his mother; he becomes increasingly individuated from her. Or stating this somewhat differently, the boy's mental representations of himself and his representations of his mother become more and more separate. As a consequence of these two developmental changes, the boy's mother becomes the primary object of his sexual urges.[2] This is understandable, given her physical proximity and availability in conjunction with the cultural and biological influences encouraging a heterosexual "object choice."

The boy's sexual impulses toward mother are, however, doomed to be largely, if not entirely, ungratified, a frustration that plays an important role in their being perceived as taboo and thus subject to defensive operations. In addition, since cues are usually available to the boy that mother is providing the sexual gratification denied him to another male—most often father—competitive and destructive wishes are mobilized toward the latter. However, fear of retaliation from this powerful male (usually fantasied as genital mutilation or castration) and often, conflicting loving feelings toward him as well motivate defensive efforts against these aggressive impulses and also motivate further defenses against the sexual urges toward mother.

As a result of this oedipal struggle, the sexual and aggressive wishes are in part modulated and in part renounced, with there being notable individual differences in the degree to which these processes are brought into play. Consequently, there are marked variations in the extent to which the behavior of adult males is still influenced by oedipal motives. In the realm of psychopathology, oedipal impulses have been proposed as underlying many kinds of symptoms, with certain types of conversion reactions, phobias (Fenichel, 1945) and homosexuality (Gillespie, 1964) being prominent examples. And even in the realm of normal behavior, derivative and otherwise regulated expressions of oedipal motives are legion. For example, everyday sexual contact can contain the disguised gratification of incestuous longings as an aspect of its meaning; and participation in competitive sports and the urge for vocational accomplishment can be motivated by unconscious impulses to defeat father.

A number of specific psychoanalytic propositions regarding the oedipus complex have been advanced by psychoanalysts and these can be grouped under three headings. One group, which can be termed "developmental propositions," relates to the emergence of the oedipus complex in childhood; for example, a mother's seductive behavior toward her son during the years when the oedipus complex is developing will make it more difficult for the boy to manage his competitive feelings toward his father.

A second group, "genetic propositions," concerns the effect of the childhood oedipus complex on later behavior. An example of this type is the postulate that male homosexuals, in contrast to male heterosexuals, are considerably more apt to have had mothers who behaved seductively toward them in early childhood.

The third group, "dynamic (or psychodynamic) propositions," refers to currently active oedipal motives—that is, unconscious incestuous and patricidal wishes, and anxieties and defenses stimulated by these wishes that are operating in the "here and now." An example is the postulate that male homosexuals are often motivated toward homosexual behavior by the need to ward off conflict over incestuous wishes and the castration anxiety these engender.

Of these three types of propositions, dynamic propositions emanate from the best "data base" available to the psychoanalyst—his or her observation of adult patients' productions in the treatment situation. Developmental and genetic propositions,[3] on the other hand, are based primarily on "secondary sources"—patients' recollections and reconstructions of events earlier in their lives. In the current article, we shall limit ourselves to research on dynamic propositions related to the oedipus complex.

STUDIES OF THE OEDIPUS COMPLEX AS A MOTIVATOR OF ADULT BEHAVIOR

In considering the studies that have been carried out on the oedipus complex as a motivator of adult behavior, an earlier and later phase of research activity can be delineated. The first phase, which largely predated the second and lasted until the 1960s, consisted of studies that can be characterized in the following way: (1) almost all of the investigations involved a correlational rather than an experimental approach; (2) there were no attempts at replication using the same instruments and measures on the same type of population; and (3) no consideration was given to the possibility that positive results were attributable to such artifacts as experimenter bias and subject expectations.

In the second phase of research activity, which was ushered in about two decades ago, two independent research programs were initiated that were characterized by experimental study in which replictions were sought and the influence of artifacts was explicitly addressed.

Phase 1

As noted above, the research during this phase mainly consisted of what traditionally has been called correlational studies and what Holt (1978: 221) recently has retermed "observational-statistical" investigations.[4] In these studies, the investigator, rather than introducing an experimental manipulation to influence the independent variable he wishes to study, accepts the naturally occurring variation in this variable, measures it, and then statistically seeks its relationship to one or more dependent variables.

As applied to the oedipus complex as a motivator of behavior, these studies typically have involved attempts at measuring an unconscious aspect of the oedipus complex—usually either incestuous wishes or castration anxiety (independent variable)—and correlating the degree to which this is present with some aspect of overt behavior that psychoanalytic theory views as related to this oedipal motive (dependent variable).

In these investigations, two types of subjects typically have been used: homosexuals and unselected college students. The former have been chosen for study since, as noted earlier, homosexuality in males is viewed psychoanalytically as most often rooted in oedipal motives—more specifically, as expressing a need to defend against strong incestuous wishes and the castration anxiety these engender. The question has been asked in these studies if homosexuals, more than heterosexuals, are characterized by the aforementioned motives.

These investigations can be divided into two groups; in one, the intensity of oedipal wishes has been the psychodynamic motive assessed and in the other, the focus has been on castration anxiety. In studies that have been carried out in the first group, there have been a few reports (Hart, 1951; Lindner, 1953; Thomas, 1951) that the homosexual group manifested stronger oedipal wishes than the controls, while less often (DeLuca, 1967) the results were negative. In the castration anxiety studies there also have been more often positive results—that is, greater castration anxiety in the homosexuals than in the heterosexual controls—(Davids, Joelson, & McArthur, 1956; Hammer, 1957; Lindner, 1953; Schwartz, 1956) than negative results (DeLuca, 1967; Thomas, 1951).

There also have been several observational-statistical studies using "normal" subjects—that is, unselected (male) college students. Here too, an aspect of the oedipus complex has been assessed and related to the presence of a type of behavior than can be psychoanalytically understood as rooted (in part) in this complex. Thus Sarnoff and Corwin (1959) found a significant relationship between castration anxiety (as assessed from a projective test) and fear of death (assessed from a self-report questionnaire), which they viewed as supporting the hypothesis that the latter is rooted in the former. McElroy (1950) found a significant correlation between male subjects' physical description of their mothers and their physical description of their wives. This was taken as support for the hypothesis that choice of mate expresses (in part) remnants of incestuous fixations on the opposite sex parent. And finally, there was a series of studies investigating the relationship between radical social attitudes of male adults and inferential evidence of oedipal hostility toward father. Three of these (Klein, 1925; Krout, 1937; Krout & Stagner, 1939) reported positive results and one (Gellerman, 1951) reported negative findings.

It would be reasonable to conclude from the above-cited observational-statistical studies bearing on the role of the oedipus complex as a motivator of adult behavior that the support they generated for this central psychoanalytic proposition is far from compelling. Although reports of positive findings were more than twice as frequent as negative ones, none of these studies was independently replicated, a shortcoming that must be viewed as serious since experimenter bias (Rosenthal, 1966) was not ruled out. (That is, whereas the judges evaluating the dependent variables in these studies typically were blind as to the status of the subjects, the experimenters who collected the data were not.) Also, the possibility that the subjects' expectations (Orne, 1962) might be influencing their responses was not considered.

Even if the above shortcomings were not present, data emanating from observational-statistical studies of this kind have very limited value. Negative results at best (i.e., even when the independent variables can be taken as *valid* measures of the psychodynamic motives) simply indicate that the experimental subjects manifest no more of these particular motives than do the controls—for example, that a particular homosexual group shows no more indication of oedipal wishes or castration anxiety than does the heterosexual comparison group. However, psychoanalytic formulations regarding the oedipus complex do not posit that homosexuals are unique by virtue of notable oedipal wishes and castration anxiety (these are understood as present in certain types of heterosexuals as well) but that these characteristics motivate homosexual reactions. Similarly, positive findings only indicate that homosexuals possess more of these characteristics than the particular control subjects with whom they are compared, but again what is crucial for the psychoanalytic formulation is their motivational role in the homosexuality.

Observational-statistical studies, in general, are limited in this way. Even when significant relationships are found, they do not necessarily imply that the dependent variable has been affected by the independent variable as the psychoanalytic formulation would have it. Thus, returning to the studies of homosexuals to exemplify this point, the presence of strong oedipal wishes or castration anxiety may be the result rather than the cause of the homosexuality; or both the homosexuality and these oedipal motives may be a consequence of some third variable. These are not just logical possibilities but clinically viable ones as well. Instances have been reported in the clinical literature in which homosexuality has stirred castration anxiety and other instances in which both homosexuality and a strong incestuous fixation are understood as a consequence of what has been termed in the psychoanalytic literature a "symbiotic fixation."[5]

Whereas observational-statistical studies can play a useful supplementary role in the testing of psychoanalytic psychodynamic propositions,[6] experimental studies must carry the brunt of the validation responsibility.

To compellingly demonstrate that oedipal motives underlie homosexual behavior (or any behavior for that matter), one must attempt to "manipulate" an oedipal motive and observe the consequences of this manipulation on the behavior.

Since the importance of an experimental paradigm for demonstrating causal relationships is generally well-recognized, it is of interest that prior to the initiation of the two research approaches that comprise what we are terming "phase 2 research," nearly all studies of the oedipus complex as a motivator of adult behavior were observational-statistical investigations. Shortly, we will suggest why this has been the case, but first let us review the few experimental studies that *were* carried out during phase 1.

Three studies could be found in phase 1 research in which experimental manipulations were employed. In the first of these, Schwartz (1955) obtained from college students pre- and postmeasures of various behaviors that psychoanalytically could be viewed as resulting from the presence of castration anxiety—for example, a sense of personal inadequacy, a reluctance to take risks, a damaged body image, and so on. Subjects were randomly assigned to one experimental and two control groups each of which viewed a film. For the experimental group, the film depicted subincision rites in an Australian Aborigine tribe. The control groups were shown films of equal length: for one, a semidocumentary of a lonely unhappy boy designed to stimulate anxiety over loss of love; and for the other, a comedy aimed at evoking only positive emotions. On six variables, the experimental group manifested a greater increase on the dependent measures after the film watching, than did the two control groups.

In a second study, Sarnoff and Corwin (1959) tested the proposition that fear of death is motivated by unconscious castration anxiety over incestuous wishes. Four groups of male undergraduates were seen, two who scored high in castration anxiety (HCA) and two low (LCA), in their responses on a projective test. For each, a fear of death questionnaire was filled out before and after an intervention—an experimental manipulation for one HCA and one LCA group and a control manipulation for the other two groups. The experimental condition consisted of subject viewing pictures of nude women with the cover task being to rate each picture for its aesthetic qualities. The control condition involved the viewing and rating of pictures of clothed fashion models. As predicted, the HCA subjects who received the experimental condition manifested the greatest increase in fear of death from the pre- to the postmeasure.

Finally, Imber (1969) attempted to stimulate oedipal anxiety in college males by (mildly) shocking them for "wrong" responses during a classification task in which they were asked to classify both experimental words ("mother" and "father") and control (neutral) words. Subjects had been divided into a high and low oedipal conflict group on the basis of projective test responses. The principal finding was that the former subjects showed a greater increase in anxiety after the experimental words than did the low oedipal conflict subjects.

Thus, prior to the phase 2 research that will be discussed in the next section, we could find only three experimental studies in the psychological literature bearing on the oedipus complex—about one-fifth the number of observational-statistical studies that we found. We shall now suggest that this dearth of experiments was the result of the unavailability of an adequate method for experimentally manipulating oedipal motives. The special problem that had to be addressed was to find a simple and reliable experimental technique that would allow for the stimulation of these motives *without bringing them into consciousness*. For according to psychoanalytic understanding, the influence of oedipal motives (and, for that matter, all psychodynamic motives) on behavior depends on these motives remaining unconscious.

As we shall now detail, such a method was provided by each of the two research programs that comprise what we have termed phase 2 research. In addition, these two programs have addressed the other methodological issue referred to earlier that also poses problems for experimenters who wish to test psychoanalytic psychodynamic propositions: the elimination or at least the control of experimenter bias, subjects' expectations, and other artifacts that contaminate experimental results. Before discussing both these methodological issues further, let us first describe the two approaches used in the phase 2 research and cite the data that bear on oedipal motives underlying adult behavior.

THE SUBLIMINAL PSYCHODYNAMIC ACTIVATION METHOD

This method (see Silverman, 1976, for its background) was developed at New York University and the Northport Veterans Administration Hospital to study the relationship between manifest psychopathology and psychodynamics. It involves subliminal exposures of psychodynamic-related and neutral (control) stimuli, usually to subjects manifesting a particular kind of pathology that the clinical psychoanalytic literature has linked to the psychodynamic content of the experimental stimuli. The rationale that prompted the use of subliminal stimulation for studying psychoanalytic dynamic relationships was the following. A stimulus containing psychodynamic content first should make contact with the related motives if they are currently active in an individual. Then, in line with what researchers in the subliminal area have reported occurs after subliminal registration of *any* stimulus (see Pine, 1964), the emerging ideas and images are likely to be transformed so that their psychodynamic character is obscured. Such would be the case particularly in anyone for whom the dynamic content is highly conflictual, that is, subjects whose psychopathology was based on these psychodynamic motives. For them it seemed especially unlikely that the dynamic content would gain access to awareness. Instead, the content could be expected to press for expression without the person's awareness, and it is in just such a circumstance that psychoanalytic theory would predict that the level of psychopathology will be affected.

The following is a description of the experimental procedure. Subjects are seen for two or more sessions, at least one of which is experimental and another, control. At the beginning of the first session, the experimenter briefly explains to the subject the purpose of the study and the tasks to be administered; he adds that on several occasions during these tasks, the subject will be asked to view flickers of light through an eyepiece of a machine—a tachistoscope—that will be made by the subliminal exposure of verbal messages or pictures. (See Silverman, 1977, for a discussion of the issue of informed consent and other ethical considerations relating to subliminal psychodynamic activation research.) Then the session proper begins with a "baseline" measure obtained for the subject's propensity for whatever behavior is being studied. This is followed by the subject being asked to look at the flickers of light that appear in the tachistoscope. Four exposures follow of either a stimulus with psychodynamic content (experimental session) or a stimulus with neutral content (control session), each exposure for a four millisecond duration. Then there is a reassessment of behavior for a determination of how the subject had been affected by the particular stimulus that had been subliminally exposed.[7]

The procedure for the other session(s) is identical to that just described, except that a different stimulus is exposed between the baseline and reassessment task series, with the order of sessions counterbalanced. The laboratory arrangement is such that the experimenter who works the tachistoscope and administers the assessment procedures never knows which stimulus is being exposed; and other members of the research team who evaluate the material for the behavior under study are "blind" also.

In over 50 studies completed to date (summarized in Silverman, 1976, in press), the subliminal presentation of dynamically related stimuli has affected degree of psychopathology in a way that subliminal neutral stimuli have not.[8] In a number of these investigations, the experiments carried out have had bearing on oedipal motivators of behavior. These can be put under two headings: studies of male homosexuals and studies of male college students engaged in a competitive activity. We will describe each of these in turn.

INVESTIGATIONS OF MALE HOMOSEXUALITY

As we implied earlier, psychoanalysis considers homosexuality in adults, at least when it is the exclusive or preferred form of sexual activity, as something more than a means of obtaining sexual gratification or as a way of expressing feelings of affection or love. Rather, such a sexual orientation is viewed as a more complex phenomenon in which important unconscious motives are being expressed. (Heterosexual behavior *can* be similarly motivated, but "obligatory homosexuality," according to psychoanalytic thinking, is *necessarily* classified as unconsciously motivated.)

One crucial psychodynamic determinant of homosexuality in males is the presence of unconscious incestuous wishes that are understood as stimulating a defensive fight from heterosexuality (Fenichel, 1945). According to this aspect of the psychoanalytic formulation, the male homosexual has remained sexually attached to his mother, and in response to the particular anxieties that he is vulnerable to and defenses that he employs, finds himself uninterested in or repelled by females as "sexual objects" and instead is attracted to males.

In three experiments utilizing the subliminal psychodynamic activation method, the above formulation was directly supported. In each, a group of male homosexuals was assessed for "homosexual orientation"[9] before and after exposure to a subliminal "incest stimulus" (the caption FUCK MOMMY accompanying a picture of a man and a woman in a sexually suggestive pose) and a subliminal "neutral stimulus" (the caption PEOPLE THINKING with a picture of two bland-looking men). In all three experiments, homosexual orientation was found to intensify after the stimulation of the incest-related content (Silverman, Kwawer, Wolitzky, & Coron, 1973; Silverman, Bronstein, & Mendelsohn, 1976).

Could the intensification of homosexual orientation resulting from the incest condition be attributed to some other quality of the stimulus than its specific incest content? One step toward making this determination was taken in the last of the three experiments (Silverman, Bronstein, & Mendelsohn, 1976). A third condition was added to the other two (in counterbalanced order) consisting of a stimulus designed to stimulate destructive rather than sexual wishes toward mother (the caption DESTROY MOTHER with a picture of a man with teeth bared about to stab a woman). This aggression condition, which in other experiments had affected other behaviors (e.g., depressive feelings), had no effect on homosexual orientation. This result was interpreted as implying that it was more than the general emotional loading or conflict-activating potential of the incest stimulus that intensified homosexual orientation since the aggressive stimulus had these qualities as well.[10]

STUDIES OF COLLEGE MALES IN A COMPETITIVE SITUATION

These experiments studied the effects of stimulating oedipal dynamics in "normal" college males in a competitive situation. The underlying assumption was that any competitive situation is likely to activate remnants of oedipal wishes and anxieties—remnants that can be found in most people.

Male college students were recruited for a dart-throwing tournament for which cash prizes were awarded. Before the dart throwing began, subjects were put through a "priming" procedure designed to activate strong competitive motives. Then there were several sessions, each comprised of a baseline and critical dart throw series (8 throws to a series), and between each series, the subject was exposed to a different subliminal condition. There were three main conditions, the effects of which were to be compared. One contained the verbal message BEATING DAD IS WRONG (BEATING in the context of competition connoting "triumphing over"), which was intended to stimulate oedipal guilt and thus impair dart-throwing performance. In a second, the message was BEATING DAD IS OK, intended to sanction oedipal wishes and thus improve performance; and in the third, the message was PEOPLE ARE WALKING intended as a relatively neutral (control) stimulus. Each of these verbal messages was accompanied by a congruent picture so that for the WRONG stimulus, the depiction was of a father and a son figure looking unhappily at each other; while for the OK message, an almost identical picture was used but with the figures' lips turned up rather than down so that they appeared to be smiling. In each of three experiments carried out at New York University

(Silverman, Ross, Adler, & Lustig, 1978), the OK stimulus produced the highest score and the WRONG stimulus the lowest, with the difference between these two conditions significant in each instance. In two experiments performed in other laboratories, this finding was both replicated and its meaning clarified by the introduction of other stimulus conditions. In one of these (Lonski & Palumbo, 1978), the messages BEATING MOM IS OK and BEATING MOM IS WRONG (with congruent pictures) were presented as well as the BEATING DAD and control stimuli. Only the BEATING DAD stimuli affected the (male) subjects, so that it could be concluded that their effect was due to more than the words OK and WRONG, with their general implication of sanction and condemnation, respectively. Stated otherwise, this finding supported the conclusion that when the subjects were affected by the BEATING DAD stimuli, both in this study and in the earlier ones, this effect was due to the specific stirring of oedipal motives.

This conclusion was further supported in experiments by Hayden and Silverstein (1978). After first replicating the BEATING DAD results, they ran another experiment in which they introduced the stimuli WINNING MOM IS OK and WINNING MOM IS WRONG. They intended these to address the incest side of the oedipus complex, in contrast to the BEATING DAD stimuli that addressed the competitive side. The new stimuli produced the hypothesized effect—WINNING MOM IS OK resulting in significantly higher dart scores than WINNING MOM IS WRONG. Since Hayden and Silverstein (1978) included as an additional control the stimuli WINNING DAD IS OK and WINNING DAD IS WRONG and found that these did *not* differentially affect dart scores, it could be concluded that it was the specifically oedipal implications of the WINNING MOM stimuli that were responsible for their impact on the subjects.[11]

THE HYPNOTIC INDUCTION OF CONFLICT METHOD

The other phase 2 research program was developed by Reyher and his coworkers at Michigan State University. In order to investigate the effects of oedipal dynamics on psychopathology, they have used hypnotic induction with college students without apparent psychiatric disturbance. A false memory of a made-up story (a paramnesia) that is designed to activate oedipal wishes is implanted under hypnosis. Then the posthypnotic suggestion is given that after the subject awakes, sexual feelings (related to the oedipal figure in the paramnesia—an older married woman) will become aroused when words associated to the paramnesia are mentioned, followed by an impulse to express these feelings. The subject is then awakened and is presented visually with a series of words, some of which are associated with the paramnesia. After each presentation, a standard nondirective probe–"how are you doing"–is employed, with reactions recorded and later scored for the appearance and intensity of symptoms.

Seven studies have been carried out by Reyher and his associates in which the oedipal paramnesia has been used (Byrnes, 1972; Karnilow, 1973; Larison, 1974; Perkins & Reyher, 1971; Reyher, 1958, 1967; Sommerschield & Reyher, 1973). In each of these investigations, a large number of symptoms were reported by the great majority of hypnotized subjects (75% or more) in whom the oedipal paramnesia was implanted. These symptoms have included disturbances of the autonomic nervous system (feelings of nausea, headaches, tachycardia, and so on); disturbances of the somatic and muscular nervous systems (stiffness, pains, tremors, and so on); disturbances of affect (lack of feeling, feelings of guilt, shame, disgust, and so on); states of confusion and disorientation; and dissociative reactions (limbs feeling detached, compulsive urges, and so on).

Two kinds of controls have been reported to demonstrate that these symptomatic reactions were in response to the hypnotic induction: (1) in five of the studies (Karnilow, 1973; Perkins & Reyher, 1971; Reyher, 1958, 1967; Sommerschield & Reyher, 1973) unrelated as well as paramnesia-related words were presented to subjects after they had been awakened from the hypnotic state and, in all five, significantly fewer symptomatic reactions were in evidence under the former condition and (2) in four of the studies (Byrnes, 1972; Perkins & Reyher, 1971; Reyher, 1967; Sommerschield & Reyher, 1973), "simulators" were put through the same procedures as the hypnotic subjects but were instructed not to allow themselves to go into a hypnotic state. In all four investigations, the simulators produced significantly fewer symptoms than the hypnotized subjects; in fact, many of them produced no symptoms.

In one of these studies (Karnilow, 1973) the specific pull of the oedipal elements of the paramnesia was assessed. Hypnotic subjects were randomly assigned to one of two groups. One of these received the oedipal paramnesia already described while the other received an almost identical paramnesia except that the woman in the story was described as single and around the same age as the subjects rather than married and older. The crucial finding was that this latter group manifested significantly fewer symptoms than did those who received the oedipal paramnesia.

METHODOLOGICAL ISSUES

Let us return to the two methodological issue outlined earlier and focus on how these were handled in the experimental research that has been described: (1) the problem of activating psychodynamic processes without interfering with their unconscious status and (2) the problems in controlling for artifacts.

The Problem of Activating Psychodynamic Motives

It was our contention that prior to the phase 2 research programs, the sparcity of experimental studies of the oedipus complex was due to the difficulty in devising a simple and reliable method for stimulating oedipal motives without allowing them into consciousness. Or to state the problem somewhat differently, for most experimental interventions, the more successfully the intervention stirs up an oedipal wish, the more likely a derivative of the wish would come into consciousness, which according to psychoanalytic understanding would eliminate or at least lessen its influence on behavior. For example, if an older male experimenter acted provocatively toward younger male subjects as a way of stirring hostility toward a father figure, it is more likely than not, the subjects would be aware of this derivative oedipal hostility with the consequence just stated. Or, if such subjects were shown a movie in which young men were having sexual relations with older women to stir up derivatives of incestuous wishes, it is likely that the resulting sexual arousal would be conscious, which again would lessen its influence on the behavior being studied. (See Silverman, 1972, and Silverman & Frank, 1978, for further discussion and documentation.)

There are three ways out of this dilemma, one of them in our opinion clearly more satisfactory than the other two. The less satisfactory ways are: (1) using a more indirect intervention in the hope that its weaker impact on oedipal motives would allow them to remain unconscious even when activated and (2) using a direct intervention but accompanying it with an additional manipulation designed to keep the activated motives out of consciousness. An example of the first of these was the film study of Schwartz (1955) cited earlier, in which the subincision rites that the experimental subjects viewed can be conceptualized as a symbolic castration designed to stimulate castration anxiety in the subjects through their identification with the "victims" in the movie. An example of the second approach was the study of Sarnoff and Corwin (1959) in which subjects were asked to look at pictures of nude women (to stimulate sexual impulses) but at the same time were requested to rate the pictures for their aesthetic value, a task that was distracting enough so that the stimulated incest derivatives were not apt to be conscious.

There are two problems with both of these approaches. First, the intervention may not accomplish its aim. With regard to indirect interventions, their very indirection may prevent the intervention from having the intended impact. Thus, in the subincision rites experiment, subjects might identify with the men performing the subincision rather than those to whom it was being done, resulting in the stimulation of aggressive impulses rather than castration fears; and in the dual manipulation studies, what is intended to keep the oedipal derivatives out of consciousness may not do so. Thus, in the Sarnoff and Corwin (1959) experiment, subjects might become sexually aroused despite the instructions that they concentrate on rating the pictures for aesthetic value.

Second, even where the intervention succeeds, each study that investigates a different psychoanalytic proposition related to the oedipus complex will require a new solution to the problem posed. The ingenuity required each time and the variety of manipulations that are needed have, we believe, a discouraging effect on experimenters, particularly those interested in a program of linked research studies.

The third strategy for stimulating unconscious motives without changing their unconscious status has been used in studies involving subliminal psychodynamic activation and hypnotic induction. Both methods use stimulation that is direct but with a technique that has built into it a means to prevent these motives from becoming conscious: the subliminal presentation of stimuli in the first instance and the nature of the hypnotic suggestion in the second. With regard to the former, it has been contended elsewhere (Silverman, 1976: 628) that when a stimulus is presented subliminally, because subjects are (by definition) unaware of its content, subjects are typically unaware of the psychodynamic motives the stimulus has stirred up. And with regard to the hypnotic induction method, note that the hypnotic suggestion included the words "the only way that you could attain peace of mind was to completely push the whole experience into the back of your mind," also inducing nonawareness of the stimulated motives.

Thus each of the two methods provides a uniform means by which various oedipal (as well as other psychodynamic) motives can be stimulated, without bringing them into awareness. It is this quality, we believe, that accounts for the large number of studies that have been carried out with each of these methods investigating psychoanalytic dynamic relationships.

The Problem of Artifacts

The other methodological issue that we shall address relates to artifacts in experimental studies of dynamic propositions. The question that can be asked is whether the positive findings summarized in this article compellingly support the psychoanalytic concept of the oedipus complex as a motivator of adult behavior. We already have argued that the results of the observational-statistical studies cannot be so viewed because of the inability of their findings to support the kind of cause-and-effect relationships implicit in this concept. But what about the positive results from the experimental studies? Before these can be seen as supportive, the question must be asked whether they may be the result of artifacts rather than the experimental manipulation that was introduced.

There are three sources of artifacts, the control of which cannot be taken for granted in personality research. These are (1) subject expectations (cf. Orne, 1962); (2) experimenter bias (Rosenthal, 1966); and (3) aspects of the experimental manipulation other than that which the experimenter is studying (cf. Weber & Cook, 1972). As Sackeim (1977) has pointed out, these artifacts have proven to be a constant source of danger in personality research and there are numerous examples of how the discovery of their influence has turned what an experimenter viewed as gold into dross. Thus, let us consider the precautions that have been taken to protect against the influence of these artifacts in the experiments that have been cited.

With regard to phase 1 research, it can be simply stated that in keeping with the general lack of sophistication about these matters during the time period in which these experiments were carried out, no or insufficient steps were taken to address the influence of these artifacts. Thus, it remains to be determined if the positive results that were reported would hold up if adequate steps were taken.

With regard to the phase 2 research programs on the other hand, specific steps have been taken to address each of these artifactual influences. In the Michigan State Hypnotic Induction studies, these steps have been the following. To assess the influence of subject expectations, as noted earlier, simulators were put through the same procedure as the hypnotized subjects and manifested few if any symptoms. Since effort was expended to motivate the simulators to respond like the hypnotized subjects, it was assumed that the expectations of the former were the same as those of the latter. Thus the symptoms manifested by the hypnotized subjects that were not manifested by the simulators were understood to be free of the contaminant of subject expections. These controls over subject expectations are not airtight, but they do constitute a reasonable effort to address the problem and may be the only steps that can be taken when hypnosis is the experimental manipulation used.

As for the influence of experimenter bias, the following has been done. In several of these studies, the experimenters' interactions with both hypnotized subjects and simulators were videotaped, with judges then asked to evaluate differences in the experimenter's behavior for the subjects in the two groups. Since no differences were found, it has been concluded that experimenter bias was not operating.[12]

Finally, let us turn to the efforts of the Michigan group in addressing the question of whether their positive findings can be attributed to an aspect of the experimental manipulation other than the oedipal content of the paramnesia. As noted earlier, this question was addressed in the Karnilow (1973) study where the effects of two paramnesias were compared. Here, the only difference was in the reference to the female in the paramnesia, she being a peer for one group and a married older woman for the other. Since the use of the latter produced more symptoms that the former, the assumption was supported that the specifically oedipal aspect of the parmnesia had affected the subjects.

Let us now turn to the attempts in the subliminal psychodynamic activation method studies to rule out these artifacts. In experiments generally, the best way of ruling out experimenter bias and subject expectations is for both the experimenter and the subject to be "blind" to the experimental conditions, as in double-blind drug studies where both the patient and the person administering the capsule do not know whether a drug or placebo is being ingested. With almost all psychological interventions, it is not possible to maintain such conditions, so that the best that can be done is to deceive both into believing that the control intervention is as potent as the experimental intervention. Subliminal stimulation experiments are the exception to this generalization, for these allow both principals to be blind as they are in drug studies. It is necessary merely to take steps like the following which have been carried out in studies of subliminal psychodynamic activation. First, to maintain blindness on the part of the experimenter, either someone else has inserted the stimuli into the tachistoscope or the experimenter has been trained to insert them himself, viewing only the backs of the stimulus cards which are marked by code letters. (For a particularly convincing piece of evidence that the experimenters *have* been blind, see Silverman et al. 1978: 355, fn. 12.) Second, to determine if the subject has been blind to whether he has received an experimental or control stimulus, a discrimination task is given to each subject individually at the end of his participation in the experiment proper. Here, the experimental and control stimuli are presented in random order under the same conditions as during the experiment proper, with subject's task being simply to tell them apart. When subjects are unable to make this discrimination, as has been the case for over 90% of them, we can assume their "blindness" and can rule out the possibility that the obtained effects were caused by subjects' conscious knowledge of the independent variable. (The few subjects who *have* been able to discriminate—and none has reported seeing anything more than differences in the darkness of the flickers or at most "a line" with one flicker but not the other—have never "carried" the experimental effects.)

Finally, let us consider whether the positive findings from the subliminal experiments are caused by something other than the oedipal elements in the stimuli. This possibility has been addressed by introducing additional experimental and control stimuli, most convincingly, we believe, in the competition experiments with the college students. Here it will be recalled that Lonski and Palumbo (1978) used the stimuli BEATING MOM IS OK and BEATING MOM IS WRONG as well as BEATING DAD IS OK and BEATING DAD IS WRONG and found that the former did not differentially affect dart-throwing behavior as the latter did. These data argue for the specifically oedipal content of the DAD messages as responsible for the experimental effects. However, this conclusion is not unassailable since it could be maintained that the difference in effectiveness of the DAD and MOM messages may have resided in something other than the differences in their oedipal connotations. It is a hypothetical possibility that some connotation of the word DAD versus MOM or of the accompanying pictures *other than* the oedipal connotations was responsible for the results obtained. And it is also possible that the differential effectiveness of the two sets of stimuli was due to differential *structural* properties of the words and/or the accompanying pictures rather than to their content.

However, the experiments of Hayden and Silverstein (1978) would seem to eliminate these other possibilities. These investigators, after replicating the original findings with the BEATING DAD stimuli, ran a new group of subjects and substituted the word WINNING for BEATING in the messages involving both DAD and MOM. In this experiment they found the previous pattern of results reversed—that is, a significant difference between the two MOM stimuli (WINNING MOM IS OK producing significantly higher dart scores than WINNING MOM IS WRONG) while there was no difference between WINNING DAD IS OK and WINNING DAD IS WRONG. The conclusion—that the only thing distinguishing the four stimuli that produced experimental results from the four stimuli that did not was the oedipal content of the former—seems to us to be beyond reasonable challenge.[13]

SUMMARY AND CONCLUSIONS

This article has been concerned with psychological research on one of the most central theorems of psychoanalysis: that the oedipus complex is a motivator of adult behavior. In the first part of the article we reviewed the empirical literature, dividing the relevant studies into what we termed phase 1 and phase 2 research. In phase 1, the research consisted almost exclusively of observational-statistical studies in which replications of earlier findings were nonexistent and little, if any, attention was paid to the possibility that artifacts were responsible for positive findings.

In phase 2, two research approaches were used that allowed for the experimental study of the relationship between oedipal motives and behavior, one involving subliminal stimulation and the other hypnotic induction. Each of these has generated a considerable amount of research activity and has yielded a number of replicated findings supporting the theorem that this complex can motivate adult behavior.

The second part of the article focused on two important methodological problems that have to be solved for the adequate experimental testing of dynamic propostions such as those related to the oedipus complex: (1) the difficulties in devising an experimental manipulation that can stimulate oedipal dynamics without distrubing their status as unconscious mental contents and (2) the difficulties in finding means by which the artifactual influence of experimenter bias, subject expectations, and non-oedipal stimulus qualities can be ruled out or at least controlled for.

In contrast to the phase 1 studies, the phase 2 approaches appear to have solved these problems and thus have offered an excellent vehicle with which to test the theorem under consideration. Many studies have been carried out with these approaches that provide support for the role of oedipal motives in adult behavior. Two of these (Karnilow, 1973; Hayden & Silverstein, 1978) deserve special attention in that they appear to have ruled out all major artifactual influences including the possibility that some non-oedipal quality of the experimental manipulation was responsible for the positive findings. These investigations can be viewed as models for the experimental testing of psychoanalytic psychodynamic propositions in general and propositions involving the oedipus complex more specifically.

NOTES

1. See Fleigel (1973) for a discussion of the controversy that exists today among psychoanalytic theorists and clinicians on the oedipus complex in females—particularly in relation to the concept of penis envy.

2. Two definitional points are in order: (1) "mother" refers to the chief mothering figure in the boy's life whether or not this is his biological mother and (2) in line with the suggestion of Klein (1972), that which Freud referred to as "sexuality"—pleasurable bodily feelings particularly in the erotogenic zones (mouth, anus, and genitals)—is being referred to here as "sensuality" with the term *sexual* being restricted to pleasurable genital feelings.

3. Psychoanalytic, developmental, and genetic propositions require different research strategies to test their validity than do dynamic propositions. Developmental propositions call for systematic observations of children and mother-child interactions such as those reported by Mahler, Pine, and Bergman (1974). Genetic propositions, on the other hand, can best be researched through longitudinal studies (e.g., Escalona and Heider, 1960) and cross-cultural investigations (e.g., Whiting, 1959). See also Zern (1970) for a study using both these methods in complementary fashion.

4. Holt has introduced this new term because, as he correctly points out, these studies do not necessarily employ correlational statistics.

5. It may be possible to obtain observational data that would not be vulnerable to the above criticism if a person is assessed many times during his life (though, needless to say, obtaining such data would not be easy). Then one might find, for example, that the appearance of castration anxiety antedates the emergence of indicators of homosexuality that then would argue against the former being the result of the latter. However, such a finding would not necessarily imply that the castration anxiety *generated* the homosexuality since the other possibility cited above—that a third variable such as a symbiotic fixation led to *both* castration anxiety and homosexuality—still would be tenable. It may also prove possible in the future for

observational data to shed light on the nature of the relationship between psycho-
dynamically relevant variables through the application of recently developed "causal
models" and their associated statistical techniques (Kenny, 1979). It is too early,
however, to judge the utility of this approach for the question at hand.

6. For example, once experimental studies have demonstrated a causal relationship, observational-statistical studies can speak to the question of the degree to which
the difference between homosexual and heterosexuals is due to the greater amount of
castration anxiety characterizing the former or to some other factors—for example,
the homosexuals' use of particular defenses to ward off the castration anxiety. For a
discussion of the complementary and supplementary role that different types of data
can play in validating psychoanalytic hypotheses, see Silverman (1975).

7. The designation *subliminal* in these experiments refers to the following. At
the tachistoscopic exposure level that is used, over 90% of subjects cannot distinguish, at better than a chance level, one stimulus from another in a "discrimination
task" given at the end of each experiment, not even when they are forced to make a
response or when they are offered a monetary incentive for discriminating between
stimuli. Moreover, the few subjects who *do* make a better than chance discrimination,
when questioned closely, maintain that either they have guessed or have made
judgments on the basis of slight differences in the color or size of the flashes; and,
most important of all, the results supporting the hypotheses are never dependent on
this small group of subjects. It also should be noted that when the stimuli are
presented at a supraliminal level, the effects that now will be described are typically
eliminated. For an extended discussion of how these experimental results support the
concept of subliminal registration strictly defined, see Silverman and Spiro (1967)
and Silverman (1968).

8. As is summarized in Silverman (in press), many of these confirmatory studies
have been carried out by independent investigators and, whereas there have been a
few reports of negative findings, the ratio of positive to negative outcomes among
them has been better than 3:1.

9. The homosexual orientation assessment consisted of the subject rating pictures of 10 males and 10 females on a 20-point scale for "how sexually attracted you
feel toward the person in the picture." The higher the ratings for males and the lower
the ratings for females, the stronger the subject's "homosexual orientation."

10. However, it could still be asked if it was the specific incestuous content that
had this effect. Before this question could be confidently answered, a number of
other stimuli would have to be introduced into the above paradigm—both other
incest-related stimuli and other non-incest-related but otherwise emotionally loaded
stimuli. This step has not yet been taken.

11. More recently, eight other investigators have conducted studies using the dart
paradigm. Their results can be categorized under three headings: (1) clear-cut replications of the main result found in the studies by Silverman et al. (1978), Hayden and
Silverstein (1978), and Lonski and Palumbo (1978)—BEATING DAD IS OK producing significantly higher scores than BEATING DAD IS WRONG; (2) partial
replications in which there were the hypothesized effects for the first four dart
throws, but not for all eight dart throws as there were in the earlier studies; and (3)
nonreplications. In the first category were samples reported by Carroll (1979),

Glennon (1981), and Palumbo (1979). Citrin (1979), Shaver (1979), and Swanson (1980, 1980a) ran samples that produced results in the second category. And in the third category were Haspel (1979), Heilbrun (1980), Swanson (1980), and Shaver (1979), the latter two appearing in this category as well as the second because they ran more than one sample.

As to what the negative findings could be due to, Carroll (1979) and Glennon (1981) have offered some interesting leads. Each of them independently examined subject variables that correlated with their experimental effects and reached a similar conclusion: The overall group effects that they obtained were carried by subjects whose defenses could be characterized as relatively "ineffective or unsuccessful" (Carroll, 1979: 31). It is thus possible that the populations in which there have been negative findings contained subjects who had particularly strong defenses. It is also possible that the effectiveness of subjects' defenses against the oedipal motives that were stimulated varies as a function of other variables, for example, the varying personalities of the experimenters or subtle differences in procedure. Clearly, further study is called for.

12. The above finding is not decisive, however, since the hypnotist's differential behavior toward the two kinds of subjects may simply have gone undetected. A tighter control would be to use two experimenters. One of them would assign subjects to the hypnosis and simulator groups and the other, who is "blind" to this information, would administer the experimental intervention. In a study by Smyth (1978) in which the Reyher type of hypnotic induction was used (though one designed to investigate non-oedipal motives), a related two-experimenter procedure was used. The addition of this blindness control did not prevent the same significant differences from emerging in the responses of the experimental and control subjects as they did in the earlier, somewhat less tightly controlled, experiments with this technique.

13. A more recent finding that also supports the specifically oedipal interpretation of the experimental effects was reported by Palumbo (1979). Whereas he obtained significant differences between the effects of BEATING DAD IS OK and BEATING DAD IS WRONG, he found no difference between the effects of two new messages: BEATING HIM IS OK and BEATING HIM IS WRONG.

REFERENCES

Burns, B. *The activation of posthypnotic conflict via free imagery: A study of repression and psychopathology.* Unpublished doctoral dissertation, Michigan State University, 1972.

Carroll, R. *Neurophysiological and psychological mediators of response to subliminal perception: The influence of hemisphericity and defensive style on susceptibility to subliminally presented conflict-laden stimuli.* Unpublished doctoral dissertation, St. John's University, 1979.

Citrin, M. *The effects of oedipal stimulation on dart throwing competition in college males and females.* Unpublished doctoral dissertation, New York University, 1979.

Davids, A., Joelson, M., & McArthur, C. Rorschach and T.A.T. indices of homosexuality in overt homosexuals, neurotics, and normal males. *Journal of Abnormal and Social Psychology,* 1956, *53,* 161-172.

DeLuca, J. N. Performance of overt male homosexuals and controls on the Blacky test. *Journal of Clinical Psychology,* 1967, *23,* 497.

Escalona, S. & Heider, G. M. *Prediction and outcome.* New York: Basic Books, 1960.

Fenichel, O. *The psychoanalytic theory of neurosis.* New York: Norton, 1945.

Fliegel, Z. O. Feminine psychosexual development in Freudian theory. *Psychoanalytic Quarterly,* 1973, *41,* 385-408.

Gellerman, S. Relation between social attitudes and a projected theme of frustration by parents. *Journal of Social Psychology,* 1951, *34,* 183-190.

Gillespie, W. H. Symposium on homosexuality. *International Journal of Psychoanalysis,* 1964, *45,* 203-209.

Glennon, S. *The effect of hemisphericity on the subliminal activation of residual oedipal conflicts.* Doctoral dissertation in preparation, New York University, 1981.

Hammer, E. F. A psychoanalytic hypothesis concerning sex offenders: A study of clinical psychologic techniques. *Journal of Clinical and Experimental Psychopathology,* 1957, *18,* 177-184.

Hart, R. D. *An evaluation of the psychoanalytic theory of male homosexuality by means of the Blacky pictures.* Unpublished doctoral dissertation, Northwestern University, 1951.

Hartmann, H. & Kris, E. The genetic approach in psychoanalysis. *Psychoanalytic Study of the Child,* 1945, *1,* 11-30.

Haspel, K. *The effects of priming and subliminal oedipal stimulation on competitive behavior of college males.* Unpublished master's thesis, University of Rhode Island, 1979.

Hayden B. & Silverstein, R. *The effects of subliminal oedipal stimulation on competitive dart throwing.* Unpublished manuscript, Brown University, 1978.

Heilbrun, K. Silverman's subliminal psychodynamic activation: A failure to replicate. *Journal of Abnormal Psychology,* 1980, *89,* 560-566.

Holt, R. R. *Methods in clinical psychology, Volume 2: Prediction and Research.* New York: Plenum, 1978.

Imber, R. *An experimental study of the oedipus complex.* Unpublished doctoral dissertation, Rutgers–The State University, 1969.

Jahoda, M. *Freud and the dilemmas of psychology.* New York: Basic Books, 1977.

Klein, G. S. The vital pleasures. In R. R. Holt and E. Peterfreund (eds.), *Psychoanalysis and Contemporary Science,* 1972, *1,* 181-205.

Krout, M. A controlled study of attitudes of radicals. *Psychological Bulletin,* 1937, *34,* 706-707.

Krout, M. & Stagner, R. Personality development in radicals: A comparative study. *Sociometry,* 1939, *2,* 31-46.

Larison, G. R. *Spontaneous repression of impulses and psychopathology.* Unpublished master's thesis, Michigan State University, 1973.

Larison, G. R. *The use of free imagery, non-directive interviewing and selected drugs to lift posthypnotic repression.* Unpublished doctoral dissertation, Michigan State University, 1974.

Lindner, H. The Black Pictures Test: A study of sexual and nonsexual offenders. *Journal of Projective Techniques,* 1953, *17,* 79-84.

Lonski, M. & Palumbo, R. The effects of subliminal stimulation on competitive dart *throwing performance.* Unpublished manuscript, Hofstra University, 1978.

Mahler, M., Pine, F., & Bergman, A. *The psychological birth of the infant.* New York: Basic Books, 1974.

McElroy, E. Methods of testing the oedipus complex hypothesis. *Quarterly Bulletin of British Psychological Society,* 1950, *1,* 364-365.

Orne, M. On the social psychology of the psychological experiment. *American Psychologist,* 1962, *17,* 776-783.

Palumbo, R. *The fear of success in adult males: The effects of subliminal messages derived from two theoretical models.* Unpublished doctoral dissertation, Hofstra University, 1979.

Perkins, K. A. & Reyher, J. Repression, psychopathology and drive representation: An experimental hypnotic investigation of impulse inhibition. *American Journal of Clinical Hypnosis,* 1971, *13,* 249-258.

Pine, F. The bearing of psychoanalytic theory on selected issues in research on marginal stimuli. *Journal of Nervous and Mental Disease,* 1964, *138,* 205-222.

Reyher, J. Hypnosis in research on psychopathology. In J. E. Gordan (ed.), *Handbook of clinical and experimental hypnosis.* New York: Macmillan, 1967.

Reyher, J. *Hypnotically induced conflict in relation to subception, repression, antisocial behavior and psychosomatic reactions.* Unpublished doctoral dissertation, University of Illinois, 1958.

Rosenthal, R. *Experimenter effects in behavioral research.* Englewood Cliffs, N.J.: Prentice-Hall, 1966.

Sackeim, H. *Self-deception: Motivational determinants of the nonawareness of cognition.* Unpublished doctoral dissertation, University of Pennsylvania, 1977.

Sarnoff, I. & Corwin, S. M. Castration anxiety and the fear of death. *Journal of Personality,* 1959, *27,* 374-385.

Schwartz, B. The measurement of castration anxiety and anxiety over loss of love. *Journal of Personality,* 1955, *24,* 204-219.

Schwartz, B. An empirical test of 2 Freudian hypotheses concerning castration anxiety. *Journal of Personality,* 1956, *25,* 318-327.

Shaver, P. A study of dart throwing and oedipal stimulation carried out at New York University, 1978. Personal communication.

Silverman, L. H. Further comments on matters relevant to investigations of subliminal phenomena: A reply. *Perceptual and Motor Skills,* 1968, *27,* 1343-1350.

Silverman, L. H. Drive stimulation and psychopathology: On the conditions under which drive-related external events evoke pathological reactions. In R. R. Holt and E. Peterfreund (eds.), *Psychoanalysis and contemporary science* (Vol. 1). New York: Macmillan, 1972.

Silverman, L. H. On the role of data from laboratory experiments in the development of the clinical theory of psychoanalysis. *International Review of Psychoanalysis,* 1975, *2,* 1-22.

Silverman, L. H. Psychoanalytic theory: The reports of my death are greatly exaggerated. *American Psychologist*, 1976, *31*, 621-637.

Silverman, L. H. Ethical considerations and guidelines in the use of the subliminal psychodynamic activation method. Research Center for Mental Health, New York University, 1977. (mimeo)

Silverman, L. H. The subliminal psychodynamic activation method: An overview. In J. Masling (ed.), *Empirical studies of psychoanalytic theory* (Vol. 1). Hillsdale, N.J.: Erlbaum, in press.

Silverman, L. H., Bronstein, A., & Mendelsohn, E. The further use of the subliminal psychodynamic activation method for the experimental study of the clinical theory of psychoanalysis: On the specificity of relationships between manifest psychopathology and unconscious conflict. *Psychotherapy: Theory, Research and Practice*, 1976, *13*, 2-16.

Silverman, L. H. & Frank, S. J. Aggressive stimulation, aggressive fantasy and disturbances of ego functioning: Some heretofore unexplored considerations of the effects of aggressive film viewing. In G. D. Goldman and D. S. Milman (eds.), *Psychoanalytic perspectives on aggression*. Dubuque, Iowa: Kendall/Hunt, 1978.

Silverman, L. H., Kwawer, J. S., Wolitzky, C., & Coron, M. An experimental study of aspects of the psychoanalytic theory of male homosexuality. *Journal of Abnormal Psychology*, 1973, *82*, 177-188.

Silverman, L. H., Ross, D., Adler, J., & Lustig, D. Simple research paradigm for demonstrating subliminal psychodynamic activation: Effects of oedipal stimuli on dart-throwing accuracy in college males. *Journal of Abnormal Psychology*, 1978, *87*, 341-357.

Silverman, L. H. & Spiro, R. H. Some comments and data on the partial cue controversy and other matters relevant to investigations of subliminal phenomena. *Perceptual and Motor Skills*, 1967, *25*, 325-338.

Smyth, L. Personal communication, 1978.

Sommerschield, H. & Reyher, J. Posthypnotic conflict, repression and psychopathology. *Journal of Abnormal Psychology*, 1973, *82*, 278-290.

Stern, R., Horowitz, L., & Lyness, J. (eds.). *Science and psychotherapy*. New York: Haven, 1977.

Swanson, R. J. Personal communication, 1980.

Thomas, R. W. *An investigation of the psychoanalytic theory of homosexuality*. Unpublished doctoral dissertation, University of Kentucky, 1951.

Weber, S. & Cook, T. Subject effects in laboratory research. *Psychological Bulletin*, 1972, *77*, 273-295.

Whiting, J. W. Sorcery, sin and the superego: A cross-cultural study of some mechanisms of social control. In M. R. Jones (ed.), *Nebraska Symposium of Motivation*. Lincoln: University of Nebraska Press, 1959.

Zern, D. The influence of certain child-rearing factors upon the development of a structured and salient sense of time. *Genetic Psychology Monographs*, 1970, *31*, 197-254.

3

Sociobiology as a Supplementary Paradigm for Social Psychological Research

MICHAEL R. CUNNINGHAM

Michael R. Cunningham is a Social-Personality Psychologist at Elmhurst College, Elmhurst, Illinois. He took his B.A. at Carleton College and his Ph.D. at the University of Minnesota. His research focuses on the effects of mood and motivational variables on social behaviors and on unobtrusive measures of personality.

Kuhn (1962) noted that a new scientific paradigm typically generated hostility rather than enthusiasm from the established scientific community. While sociobiologist Edward O. Wilson has not been invited to recant before Rome, it is surprising how little empirical attention has been devoted to sociobiology by social psychologists in the years since Wilson's (1975) major volume was published. Despite Trivers's (1977) gauntlet-tossing prediction "sooner or later, political science, law, economics, psychology, psychiatry and anthropology will all be branches of sociobiology," few social psychologists have investigated the theoretical propo-

AUTHOR'S NOTE: I would like to thank Marilyn Brewer, William Graziano, Michael Lougee, Victoria Mandell, Katherine Noll, Harry Triandis, Paul Rosenblatt, Brendan Rule, and Michele Tomarelli for their helpful comments on an earlier draft. Address requests for reprints to the author, Department of Psychology, Elmhurst College, Elmhurst, Illinois 60126.

sitions of sociobiology. In the *Social Science Citation Indices* for 1975 through 1979, Wilson received zero citations in empirical social psychological journal articles.

Silence is the sovereign contempt, as Sainte-Beuve observed, and this attitude may stem from a variety of negative perceptions, including views that sociobiology is just another reworking of Social Darwinism or McDougall's instinctualism, that it naively contradicts established findings on the role of learning and cognition in behavior, that it attempts to explain everything but makes no predictions that are potentially falsifiable, and that it is sexist and racist.

I am by no means a true believer in sociobiology, and this article is not meant to foster conversion. Each of the foregoing negative impressions of sociobiology has a grain of truth, yet should not obscure its heuristic value. Sociobiology has raised some stimulating new issues and has challenged traditional interpretations within many topic areas of social psychology. The present article, then, will provide an introduction to sociobiology with an emphasis on the psychological research findings relating to sociobiological hypotheses, as well as an indication of topics requiring explorations within the areas of altruism, attraction, gender differences, sexual behavior, child care, aggression, and conformity. Little attempt will be made to argue against sociobiology or to address the enormous range of philosophical, methodological, ethical, and political issues raised by the sociobiological approach and instead the reader is referred to works by Campbell (1975), Wispe and Thompson (1976), Sahlins (1977), Caplan (1978), Gregory, Silvers, and Sutch (1978), Wyers et al. (1980), and especially Ruse (1979) for such discussion. Those wishing to examine the evidence for sociobiology in more detail can find many of the research reports discussed here in the collections of Hunt (1980) and Clutton-Brock and Harvey (1978).

ORIENTATION OF SOCIOBIOLOGY

Sociobiology, in Wilson's (1975) definition, is the "systematic study of the biological basis of all social behavior." That definition is misleading, however, since it fails to indicate the differences between sociobiology and other biologically oriented disciplines. Suffice to note at this point that sociobiology does not probe deeply into neural and hormonal mechanisms as does psychobiology, into familial relatedness in psychological traits as does behavior genetics, or even into the specific motivational and stimulus determinants of animal behavior as does ethology, though findings from these disciplines are discussed by sociobiologists.

Sociobiology is instead committed to a Darwinian analysis of selfish and social behaviors. The basic assumptions of sociobiology are fourfold: (1) A large number of behaviors involve substantial genetic determination. Such genetic influence may range from complete fixed behavioral programming to a predisposition to easily learn certain broad classes of behaviors. (2) Genetically based behaviors are maintained in a population if they increase the genetic fitness (i.e., reproductive success) of the individual or his close relatives who also carry the genes for that behavior. (3) Behavior can best be studied by observing over several generations the survival and reproduction rate of individuals exhibiting that behavior as a function of alterations in environmental conditions. (4) In lieu of population genetics research, it is valuable to describe and provide mathematical models of how a given behavior might be adaptive and increase genetic fitness within certain environments.

There have been some elegant demonstrations of the genetic mechanisms involved in behavior, such as that in Rothenbuhler (1964) on the two genes involved in nest cleaning by the honey bee. Yet most sociobiological writing has been descriptive and speculative. Sociobiologists have, moreover, manifested little concern with testing the possibility that a given phenomenon could be due to learning. The logic and limitations of the sociobiological approach are both apparent in the analysis of altruism.

ALTRUISM

Kin Selection Altruism

The story is told that biologist J.B.S. Haldane was once asked if he would be willing to give up his life for his brother. No, said Haldane, he would not sacrifice himself for his brother, but he would give up his life to save three brothers or nine cousins (Barash, 1979). Such an altruistic decision would be reasonable based on the sociobiological principle of kin selection altruism. Kin selection was defined by Wilson (1978) as "the increase of certain genes over others in a population as a result of one or more individuals favoring the survival and reproduction of relatives who therefore are likely to possess the same genes by common descent." Thus, natural selection may have favored the retention of genes inclining the individual toward altruistic self-sacrifice to aid relatives possessing his genes (Hamilton, 1964). Since humans share one-half of their genes with their siblings, and one-eighth of their genes with their cousin, an individual could assure the survival of his genes if not his body by protecting the number of kin specified by Haldane.

Kin-selection-based altruism may be most likely to occur (1) among closely related rather than distantly related individuals, (2) among species with little dispersal that are therefore likely to share kinship ties with their neighbors, and (3) among species exhibiting the capacity to recognize relatives and discriminate against nonrelatives (Barash, 1977). Kin selection altruism is common in social species, including ants, many bees, certain carnivores, and many primates (Wilson, 1975). The wasp which attacks an enemy to protect its nest even though it causes its own death is one example. Another instance of kin selection was provided by Trivers and Hare (1976). Because of the complex genetics of the haplodiploid insect species, sisters are related to each other by three-quarters but are related to their brothers by only one-quarter. Trivers and Hare (1976) found that females invested three times the work in their sisters compared to their brothers, paralleling their genetic relatedness. Although alternate interpretations have been proposed for this study (Alexander & Sherman, 1977), other instances of kin selection abound.

When a predator attacks a group of zebras, all of the young are defended by the adults, but the same type of protection is not shown by wildebeests. The altruistic defense by the zebras and its absence in the wildebeest can be interpreted using knowledge of kin selection and the behavioral habits of the two species. Zebras travel in relatively small family groupings, so any offspring are likely to be related. Wildebeests, by contrast, travel in larger herds with multiple families, so there is less likelihood that any offspring is related to a given adult (West-Eberhard, 1975). An interesting human parallel is the research by Takooshian, Haber, and Lucido (1977), which found that 72% of the people approached by a lost child in a small town (with fewer families and a greater likelihood of relatedness) offered help, compared to only 46% in a large city. Diffusion of responsibility or urban stress and alienation could have, of course, produced these results.

Other investigations of helping behavior have been performed using variables that have a tenuous association with genetic relatedness. It has been found that people are often more likely to help members of their own race than members of another race (Bryan & Test, 1967; Bingham & Richardson, 1979) and a compatriot rather than a foreigner (Feldman, 1968). Yet situational and individual factors exert a substantial moderating effect (West, Whitney, & Schnedler, 1975; Gaertner & Dovido, 1977; Crosby, Bromley, & Saxe, 1980). People are also more likely to help people like themselves along the dimension of attitudinal similarity (Einswiller, Deaux, & Willits, 1971; Romer, Bontemps, Flynn, McGuire, & Gruder, 1977), although attitudinal and genetic similarity may have little association. Finally, Clark and Mills (1979) found that the patterns of helping demonstrated in induced close or "communal" relationships differed from those in more distant "exchange" relationships.

Informal observation suggests that people are more likely to exchange presents, loans, and help with parents, children, and siblings than with aunts, uncles, or cousins who are more distantly related. Some cultures and ethnic groups do, however, make greater use of extended family ties than others (McAdoo, 1978; Thernstrom, 1980). I know of no psychological experiment exploring help giving among relatives, but research on trust, cooperation, and reciprocity with people of varying degrees of relatedness and norms of family commitment might produce different patterns of results than the studies involving strangers or casual acquaintances (cf. Shapiro, 1980). It would also be interesting to see if more helping was given to someone with the same last name (which suggests a distant relation) or physical phenotypic appearance (height, build, coloration) as the potential helper than to others.

Reciprocal altruism

Trivers (1971) suggested that there may be genetic predispositions toward reciprocal altruism, the trading of favors and help with nonrelated individuals, since aid in times of danger or scarcity could increase the individual's likelihood of survival. Rhesus, macaques, baboons, and anthropoid apes are known to form coalitions or cliques and to aid one another in a reciprocal manner, while chimpanzees, gibbons, African wild dogs, and wolves beg food from each other reciprocally (Wilson, 1975). Reciprocal altruism may be most likely to occur when the situation involves (1) low risk for the helper; (2) high benefit for the recipient; (3) high expectation that the situation will be reversed; and (4) the helper and helpee can recognize each other in the future (Barash, 1977).

Supporting these predictions, psychological research has found that the cost/benefit ratio generally affected the likelihood of human helping (Piliavin & Piliavin, 1972; Weyant, 1978). Similarly, the possibility of reciprocity has been found to facilitate helping (Regan, 1971; Romer et al., 1977). Such findings are also interpretable using reinforcement exchange and equity formulations.

An inability to recognize past helpers or beneficiaries was predicted to reduce the likelihood of helping, and it should be noted in this context that both whites and blacks were poorer at identifying previously seen members of other races than members of their own race (Malpass & Kravitz, 1969) even with substantial cross-racial experience (Luce, 1974) and age (Brigham & Williamson, 1979). Such inability could lower cross-racial and intraurban helping apart from any effect of kin selection.

The sociobiological emphasis on reciprocity provides insight into the ambivalence people manifest toward the disabled, the stigmatized, and the aged. Katz, Gloss, Lucido, and Forbes (1979) suggested that people see the physically handicapped and minorities both as victims of misfortune and discrimination and as "lacking some attributes of full creditable human beings." Such perceptions may produce positive or negative responses depending on the costs of helping. Less high cost helping may be directed toward the stigmatized because they may be seen as less fit and possessing fewer resources to reciprocate in the future. Thus, Ungar (1979) found that no difference in helping was displayed toward a person with and without an eyepatch when the helping required little effort, but significantly less helping was given to the stigmatized person when helping involved high effort. There is an ironical converse to this analysis, that people should be most willing to help the most fit. This has been demonstrated in numerous studies in which high status (Pandey, 1979) and highly physically attractive individuals (Benson, Karabenick, & Lerner, 1976) were more likely than others to receive aid.

Trivers (1971) suggested that in a social system involving reciprocity, an individual could gain an advantage by subtle cheating. To combat this tendency, humans may have evolved a complex regulatory system involving emotions of liking, guilt, and gratitude (Tesser, Gatewood, & Puver, 1968), as well as the ability to detect duplicity and moralistic aggression to punish "sneaky cheaters." People do seem to be quite capable of detecting lying from nonverbal cues (Kraut, 1978). Nonetheless, individualistic treacherous behavior is frequent in situations such as the Prisoner's Dilemma and Commons Problem (Edney, 1980) even though retaliation is also evident. It would be useful to have additional information on the specific determinants of treachery and responses to perceive deviancy.

There are numerous situations in which people act cooperatively or helpfully with low likelihood of reciprocity. In fact, most social psychological studies on altruism involve helping between strangers in a setting where there are minimal chances of either relatedness or reciprocity. Sociobiology has no theoretical machinery to account for such helping and might regard it as a nonadaptive, vestigal response pattern. Helping stimulated by irrelevant positive mood (Cunningham, 1979; Cunningham, Steinberg, & Grev, 1980), for example, may once have been useful to initiate liking and reciprocal relationships in small-scale societies. Similarly, guilt-induced helping may once have aided the individual in avoiding moralistic aggression following transgression. Thus, emotion-activated helping may historically have increased the individual's fitness, but frequent altruism toward strangers may simply represent a genetic pattern which has not yet been bred out of the species (like our taste for sugar and saturated fats). The critical test, of course, would be to determine whether selfish or altruistic urban dwellers live longer and have more children, in other words, see whether nice guys do finish last.

There is currently little direct evidence for any innateness in altruistic responding, although Zahn-Waxler, Radke-Yarrow, and King (1979) reported instances of empathic responding in children as young as 18 months. Other investigators have viewed helping as a developmental phenomenon (Bryan & London, 1970; Cialdini & Kenrick, 1976); positive evaluation of reciprocity, for example, was more evident in older children than younger children (Berndt, 1979). Sociobiology is, however, rather willing to ascribe a large role in altruistic behavior to learning and cultural norms. Trivers commented:

> Selection should favor learning about the altruistic and cheating tendencies of others indirectly, both through observing interactions of others and, once linguistic abilities have evolved, by hearing about such interactions or hearing characterizations of individuals [1971: 36].

The impression is conveyed, then, that natural selection in humans has favored genes that make it particularly easy to acquire altruistic behaviors and moral norms, although the forms may vary depending on the social conditions. This position is very similar to the concept of preparedness advanced by Seligman (1970) to account for the rapid acquisition of conditioned taste aversion.

INTERPERSONAL ATTRACTION

Facial Attractiveness

Sociobiologists argued that many aspects of attraction in humans are controlled by genetic factors. Ethologists such as Lorenz (1943) and Eibl-Eibesfeldt (1970) noted that infants across a wide range of species tended to have in common such characteristics as large eyes and head compared to the rest of the body, rounded features, softer skin, and a coloration (usually lighter) which differed from that of adults. These infantile features were believed to elicit instinctive caretaking responses from adults, and exaggerated versions of these features elicited even stronger positive responses.

There is abundant evidence that stereotypical infant features are associated with positive evaluations from adult humans (Huckstedt, 1965; Gardner & Wallach, 1975; Sternglanz, Graz, & Murikami, 1977). A study using photographs of infants was conducted by Hildebrandt and Fitzgerald (1977), for example, who measured the size of various facial features and correlated them with ratings of "cuteness." They found that larger eye width and height, larger forehead height, and larger cheeks were positively associated with cuteness while larger nose width, ear height, and mouth height were negatively correlated. It seems clear, then, that certain infantile features are associated with attractiveness, although the genetic basis and relationship to caretaking have not been fully established. Malmuth, Shayne, and Pogue (1978) did find, however, that adults demonstrated more unrelated prosocial behavior when an infant was present than when an infant was not present.

Physical attractiveness is as important in judgments of adults as in judgments of children (Berscheid & Walster, 1974), but whether there are any universally attractive stimuli in adults cannot be determined from the published literature. Ford and Beach (1951) reported wide cross-cultural variations in preferred female physiques. Variability in preferences and associations with personality were reported for males judging female silhouettes (Wiggins, Wiggins, & Conger, 1968) and females judging males (Beck, Ward-Hull, & McLear, 1974). In judgments of faces, however, rough agreement in preferences was shown in judgments made by Asian-American and Caucasian females (Wagatsumo & Kleinke, 1979), Chinese, Indian, and English females judging Greek males (Thakevar & Iwawaki, 1979), and South African and American males and females (Morse, Gruzen, & Reis, 1976), although the studies tended to highlight differences.

There is no published study specifying adult facial attractiveness cues. Yet if certain infant features are inherently attractive to adults, people may also be attracted to other adults displaying infantile features. To investigate this hypothesis, I conducted a study (Note 1) to determine what facial features were most closely associated with attractiveness ratings of females by males. It was found, parallel with the infant results, that large eyes, small nose, and small chin were associated with attractiveness in adult females. In addition, a larger smile, higher eyebrows, and wider cheekbones were also related to attractiveness ratings. Further, the size of various features was significantly associated with a range of subject's behavioral preferences. Women with larger eyes were significantly more often chosen to give a ride to, hire for a job, save if drowning, date, have sex, and have children with than other women, suggesting that such features may contribute to the individuals' likelihood of survival and reproduction.

Williams (1975) argued that the major variable influencing male's perception of female attractiveness was age. Men may prefer women with infantile features because they appear young. Youth (and health) is allegedly preferred since it entails the greatest number of fertile years. In the United States, males do tend to choose females younger than themselves in their first and especially in later marriages (Bureau of the Census, 1975). It would be interesting to examine cases of older woman-younger man relationships to determine the relative importance of physical appearance, personality, desire for infertility, and expectation of inheritance as a basis for attraction.

If certain features are attractive, it would not be surprising to find individuals altering their appearance to match the ideal; and women and some men do use cosmetics to achieve that end. Such behavior, however, is a form of deceit in the sense that the individuals may present a visual phenotype without possessing the corresponding genotype for those features. It was found that women using lipstick were perceived as more frivolous than women who did not (McKeachie, 1952). It could be revealing to know whether those who attempt to alter their apparent genetic fitness using hair tint, orthodontics, cosmetic surgery, contact lenses, or padded clothing are seen as dishonest by males or females.

Male Attractiveness

Ethologists such as Guthrie (1976) have suggested that certain male features may have biological survival value as symbols of power. A beard and large chin were said to exaggerate the jaw-weapon display while grey hair was believed to convey social rank and maturity (Freedman, 1979). Baldness was said to be a "badge of leadership and dominance" and was found in mature chimpanzees, Uakari monkeys, macaques, and orangutans, as well as humans. Finally, darker complexion and height were believed by Guthrie (1976) to convey dominance.

Feinman and Gill (1978) confirmed part of the former hypotheses with the finding that women preferred men with relatively dark coloration while men preferred women with lighter coloration. The effect of height is more complex. Taller men have had an advantage in employment interviews and career salaries (Feldman, 1979), and higher status men were presumed to be taller (Wilson, 1968). Yet Graziano, Brothen, and Berscheid (1978) found that independently of their own height, women preferred men of medium height over men of short or tall stature. Men, by contrast, indicated greatest liking for short men, perhaps because such men were seen as less intimidating and more easily dominated than others.

In species employing intrasexual selection (male combat), such as the elephant, seal, elk, and bighorn sheep, the male's social rank is the primary signal for female attraction. Social rank is based on direct male competition and tends to favor males possessing abundant aggressiveness, strength, and size. In epigamic selection, or female choice species such as the peacock and lyre bird, males are more highly ornamented than the females and the female tends to respond to the male's sexual ornamentation, courtship signals, and possession of territory.

Humans do not neatly fit into either category, but there are indications that physical attractiveness is particularly important in evaluations of females, while males tend to be evaluated on their social status and competence (Rosenblatt, 1974). Berscheid and Walster (1974) reported that physical attractiveness was more closely associated with the number of dates the person had recently had for females than for males; and

Morse, Gruzen, and Reiss (1976) reported that physical char\ were more important in males' overall ratings of females while   .ales placed more emphasis on the male's personality.

If males are attracted by youth and potential fertility while females are attracted by status and capabilities, it might be predicted that males will expend more friendliness, attention, and resources in the earlier stages of the relationship to establish his fitness in the eyes of the woman. Once the woman has consented to sexual intercourse, it would be expected that the man would become more conservative in his attention and expenditures, either because he feels he has less to gain, in which case he may resist further commitment, or to maintain resources for potential offspring. Since as the next selection will indicate, females have more to lose by making a poor mate selection, there may also have been selection pressure for females who were discriminating of men with the best genetic combinations and who were not deceived by false displays of fitness. Yet while females have been found to be more sensitive than males to nonverbal signals of emotion (Cunningham, 1977), it is not yet clear that females are generally more accurate in judging personality or status.

Postsexual Attraction

Once initial heterosexual contact has taken place, two sociobiological variables might contribute to the maintenance of a heterosexual relationship: the emotions generated by sexual intercouse and attraction to the offspring. Wilson (1978) suggested that the female's virtually constant receptivity and the pleasure which males and females derive from orgasm help to maintain pair bonding. It is interesting to note that a female lion, leopard, and cougar may copulate 50 times a day with the same male and maintain this level for as long as seven days; Barash (1979) suggested that such hypersexuality prevented the male from becoming involved with other females during the breeding season. In humans, such singleminded sexuality is seldom seen even among newlyweds, but Howard and Dawes (1976) have found that when the frequency of sexual intercourse exceeded the frequency of fighting in marriage, the relationship was reported to be a happy one. The causal effect of sex in relationships, however, remains unknown.

The occurrence of offspring may also contribute to the stability of a relationship (Rosenblatt & Skoogberg, 1974). Among the kittiwakes, a European gull, pairs that failed to hatch any offspring the previous year were three times as likely to separate as successful pairs (Coulson, 1966). In human couples, involuntary sterility or the loss of children is often associated with tension and marital dissatisfaction (Mazor, 1980; Barash, 1979) although voluntary childlessness is associated with marital happiness (Renne, 1976; Poston, 1976). In this context, it can be noted that the passionate love stage of relationships averages about 15 months (Walster & Walster, 1978), which would be enough time for a couple not practicing contraception to conceive and bear a child. It is interesting to speculate that the decline in the intensity of passion may have adaptive significance to motivate couples not producing offsping to diminish their commitment to the relationship and seek fertile ground elsewhere. By contrast, married couples with their first (planned) baby often seem more in love than others, but I have seen no studies documenting such phenomenon, nor addressing the significance of passion's maintenance and decline.

GENDER DIFFERENCES

Male Versus Female Sexual Behavior

The amount of investment which each gender contributes to their offspring, in terms of time, nutrition, energy, and increased vulnerability to predators, varies widely across species. In the waterbug, the male carries the eggs deposited by the female to term on his back. In the stickleback, the male fertilizes eggs left by a number of females and cares for them in his nest, while in the seahorse, the male carries the eggs in a pouch (Barash, 1977). Human females produce a limited number of ova, which require substantial investment to carry to term and which result in offspring requiring a great deal of parental care. Human males, by contrast, need only to contribute sperm, which is produced in sufficient quantity to fertilize a large number of females.

Sociobiologists suggested that the difference in reproductive investment between males and females could result in selection pressure favoring different sexual patterns between the human genders (Trivers, 1972; Wilson, 1975; Symons, 1979). The forms these differences take are described by Wilson:

If males are able to court one female after another, some will be big winners and others will be absolute losers, while virtually all healthy females will succeed in being fertilized. It pays males to be aggressive, hasty, fickle and undiscriminating. In theory it is more profit-able for females to be coy, to hold back until they can identify males with the best genes. In species that rear young, it is also more important for the females to detect males who are more likely to stay with them after insemination. Humans obey this biological principle faithfully [1978: 100].

Data on male sexual aggressiveness, haste, arousability, and promiscuity are rather sparse. No study is known showing that men compete more aggressively for attractive women than women compete for attractive men. Recent research on jealousy, however, indicated that males are more likely to verbally threaten a potential interloper and become sexually aggressive with others when faced with potential disaffection, while women were more likely than males to make themselves appear more attractive to their partner or pretend they did not care (Shettel-Neuber, Bryson, & Young, 1978).

On the issue of male versus female sexual arousability, some studies have found that males were more easily aroused by pornography (reviewed by Symons, 1979), but other studies found no differences (Fisher & Bryne, 1978). The possibility that males may be easily aroused by a novel partner even when sexually sated, called the Coolidge effect, has been examined with sheep, cattle, hamsters, and rats, but the results are not conclusive, and few studies have examined the converse effect with females so conclusions about gender differences in sexual arousability seem premature (Dewsbury, 1981). Comparison of male and female satiation rates to pornography (cf. Mann et al., 1974) may, however, allow additional insights.

It is not clear that males are more promiscuous than females, although men in general have sexual intercourse with more partners than do women (Hunt, 1974), a difference which is particularly evident when male homosexuals are contrasted with lesbians. The difference in number of partners is even evident in permissive cultures, such as Mangaia where female premarital sexuality is encouraged (Marshall, 1971). Males are also more likely than females to have extramarital affairs and to have more partners than females who have extramarital affairs (Symons, 1979). These differences may be due to opportunity and socialization, however, since younger women were more likely to have had extramarital affairs than older women (Hunt, 1974).

There is little evidence for instinctive female coyness. Sorenson (1973) found that 58% of the males versus only 19% of the females thought that sex was "all right with someone known for only a few hours." Yet in a nonrepresentative urban sample of over 106,000 women conducted by *Cosmopolitan* magazine, 69% reported sexual intercourse with a man on the first date (Wolfe, 1980). Although that figure seemed rather high, in a small-scale study I conducted in 1980 of 38 randomly selected teen-age women at a suburban high school, 50% of the women were nonvirgins and 33% of nonvirgins had engaged in sex on a first date. It would appear that not all females hold back to identify males with the best genes.

Monogamy and Polygamy

There are, of course, cultural double standards affecting sexual behavior, such that it is more acceptable for a man to have multiple partners, for an older man to be involved with a younger woman, and in many cultures for a man to have more than one wife. Roughly 70% of the world's cultures are polygynous while less than 1% are polyandrous (Ford & Beach, 1951). When polyandry does occur, as in the Todas, Tubi-Kawahil, Tre-ba, and some Pahau-speaking people of North India, it seems to be found among poor men and entails two brothers sharing a wife, which ensures that both husbands are related to the offspring (Barash, 1979). Polyandry is also extremely rare in nature although it is found in the jaconas and a few other species (Orians, 1969).

While prevalence of a double standard could be due to the fact that men control the political and economic institutions worldwide, and thus make rules to suit themselves, cross-species comparison produces a more complicated picture. Orians (1969) studied the conditions favoring monogamy and polygamy and found close relationships with parental investment and infant care dynamics. Monogamy was much more common in birds than in mammals, more common in birds inhabiting harsh environments than those occupying more abundant environments, and in birds whose young were slow to develop. Among mammals, monogamy was more common among carnivores (e.g., foxes, badgers) than among herbivorides. In each of the monogamous species, the ecology required the male to make a greater investment in the care of the offspring than in polygymous species, thus making the male less able to divide his attention and resources among the offspring by several females. While this analysis implies that the environment has determined the males' mating behavior, polygamy may also benefit the female. Altmann, Wagner, and Lenington (1977) discussed studies of redwing blackbirds that found that the number of chicks fledged per female was positively associated with the number of females in the harem. Because of various advantages of group life, a female "may obtain a higher fitness by mating polygamously with a given male than monogamously with the same male."

It is not clear whether the same dynamics operate in humans, although ecology-economic factors do affect human mating systems. Coppinger & Rosenblatt (1966), for example, found cross-culturally that when spouses were dependent on each other for economic subsistence, the institution of romantic love was less strongly present. Heath (1958) reported cross-cultural data indicating that when the female in a society made a substantial contribution to the couple's economic subsistence, the groom paid a bride price, but when the female made less of an economic contribution, the groom received a dowry. Finally, Ember (1978) reported that men were more likely to fear sex with women in cultures in which population pressures on resources made the avoidance of pregnancy desirable, again suggesting human sensitivity to ecological dynamics.

Other data, however, seem less congruent with the sociobiological analysis stressing positive economic and environmental factors in multiple-partner sexuality. Osmond (1965) indicated that monogamy is favored by societies with more complex socioeconomic structures, whereas polygyny is favored by cultures with simpler economics. If a complex economy is assumed to offer a more benign environment for offspring and demand less resource contribution from the male, this would seem to be directly counter to the sociobiological prediction. It is not clear, however, that offspring born in a complex economy are less needful of the contribution of the father. There is also little evidence of a relationship between human monogamy and environmental climate (Munroe & Munroe, 1980). Also contrary to the analysis linking diminished need for male resources with polygamy are the findings of Edwards (1973) on attitudes toward extramarital sex. Upper- and middle-class individuals, who would be in better positions to support multiple partners and their offspring, were less likely than lower-class people to endorse extramarital sex. It would appear that sociobiology cannot adequately account for human polygamy.

Trivers (1972) has extended the analysis of the evolution of polygamy with the suggestion that when one of the genders invests considerably more resources in the offspring, members of the other gender will compete among themselves for polygamous mating with the contributing gender. The reason is that if one gender makes most of the investment in the offspring, the other gender can reproduce with multiple partners, increasing the number of its surviving offspring. This makes the opposite sex worth fighting for. The more competition there is, the more selection pressure there will be for large, strong, and aggressive competitors (and a small number of "sneaky cheaters"). Of course, such selection pressure would only operate on the competing gender, which is usually the male, and it tends to produce sexual dimorphism or a difference in size, form, ornamentation, or weaponry between males and females. Alexander, Hoagland, Howard, Noonan, and Sherman (1980) have found a linear relationship between the magnitude of sexual dimorphism and the average number of females per successful male across a variety of species. In humans, males are somewhat but not substantially larger than females, and when this difference is interpolated with that of other species, it predicts a ratio of greater than one, but less than three females per male. As Wilson (1978) observed, "This prediction is close to reality; we know we are a mildly polygamous species."

Although sexual dimorphism may have been the result of selection pressure resulting from male combat, there is also some evidence that sexual dimorphism is associated with competition between the genders in the form of rape. Berry and Shine (1980) studied a number of species of turtles and found that the greater the sexual dimorphism, the greater the likelihood of forced insemination. While it is interesting to note that in humans, males rarely marry females larger than themselves (Gillis & Avis, 1980), there is no evidence that this pattern developed to facilitate male sexual dominance. Further discussion of human rape will be made in the section on aggression.

Sexual dimorphism does not always favor the male, of course. Ecological factors and the demands of pregnancy and lactation can result in cases where the female of the species (e.g., the brown bat) is larger than the male (Ralls, 1977). There may be definite risks to males when females become larger than the male, for in species such as the mantis, black widow spider, and ampid fly, the female cannibalizes the male after she has accepted his genetic contribution.

Gender Roles

As a consequence of their greater parental investment, human females are predicted by sociobiologists to demonstrate greater commitment to the offspring than males (Symons, 1979). Cross-culturally, women have had primary responsibility for the care of children and the performance of domestic tasks, whereas men performed most political, military, and trade activities (Murdock & Provost, 1973; Whyte, 1978). While Goldberg (1977) and others have argued that selection pressure favored individuals with personality traits appropriate for their gender roles, there is little evidence that differences between males and females in child care personality are genetically based. While studies have found that wives invested more time in their infants than their husbands (Rebelsky & Hanks, 1973), in Berman's (1980) review of responsiveness to the young it could not be concluded that women were necessarily more responsive to children than were men.

Rosenblatt and Cunningham (1977) suggested that gender patterning of personality and division of labor were based on female mobility restrictions occurring with pregnancy and nursing. With ineffective controls on fertility, high infant mortality rates, and short life spans, a substantial portion of the woman's life in a small-scale culture was devoted to child care. It is not surprising, then, that cross-culturally women have been socialized to be nurturant, responsible, and obedient rather than self-reliant and achievement oriented (Barry, Bacon, & Child, 1957). In current Western society, however, families are smaller, new institutions are developing for child care, females live longer past their child care years, and obtain employment in many formally male roles. While it may take several decades for socialization practices to reflect this reality, this natural experiment may prove the best test of the relative contribution of gender genetics and learning to personality.

CHILD CARE

Extent of Parental Investment

Although evolutionary theory predicts that individuals will act to maximize the number of reproducing offspring, there are two ways of doing this, termed by some population geneticists 'r-selection' and 'K-selection' (Pianka, 1970). The pattern of r-selection essentially involves producing many offspring and investing as little resources as possible in each. The r-selection pattern is more common in variable, unpredictable, temperate environments. The alternate pattern, K-selection, involves producing fewer total offspring, but investing more resources in each. K-selection is more common in predictable, high-density, and tropical environments.

With its small litter size, slow gestation, and long time necessary for offspring to reach reproductive age, humans are clearly a K-selection species. Yet some humans, such as those low in IQ, evidence higher fertility than others (Udry, 1976), leaning toward an r-selection pattern. In addition to contraceptive use and attitudes (Eagly & Anderson, 1974), researchers might explore the ecology, including perceived infant mortality rates and economic stability of different groups, to understand the motivation for high and low fertility rates.

Trivers and Willard (1973) suggested that ecological factors not only affect fertility rates but also the type of offspring produced. They indicated that when the condition of the environment and thus the mother was poor, male offspring would be less fit after the period of parental investment, and this would affect the male's ability to compete for females, and thus his reproductive success. It was predicted and found that in poor environments there was a higher ratio of births of females to males, perhaps due to higher male infant mortality. Under positive environmental circumstances, a well-bred male can produce more offspring than a female. Males are preferred over females as offspring in many human societies. In the United States, couples with a son are less likely to be divorced than couples with only daughters, but since this effect is stronger in the less well-educated, the cause may be sexist attitudes (Spanier & Glick, 1981).

While it may be in the parents' genetic interest to reproduce copiously, this may conflict with the interests of the offspring (Trivers, 1974). During the period of dependency, each offspring may want to secure maximal parental investment, even if it is to the detriment of the siblings. To secure such favoritism, each child might be expected to exaggerate both its genetic fitness and its need for resources. The parents are equally related to all their offspring, and their inclusive fitness might be maximized if the children behave altruistically, rather than egotistically toward each other leading to battles involving issues of sharing, fairness, and moral development. Sibling squabbling might be expected to subside when parental investment is no longer needed, although little seems to be written on such conflict and its reconciliation.

Parents may not invest equally in each of their offspring. There seems to be a tendency for parents to invest most in the first born, since that offspring is closest to the age of reproduction, and next most in the last offspring, since resources are no longer needed for subsequent children (Barash, 1979). In line with the latter tendency, older parents may be more generous with their children than younger parents, again because of a reduced expectation for additional demands on their resources (Barash, 1979). Post menopausal grandmothers may follow similar dynamics, although grandparent-child interactions are all but unexplored (Feldman & Nash, 1979).

Because of their genetic and resource investment, parents may continue to try to influence the lives and especially the mate selection and reproduction of their offspring. Trivers (1974) suggested that parental involvement in the reproductive behavior of their offspring may extend to manipulating the children's sexual orientation. There may be circumstances in which the parents can maximize their inclusive fitness by concentrating their investment in selected offspring and by manipulating the other offsprings to contribute to those siblings, instead of concentrating on the sibling's own reproductive success. This could even include manipulating sons to be celibate (i.e., priesthood, military career) or homosexual. Some weak evidence for this hypothesis is provided by Suarez and Przybeck (1980), who found that male homosexuals were more likely to come from a family with a larger number of males than females. Slater (1962) also found that male homosexuals were more likely to be later born rather than first born. Both results are congruent with the hypothesis that homosexual orientation is produced only when the reproducing role for the next generation has been insured. Wilson (1978) preferred a genetic mechanism rather than parental manipulation as a cause for homosexuality but suggested that such genes could be maintained in the population due to the gain in inclusive fitness provided a homosexual who engaged in kin selection altruism. Such speculations seem to have extremely limited face validity, but may warrant research on sibling interactions and helping behavior shown by homosexuals.

Protecting Parental Investment

It is in the genetic interest of parents to invest their resources in their own offspring, but not in other parents' offspring. Some species, such as the cuckoo bird, actually deposit eggs in the nests of other birds so they will not have to do the investing (hence the term *cuckold*), while in other species such as certain acanthocephalan worms, the wombat, and many primates, the male deposits a copulatory plug after sex to insure certainty of paternity (Wilson, 1975; Barash, 1979).

Erickson and Zenone (1976) have found that ring dove males engaged in more vigorous courting and displayed less aggression to "virgin" females who had not been exposed to other males, and who would thus entail a minimal risk of prior fertilization or commitment compared to other females. In some species the male insures his paternity by allowing no other male to enter his territory during breeding season. Male primates with well-defended territories, such as the siamang, incidentally, tend to spend a great deal of time with their young, while less territorial species such as baboons, macaques, and chimpanzees show less paternal care (Barash, 1979). Avoiding investments in unrelated offspring sometimes takes extreme forms; the bluebird neglects to feed or defend unrelated offspring of a new mate while the langur usually kills his potential stepchildren after deposing a rival and securing his mate and her offspring (Wilson, 1975). In our species, at least in the United States, sexually inexperienced people are preferred as date and marriage partners primarily by other sexually inexperienced individuals, not by everyone (Istavan & Griffitt, 1980). Yet husbands do show moralistic aggression if they discover their spouses' sexual infidelity. It has even been suggested that a period of engagement prior to marriage was instiuted to insure that the female was not pregnant from a prior liaison (Dawkins, 1976). Further, the more children a divorced or widowed mother has, the less her likelihood of remarriage (Bureau of the Census, 1975).

While most adoptions in the United States involve relatives, some people are willing to adopt unrelated offspring including children of other races. Yet relatively little is known of the decision processes, adjustment outcomes, and responses of relatives, particularly to cross-racial adoption (Zastrow, 1977). Daly and Wilson (1980) reported that in the United States in 1976, children living with one natural and one stepparent were 2.2 to 6.9 times as likely to be abused as children living with two natural parents, and 1.1 to 1.4 times as likely to be neglected. While two stepparents, especially those who adopt due to infertility, could be more caring, much more needs to be learned about the dynamics of such attachments. Alexander (1977) provided some additional insight on the association of offspring genetic relatedness with social structure cross-culturally. Alexander (1977) reasoned that since fathers have a genetic overlap with their offspring of 50%, whereas the mother's brother, or maternal uncle, has an overlap of 25%, the uncle should have much less interest in his sister's offspring than her husband should have, that is, unless the offspring's paternity is in doubt. Variables that make paternal identity doubtful, such as husband absences on hunting or military trips, separation of the living quarters of spouses, and social tolerance of extramarital sexuality, appear to be associated with an increased likelihood of the institution of the avunculate. With the avunculate, the mother's brother is responsible for the discipline and support of the offspring, rather than the mother's legal husband. This institution follows the logic of kin selection altruism. Each maternal uncle can be certain that he is related to his sister's children irrespective of the identity of the father, just as he cannot be certain whether he is related to his own wife's offspring. In societies employing the avunculate, it is also common for kinship terms to be matrilineal, so that the children would take the mother's surname rather than the father's.

Alexander's (1977) sociobiological analysis is in direct conflict with main sequence kinship theory associated with Murdock (1949) and others (reviewed by Narrol, 1970). Murdock (1949) argued that systems of kinship and residence were based on the relative economic contribution of males and females. Matrilineality, matrilocality, and the prevalence of the avunculate were believed to be based on substantial subsistence contributions from the female. Further cross-cultural work to test these competing hypotheses seems indicated. At the same time, it might be useful to examine the support systems of unmarried mothers to find vestiges of the avunculate in our own society.

AGGRESSION

Resources and Aggression

The sociobiological prospective on aggression differs from those of ethologists and social psychologists. Lorenz (1965) has analyzed how aggression may serve the individual in achieving dominance and territory and thus facilitating reproduction, but has argued that aggression is restrained by submission gestures and pain cues from the defeated adversary, for the good of the species in all creatures but man.

It is interesting to note that when male children are in conflict, those not wishing to compete try to make themselves appear smaller, a submission gesture found in other species (Ginsburg, Pollman, & Wauson, 1977). Yet when humans are angered, pain cues from the victim do not always deter aggression (Rule & Leger, 1976; Baron, 1979), although an apology may reduce retaliatory aggression (Cunningham, Note 2). Nonetheless, sociobiologists point out that there is little restraint for the good of the species evident in nature (Wilson, 1975) and that other species, such as the chimpanzee, engage in fatal combat, murder, and infanticide.

Contemporary social psychological approaches to aggression (reviewed by Baron, 1977) consider internal emotional states, individual differences, and situation factors. The one variable psychologists have not considered in detail, however, is the one of most importance to the sociobiologists, the biological advantage to be gained by the individual in being aggressive. Barash (1977) stated this point succinctly: "Evolutionary theory suggests a simple answer to the question, when should an individual be aggressive? . . . Each individual should be aggressive where such behavior increases the individual's inclusive fitness."

The attainment and defense of resources appears as a major goal of human aggression in groups and is strikingly evident in the analysis of small-scale cultures such as the Maori of New Zealand. Vayda (1976) argued that the Maori went to war whenever their population density became too high. Their choice over which neighbor to expand against was based on genealogical lineage; the Maori tribes attacked whichever other tribe to which they had the least relationship. The Mundurucu similarly went to war whenever their protein supply fell below their needs, while the Yanomami conducted their wars over women or revenge for deaths caused by competition for women (Wilson 1978). Yet while these conflicts reflect sociobiological dynamics, it seems a bit naive to attribute the causes of modern war to any single class of variables. A complex interaction of social attitudes and values (misperception of the enemy, power motivation) as well as ecological variables (number of available young men, economic need for space and raw materials) is likely involved (Pruitt & Snyder, 1969).

Although the effect of crowding has been explored (Lawrence, 1974), it may be difficult to manipulate some of the other variables—such as access to a mate, control of land, and meaningful social rank—in a laboratory situation. While I can imagine experiments in which men compete to spend a night with a campus beauty queen or randomly selected property owners are told they will have to move to make way for a shopping center, there would be problems with an ethical review panel. Yet experiments on aggression which employ frustrating competition or the confederate depriving the subject of some resource, such as money, may be effective analogs (Foa, Megonigal, & Greipp, 1976).

Age and Aggression

Fox (1980) has argued that because older males have historically had control of a societies' scarce resources and through those resources had greater access to women, the interests of the young "have nots" and older "have gots" have necessarily been at conflict. Formal law making as well as implicit taboos may have been instituted to control impetuous unmated males. Fox (1980) further suggested the young man who could control himself so as not to attack a powerful, established elder was most likely to succeed. Thus, the tendency for males to mature sexually more slowly than females may have been selected for, if males who tried to compete for mates before they were full grown were injured or killed. It is interesting to note in this context that in Silverman and Maxwell's (1978) cross-cultural survey, institutionalized deference was much more commonly paid to elderly males than elderly females suggesting older males were more to be feared. No research was found indicating that attitudes toward the elderly were more negative in polygymous societies, where some older males have a disproportionate number of females. Attitudes toward the elderly did tend to be more positive when older people had valuable information on techniques of survival to share (Maxwell & Silverman, 1970).

In the United States, it is interesting to note that those who had most to gain from reduced demand on resources, the young and urban dwelling, were most likely to approve of euthanasia and suicide (Singh, 1979). It seems difficult to separate sociobiological from learned attitudinal motivations, yet it may be interesting to examine intergenerational dynamics using experimental aggression and cooperation designs. Graziano (1978), for example, found that first graders were likely to defer to third graders by overcompensating them for their performance on task, even without explicit demands.

Gender and Aggression

Males are presumed by sociobiologists to aggress against men of other societies and generations primarily in order to increase their survival and the number and survival of their offspring. The latter dynamics could, unfortunately, motivate sexual aggression by men toward women. Rape is found in other species than our own (Barry & Shine, 1980) and seems to be particularly likely with soldiers during wartime, when normal social restraints are absent (Brownmiller, 1975). As a reproductive pattern, rape would seem to be an r-selection strategy, but data on such questions as number of viable offspring sired by rapists and the number of cross-racial versus intraracial rapes were not found (Heilbrum & Cross, 1979). Cross-culturally, rape tended to be more common in societies where divorce was more difficult to obtain (Minturn, Grosse, & Haider, 1969). This could have been due to the fact that those males who desired to possess multiple women were prevented from doing so legitimately in serial monogamy, and thus resorted to rape. Alternately the association could have been due to frustrating cultural attitudes toward women, marriage, or sex.

The actual potential for rape by the average male also remains unknown. Donnerstein and Hallam (1978) have found that erotic stimuli tended to increase male's aggression toward females, while Malamuth, Heim, and Feshbach (1980) found that presentation of a film depicting a rape in which the victim experienced both pain and an orgasm proved to be sexually arousing to college males. The latter study and other experiments have found that portrayal of rape without female enjoyment was not sexually arousing to males. Somewhat disconcerting, however, is the finding by Malamuth, Haber, and Feshbach (1980) that 51% of the college males in their sample indicated that they could behave as a rapist under some circumstances if assured they would not be punished. Psychological and sociobiological dimensions of male sexual aggression require a great deal more exploration.

Men appear more willing to behave aggressively than women, although women can certainly behave aggressively (Frodi, Macauley, & Thome, 1977; Richardson, Bernstein, & Taylor, 1979). Females of other species have demonstrated extreme aggressiveness in defending their young; it would be interesting to see further examination of female protective aggressiveness in the laboratory. Little is known, as well, about the nature of female sexual aggressiveness. Females presumably are less likely to resort to violence to insure sexual intercourse, because of the gender-linked difference in size and because it may be in the male's best genetic interest to comply. A woman of independent means (inheritance, career, or welfare aid) who did not require the resources of a husband might perhaps go to some lengths to secure the genes of a particularly fit male. It might be informative to explore the sexual behavior of women in that position.

Relatedness and Aggression

To maximize inclusive fitness, an individual should be less likely to aggress against close relatives than the genetically unrelated. The fact that murder of the spouse is more common than murder of parents or offspring fits this hypothesis, but the fact that murder of offspring in humans does occur cannot easily be explained using sociobiological theory. It might be informative to explore the dynamics of such aggression using laboratory aggression and game procedures with related individuals as the subjects. It would be interesting to see, for example, if wives were more likely to shock their husband than their sister or men were willing to accept a large number of shocks to protect their children.

Human willingess to protect relatives could be used in the interests of world peace. At present, it appears that U.S. foreign policies toward Israel and a host of other countries are often shaped by pressure generated by citizens who have relatives living in those countries. Worldwide hostage exchange, similar to the practice of exogamous marriage, might be an effective way of preventing the leaders of world powers from acting precipitously. Thus, the children of the leaders of the major nations could be required to live in the capitals of their competitors. If reproduction and protection of offspring are fundamental biological motivations, then even the most cynical leaders might hesitate about launching a surprise attack if it would inevitably result in the death of their children. To insure absolute commitment to the system, it would be best if the leaders could receive vasectomies or hysterectomies so that they could produce no more off-spring if the hostages were forfeit.

It is difficult to assess to what extent there exists a predisposition to aggress against genetically distant groups. Hoetink (1973) has argued that antagonism is greatest between human groups who maintain the most discrepant body images for themselves (i.e., blue-eyed, fair-skinned, and muscular versus brown-eyed, dark-skinned, and lanky). Some racism has been evident in warfare. Of the American veteran combat troops in the Pacific, asked in 1944 what they would like to see happen to the Japanese after the war, 42% responded that they would like to wipe out the whole Japanese nation (Stouffer et al., 1949). Only 25% of the combat soldiers in Europe preferred such a fate for the Germans. The safety of prisoners has been rumored to be poor when the combatants were from different races although little data has been collected.

Effects of race in aggression have also been found in research in the United States. Inn, Sheeler, and Sparling (1977) found that white police officers were more likely to shoot at black than white suspects. Donnerstein and Donnerstein (1975) found that whites were likely to deliver more severe shocks to blacks than whites in a laboratory setting, while Wilson and Rogers (1975) found blacks in a similar procedure aggressed more against whites than blacks. Yet such racist main effects are not consistently evident. Crosby, Bromley, and Saxe (1980) reviewed this literature and concluded that racial bias in aggressive responding was "pervasive but subtle." Illustrating this trend, Rogers and Prentice-Dunn (1980) found that when there was no provocation, whites aggressed somewhat less against blacks than against whites, but when there was provocation, whites aggressed much more against blacks than whites. It should be clear from such results that racial discrimination in aggression is not reflexive, but can be elicited by the appropriate situation. To pursue the sociobiological hypothesis, it would be interesting to see if more racial biasing would be shown by individuals as a function of their ethnic origins and physical phenotypic dissimilarity to members of other races and would be stronger in competition for valued incentives than following simple insults.

CONFORMITY AND SOCIAL ORGANIZATION

Sociobiologists have argued that humans are genetically disposed toward conformity and a social structure involving religious indoctrination. Wilson (1979) speculated further that humans are physiologically programmed to participate in the process of "sacralization," which involves the learning of a cosmology and a simplified moral system, combined with deep emotional commitment to the symbols and to other believers. According to Wilson (1975), "human beings are absurdly easy to indoctrinate, they seek it."

Religious concepts and customs do seem to be found in all societies (Murcock, 1945). Further, subjects in the Asch (1951) conformity and Milgrim (1963) obedience studies demonstrated exceptionally high responsiveness to social pressure. In the model culture procedure (MacNeal & Sherif, 1973) moreover, subjects implicitly indoctrinated generations of other subjects into reporting aberrant perceptual judgments. Yet subjects also manifested substantial individual differences in response to social pressure, as well as such sensitivity to situational variables that obedience rates have varied from 80% to 0% across conditions (Tilker, 1970). While Wilson (1975) was aware of the plasticity and flexibility of human behavior, sociobiology provided no theoretical constructs to predict when humans would demonstrate autonomous and when herdlike collective behavior, and thus in its stronger conclusions on this topic seemed seriously misleading.

Tiger (1970) argued that the necessity for effective cooperation during wartime generated selection pressure that resulted in males who were more capable of organizing themselves hierarchically and establishing bonds of loyalty to each other than were women. He cited as evidence of this tendency the dominance of men in political and economic institutions and the widespread existence of men's formal social organizations such as the lodge, smoking club, and veteran's group which resembled artificial kin lineages and had few female counterparts. Tiger also argued that men preferred to exclude women from such organizations to prevent destabilizing sexual rivalry.

The tendency for people to organize spontaneously and arrange themselves hierarchically has not been a major focus of psychological research. Nonetheless, the classic Sherif (1961) Robber's Cave study on group relations might be replicated to determine if females responded to competition with the same increased stratification and outgroup hostility as males. Similarly, studies concerned with leader and follower responses under stress (e.g., Klein, 1976) might be expanded to include female subjects. Another way of examining the capacity for hierarchical discipline is in terms of response to persuasion, conformity, and obedience pressure. In Eagly's (1978) discussion of gender differences in influenceability, however, the vast majority of studies reported no significant differences.

In his discussion of social structure, Wilson (1978) also raised the issue of cross-cultural universals in social behavior. While some psychologists have discussed the question of universals (e.g., Triandis, 1977; Lonner, 1979), this has not been a prominent feature of mainstream theory and research. Murdock's (1945) list of the categories of social phenomena found in one form or another in all cultures is instructive:

> age-grading, athletic sports, bodily adornment, calendar, cleanliness training, community organization, cooking, cooperative labor, cosmology, courtship, dancing, decorative art, divination, division of labor, dream interpretation, education, eschatology, ethics, ethnobotany, etiquette, faith healing, family feasting, fire making, folklore, food taboos, funeral rites, games, gestures, gift giving, government, greetings, hair styles, hospitality, housing, hygiene, incest taboos, inheritance rules, joking, kin groups, kinship nomenclature, language, law, luck, superstitions, magic, marriage, mealtimes, medicine, obstetrics, penal sanctions, personal names, population policy, postnatal care, pregnancy usages, property rights, propitiation of supernatural beings, puberty customs, religious ritual, residence rules, sexual restrictions, soul concepts, status differentiation, surgery, tool making, trade, visiting, weaving, and weather control.

The universal existence of a general category of behavior does not necessitate genetic mechanisms and could be due to consistency in the physical environment or to learned responses which were so effective they spread universally by cultural diffusion. Of course, Wilson (1975) and other sociobiologists did ascribe a large portion of human behavior to socialization and learning. Nonetheless, the fact that some behaviors are found in all societies implies that those behaviors may be either particularly socially functional, which may reveal something of human motivation, or be particularly easy to learn, which may be evidence for genetic predispositions.

On a Social Psychological Paradigm Shift

The present social psychological paradigm was best articulated by Kurt Lewin in the statement that behavior is a function of the person and the environment. Social psychologists have generally operationalized this paradigm in the form of research on the effect of manipulated social environmental stimuli combined with paper-and-pencil measures of personality

and cognitive processes on specific overt behaviors or self-reported preferences. While sociobiologists might agree that behavior is a function of the
person and the environment, they would suggest that in addition to
stimulating learned responses, the environment has selected for certain
genetically based response dispositions and that the person is fundamen-
tally oriented toward performing behaviors which maximize the likelihood
of the survival of his genes.

The sociobiological perspective may represent concern with a deeper
level of motivation and a commitment to questions of ultimate causation
rather than issues of proximate causation (Symonds, 1979). Proximate
causation involves "how" questions concerning the specific eliciting and
processing mechanisms involved in the expression of a behavior. Social
psychology's concern with proximate causation is evident in its focus on
short-term social behavior such as spontaneous helping, attraction between
strangers, and provoked aggression in which the goal of the research is the
demonstration of the causal effect of external stimuli and internal attributions on a response. This approach can be justified on both theoretical and
practical grounds. Yet it is possible to approach behavioral questions at
another level of analysis without entering the infinite regress from psychology into physiology, chemistry, and physics.

Ultimate causation refers to "why" questions of the evolutionary
significance and function of a behavior. Sociobiology might thus ask: What
an individual would gain by enacting a behavior, why the outcome of the
behavior is experienced as rewarding, why the initial reinforcement used in
the acquisition of the behavior was motivating, how often various classes
of behaviors producing various types of outcomes are performed, and what
are the circumstances stimulating maximal performance of a behavior (i.e.,
for whom might a person risk most to save, attempt most vigorously to
seduce, or fight with greatest verocity)?

Ultimate questions involve a danger of teleology and are not always
amenable to rigorously controlled laboratory experimentation. A shift of
social psychology toward the sociobiological approach would entail greater
interest in cross-cultural and cross-species comparisons and greater concern
with obtaining actuarial frequency and simple correlational data. Psychologists have, of course, conducted this type of research in the past, such as
that by Ekman, Friesen, and Ellsworth (1972) and Izard (1977) on
Darwin's hypothesis of universals in the facial expression of emotion and
by Wheeler and Nezlek (1977) on the naturally occurring frequency of
social interactions, but such procedures remain underemployed. Research

on questions such as to whom an individual would lend most money, how rapidly males and females become infatuated, or which other group an ethnic juvenile gang would be most likely to attack might seem mundane if the behaviors are believed to be totally dependent on social training. In the light of sociobiological predictions, however, the data may prove revealing about human nature.

It should be clear from the foregoing review that sociobiology cannot provide a complete alternative paradigm for social psychology. Sociobiology simply has little to contribute on many traditional topics, such as attitude change, bargaining, dissonance, group problem solving, person perception, or self-disclosure. Actually, Wilson (1978), in contrast to Trivers (1977), believes that sociobiology will eventually be absorbed by the social sciences, rather than the reverse.

With an interest in different questions, and commitments to different methodologies, social psychologists and sociobiologist may continue to reject each other's evidence and generally talk past each other's concerns and objections. The future direction which sociobiology takes could be influenced by the results of findings by social psychologists. Yet no matter what ultimately becomes of sociobiology, social psychological knowledge can be enriched by active pursuit of the questions of altruism, attraction, sexuality, family relations, aggression, and conformity raised by sociobiology.

REFERENCE NOTES

1. Cunningham, M. R. & Graf, C. Beauty in the eyes of the beheld: The sociobiological basis of female facial physical attractiveness. Manuscript in preparation.

2. Cunningham, M. R. The behavioral differentiation of emotion: Anger, guilt and sometimes having to say you're sorry. Under editorial review.

REFERENCES

Alexander, R. D. Natural selection and the analysis of human sociality. In C. E. Goulden (ed.), *Changing scenes in natural sciences.* Philadelphia: Academy of Natural Sciences, 1977.

Alexander, R. D., Hoogland, T. L., Howard, R. D., Noonan, K. M., & Sherman, P. W. Sexual dimorphisms and breeding systems in pinnipeds, ungulates, primates and humans. In N. A. Chagnon and W. G. Ivons (eds.), *Evolutionary biology and human social organization*. Scituate, Mass.: Duxbury Press.

Alexander, R. D. & Sherman, P. W. Local mate competition and parental investment in social insects. *Science*, 1977, *196*, 494-500.

Altman, S. A., Wagner, S. S., & Lenington, S. Two models for the evolution of polygyny. *Behavioral Ecology and Sociobiology*, 1977, *2*, 397-410.

Asch, S. Effects of group pressure upon the modification and distortion of judgement. In H. Guetzkow (ed.), *Groups, leadership and men*. Pittsburgh: Carnegie Press, 1951.

Barash, D. P. *Sociobiology & behavior*. New York: Elsevier, 1977.

Barash, D. P. *The whisperings within*. New York: Harper & Row, 1979.

Baron, R. A. *Human aggression*. New York: Plenum Press, 1977.

Baron, R. A. Effects of victim's pain cues, victim's race, and level of prior instigation upon physical aggression. *Journal of Applied Social Psychology*, 1979, *9*, 103-114.

Barry, H., III, Bacon, M. K., & Child, I. L. A cross-cultural survey of some sex differences in socialization. *Journal of Abnormal and Social Psychology*, 1957, *55*, 327-332.

Beck, S. P., Ward-Hull, C. I., & McLear, P. M. Variables related to women's somatic preferences of the male and female body. *Journal of Personality and Social Psychology*, 1976, *34*, 1200-1210.

Benson, P. L., Karabenick, S. A., & Lerner, R. M. Pretty pleases: The effects of physical attractiveness, race and sex on receiving help. *Journal of Experimental and Social Psychology*, 1976, *12*, 9-25.

Berndt, T. J. Lack of acceptance of reciprocity norms in preschool children. *Developmental Psychology*, 1979, *15*, 662-663.

Berry, J. F. & Shine, R. Sexual size dimorphism and sexual selection in turtles (order Testudines). *Occologia*, 1980, *44*, 185-191.

Berscheid, E. & Walster, E. Physical attractiveness. In L. Berkowitz (ed.), *Advances in experimental social psychology*. New York: Academic Press, 1974.

Berscheid, E. & Walster, E. *Interpersonal attraction*. Reading, Mass.: Addison-Wesley, 1978.

Brigham, J. C. & Richardson, C. B. Race, sex and helping in the marketplace. *Journal of Applied Social Psychology*, 1979, *9*, 314-322.

Brigham, J. C. & Williamson, N. L. Cross-racial recognition and age: When you're over 60, do they still "all look alike?" *Personality and Social Psychology Bulletin*, 1979, *5*, 218.

Brownmiller, S. *Against our will: Men, women and rape*. New York: Simon & Schuster, 1975.

Bryan, J. H. & London, P. Altruistic behavior by children. *Psychological Bulletin*, 1970, *13*, 200-211.

Bureau of the Census, *Current Population Reports, Series P-20, No. 312*. Washington, D.C.: Government Printing Office, 1975.

Campbell, D. T. On the conflicts between biological and social evolution and between psychology and moral tradition. *American Psychologist*, 1975, *30*, 1103-1112.

Cialdini, R. B. & Kenrick, D. T. Altruism or hedonism: A social development perspective on the relationship of negative mood state and helping. *Journal of Personality and Social Psychology,* 1976, *34,* 907-914.

Clark, M. S. & Mills, T. Interpersonal attraction in exchange and communal relationships. *Journal of Personality and Social Psychology,* 1979, *37,* 12-24.

Clutton-Brock, T. H. & Harvey, P. H. *Readings in sociobiology,* Reading, Mass.: W. H. Freeman, 1978.

Coppinger, R. M. & Rosenblatt, P. C. Romantic love and subsistence dependence of spouses. *South West Journal of Anthropology,* 1968, *24,* 310-331.

Coulson, J. C. The influence of the pair-bond and age on the breeding biology of the kittiwake, gull, Rissa Tridactyla. *Journal of Animal Ecology,* 1966, *35,* 269-279.

Crosby, F., Bromley, S., & Saxe, L. Recent unobtrusive studies of black and white discrimination and prejudice: A literature review. *Psychological Bulletin,* 1980, *87,* 546-563.

Cunningham, M. R. Personality and the structure of the nonverbal communication of emotion. *Journal of Personality,* 1977, *45,* 564-584.

Cunningham, M. R. Weather, mood and helping behavior: Quasi experiments with the sunshine samaritan. *Journal of Personality and Social Psychology,* 1979, *37,* 1947-1956.

Cunningham, M. R., Steinberg, J., & Grev, R. Wanting to and having to help: Separate motivations for positive mood and guilt induced helping. *Journal of Personality and Social Psychology,* 1980, *38,* 181-192.

Daly, M. & Wilson, M. Discriminative parental solicitude: A biological perspective. *Journal of Marriage and the Family,* 1980, *42,* 277-288.

Dawkins, R. *The selfish gene.* New York: Oxford University Press, 1976.

Dermer, M. & Theil, D. When beauty may fail. *Journal of Personality and Social Psychology,* 1975, *31,* 1168-1177.

Dewsbury, D. A. Effects of novelty on copulatory behavior. *Psychological Bulletin,* 1981, *89,* 464-482.

Donnerstein, E. & Donnerstein, M. The effects of attitudinal similarity on interracial aggression. *Journal of Personality and Social Psychology,* 1975, *43,* 485-502.

Donnerstein, E. & Hallam, J. Facilitating effects of erotica on aggression against women. *Journal of Personality and Social Psychology,* 1978, *36,* 1270-1277.

Eagley, A. H. Sex differences in influenceability. *Psychological Bulletin,* 1978, *85,* 86-116.

Eagley, A. H. & Anderson, P. Sex role and attitudinal correlates of desired family size. *Journal of Applied Social Psychology,* 1974, *4,* 151-164.

Edwards, J. N. Extramarital involvement: Fact and theory. *Journal of Sex Research,* 1973, *9,* 210-224.

Eibl-Eibesfeldt, I. *Ethology, the biology of behavior.* New York: Holt, Rinehart & Winston.

Einswiller, T., Deaux, K., & Willits, J. E. Similarity, sex and requests for small favors. *Journal of Applied Social Psychology,* 1971, *1,* 284-291.

Ekman, D., Friesen, W. V., & Ellsworth, P. *Emotions in the human face.* New York: Pergamon, 1972.

Ember, C. R. Men's fear of sex with women: A cross-cultural study. *Sex Roles,* 1978, *4,* 657-678.

Erikson, C. J. & Zenone, P. G. Courtship differences in male ring dove: Avoidance of cuckoldry. *Science,* 1976, *192,* 1363-1365.

Feinman, S. & Gill, G. W. Sex differences in physical attractiveness preferences. *Journal of Social Psychology,* 1978, *105,* 43-52.

Feldman, R. E. Response to compatriot and foreigners who seek assistance. *Journal of Personality and Social Psychology,* 1968, *10,* 202-214.

Feldman, S. D. The presentation of shortness in everyday life—height and heightism in American society. Presented at the meeting of the American Sociological Association, 1971.

Feldman, S. S. & Nash, S. C. Sex differences in responsiveness to babies among mature adults. *Developmental Psychology,* 1979, *15,* 430-436.

Fisher, W. A. & Byrne, D. A. Sex differences in response to erotica: Love vs. lust. *Journal of Personality and Social Psychology,* 1978, *36,* 117.

Foa, U. G., Megonigal, S., & Greipp, J. R. Some evidence against the possibility of Utopian societies. *Journal of Personality and Social Psychology,* 1976, *34,* 1043-1048.

Ford, C. S. & Beach, F. A. *Patterns of sexual behavior.* New York: Harper & Row, 1951.

Fox, R. *The red lamp of incest.* New York: Dutton, 1980.

Freedman, D. G. *Human sociobiology: A holistic approach.* New York: Free Press, 1979.

Frodi, A., Macaulay, J., & Thome, R. R. Are women always less aggressive than men? A review of the experimental literature. *Psychological Bulletin,* 1977, *84,* 634-666.

Gaertner, S. L. & Dovidio, J. F. The subtlety of white racism, arousal and helping behavior. *Journal of Personality and Social Psychology,* 1977, *35,* 691-707.

Gardner, B. T. & Wallach, L. Shapes and figures identified as a baby's head. *Perceptual and Motor Skills,* 1965, *20,* 135-142.

Ginsburg, H., Pollman, V., & Wauson, M. An ethological analysis of nonverbal inhibitors of aggressive behavior in male elementary school children. *Developmental Psychology,* 1977, *13,* 417-418.

Goldberg, S. *The inevitability of patriarchy.* London: Maurice Temple Smith, Ltd., 1977.

Gouaux, C. Induced affective states and interpersonal attraction. *Journal of Personality and Social Psychology,* 1971, *20,* 37-43.

Graziano, W. G. Standards of fair play in same-age and mixed age groups of children. *Developmental Psychology,* 1978, *14,* 524-531.

Graziano, W., Brothen, T., & Berscheid, E. Height and attraction: Do men and women see eye-to-eye? *Journal of Personality,* 1978, *46,* 128-145.

Gregory, M. S., Silvers, H., & Sutch, D. *Sociobiology and human nature.* San Francisco: Jossey-Bass, 1978.

Guthrie, R. D. *Body hotspots.* New York: Van Nostrand Reinhold, 1976.

Hamilton, W. D. The genetical theory of social behavior, I, II. *Journal of Theoretical Biology,* 1964, *7,* 1-52.

Hansson, R. O., Slade, K. M., & Slade, P. S. Urban-rural differences in responsiveness to an altruistic model. *Journal of Social Psychology*, 1978, *105*, 99-105.

Heilbrun, A. B., Jr. & Cross, J. M. An analysis of rape patterns in white and black rapists. *Journal of Social Psychology*, 1979, *108*, 83-87.

Hildebrandt, K. A. & Fitzgerald, H. E. Facial feature determinants of perceived infant cuteness. Presented at the meeting of the Midwestern Psychological Association, Chicago, May 1977.

Hoetink, H. *Slavery and race relations in America.* New York: Harper & Row, 1973.

House, J. S. & Wolf, S. Effects of urban residence on interpersonal trust and helping behavior. *Journal of Personality and Social Psychology*, 1978, *36*, 1029-1043.

Howard, J. W. & Dawes, R. M. Linear prediction of marital happiness. *Personality and Social Psychology Bulletin*, 1976, *2*, 478-480.

Huckstedt, B. Experimentelle intrsuchungen zum "Kindchenschema." *Zeitschrift fur Experimentelle un Angewandt Psychologie*, 1965, *12*, 421-450.

Hunt, J. H. *Selected readings in sociobiology.* New York: McGraw-Hill, 1980.

Hunt, M. *Sexual behavior in the 1970's.* Chicago: Playboy Press, 1974.

Inn, A., Sheeler, A. C., & Sparling, C. L. The effects of suspect race and situation hazard on police officer shooting behavior. *Journal of Applied Social Psychology*, 1977, *7*, 27-37.

Istavan, J. & Griffit, W. Effects of sexual experience on dating desirability and marriage desirability: An experimental study. *Journal of Marriage and the Family*, 80, *42*, 377-386.

Izard, C. E. *Human emotions.* New York: Plenum, 1977.

Katz, I., Glass, D. C., Lucido, D., & Farber, J. Harm doing and victim's racial or orthopedic stigma as determinants of helping behavior. *Journal of Personality*, 1979, *47*, 340-364.

Klein, A. L. Changes in leadership appraisal as a function of the stress of a simulated panic situation. *Journal of Personality and Social Psychology*, 1976, *34*, 1143-1154.

Kraut, R. E. Verbal and nonverbal cues in the perception of lying. *Journal of Personality and Social Psychology*, 1978, *36*, 380-391.

Kraut, R. E. & Johnston, R. E. Social and emotional messages of smiling: An ethological approach. *Journal of Personality and Social Psychology*, 1979, *37*, 1539-1553.

Kuhn, T. *The structure of scientific revolutions.* Chicago: University of Chicago Press, 1962.

Lawrence, T.E.S. Science and sentiment: Overview of research on crowding and human behavior. *Psychological Bulletin*, 1974, *81*, 712-720.

Levine, M. E., Vilena, T., Altman, D., & Nadien, M. Trust of the stranger: An urban/small town comparison. *Journal of Psychology*, 1976, *92*, 113-116.

Lonner, W. The search for psychological universals. In H. C. Triandis and W. W. Lambert (eds.), The *handbook of cross-culture psychology* (Vol. 1). Boston: Allyn and Bacon, 1979.

Lorenz, K. Die Angeboren formen mogliche erfahrung. *Zeitschrift fur Tierpsychologie*, 1943, *5*, 245-409.

Lorenz, K. *On aggression.* New York: Harcourt Brace Jovanovich, 1966.

Luce, T. S. The role of experience in inter-racial recognition. Presented at the meeting of the American Psychological Association, New Orleans, September 1974.

MacNeil, M. K. & Sherif, M. Norm change over subject generations as a function of arbitrariness of prescribed norms. *Journal of Personality and Social Psychology,* 1976, *34,* 762-773.

Malamuth, N. M., Haber, S., & Feshbach, S. Testing hypotheses regarding rape: Exposure to sexual violence, sex differences, and the "normality" of rapists. *Journal of Research in Personality,* 1980, *14,* 121-137.

Malamuth, N. M., Heim, M., & Feshbach, S. Sexual responsiveness of college students to rape depictions; Inhibitory and disinhibitory effects. *Journal of Personality and Social Psychology,* 1980, *38,* 399-408.

Malamuth, N. M., Shayne, E., & Pogue, B. Infant cues and stopping at the crosswalk. *Personality and Social Psychology Bulletin,* 1978, *4,* 334-336.

Malpass, R. S. & Kravitz, J. Recognition for faces of own and other races. *Journal of Personality and Social Psychology,* 1969, *13,* 330-334.

Mann, J., Berkowitz, L., Sidmon, J., Starr, S., & West, S. Satiation of the transient stimulating effects of erotic films. *Journal of Personality and Social Psychology,* 1974, *30,* 729-735.

Maxwell, R. J. & Silverman, P. Information and esteem: Cultural considerations in the treatment of the aged. *Aging and Human Development,* 1970, *1,* 361-392.

Mazor, M. D. Barren couples. *Psychology Today,* 1979, *12,* 101-111.

McAdoo, H. P. Factors relating to stability in upwardly mobile black families. *Journal of Marriage and the Family,* 1978, *40,* 761-776.

McKeachie, W. Lipstick as a determiner of first impressions of personality: An experiment for the general psychology course. *Journal of Social Psychology,* 1952, *36,* 241-244.

Milgrim, S. Behavioral study of obedience. *Journal of Abnormal and Social Psychology,* 1963, *67,* 371-378.

Minturn, L., Grosse, M., & Haider, S. Cultural patterning of sexual beliefs and behavior. *Ethnology,* 1969, *8,* 301-318.

Morse, S. T., Gruzen, J., & Reis, H. The "eye of the beholder": A neglected variable in the study of physical attractiveness. *Journal of Personality,* 1976, *44,* 209-225.

Munroe, R. L. & Munroe, R. H. Perspectives suggested by anthropological data. In H. C. Triandis & W. W. Lambert (eds.), *Handbook of cross-cultural psychology* (Vol. 1). Boston: Allyn & Bacon, 1980.

Murdock, G. P. The common denominator of culture. In R. Linton (ed.), *The science of man in the world crisis.* New York: Columbia University Press, 1945.

Murdock, G. P. *Social structure.* New York: Macmillan, 1949.

Murdock, G. P. & Provost, C. Factors in the division of labor by sex: A cross-cultural analysis. *Ethnology,* 1973, *12,* 203-225.

Naroll, R. What have we learned from cross-cultural surveys? *American Anthropologist,* 1970, *72,* 1227-1288.

Orians, G. H. On the evolution of mating systems in birds and mammals. *American Naturalist,* 1969, *103,* 589-603.

Osmond, M. Toward monogamy: A cross-cultural study of correlates of type of marriage. *Social Forces,* 1965, *44,* 8-16.

Pandey, J. Effects of benefactor and recipient status on helping behavior. *Journal of Social Psychology*, 1979, *108*, 171-176.

Pianka, E. R. On r- and K-selection *American Naturalist*, 1970, *104*, 592-597.

Poston, D. L. Characteristics of voluntary and involuntary childless wives. *Social Biology*, 1976, *23*, 198-209.

Pruitt, D. G. & Snyder, R. C. *Theory and research on the causes of war*. Englewood Cliffs, N.J.: Prentice-Hall, 1969.

Ralls, K. Sexual dimorphism in mammals: Avian models and unanswered questions. *American Naturalist*, 1977, *111*, 917-938.

Rebelsky, F. & Hanks, C. Father's verbal interaction with infants in the first three months of life. *Child Development*, 1971, *42*, 63-68.

Regan, D. T. Effects of a favor and liking on compliance. *Journal of Experimental Social Psychology*, 1971, *7*, 627-369.

Renne, K. S. Childlessness, health and marital satisfaction. *Social Biology*, 1976, *23*, 183-197.

Richardson, D. C., Bernstein, S., & Taylor, S. P. The effect of situational contingencies on female retaliative behavior. *Journal of Personality and Social Psychology*, 1979, *37*, 2044-2048.

Rogers, R. & Prentice-Dunn, S. Deindividuation and aggression: Role of models, insult, and victim's race. Presented at the meeting of the American Psychological Association, Montreal, September 1980.

Romer, D., Bontemps, M., Flynn, M., McGuire, T., & Gruder, C. L. The effects of status similarity and expectations of reciprocation upon altruistic behavior. *Personality and Social Psychology Bulletin*, 1977, *3*, 103-106.

Rosenblatt, P. C. Cross-cultural perspective on attraction. In T. L. Huston (ed.), *Foundations of interpersonal attraction*. New York: Academic Press, 1974.

Rosenblatt, P. C. & Cunningham, M. R. Sex differences in cross-cultural perspective. In B. B. Lloyd and J. Archer (eds.), *Exploring sex differences*. New York: Academic Press, 1976.

Rosenblatt, P. C. & Skoogberg, E. L. Birth order in cross cultural perspective. *Development Psychology*, 1974, *10*, 48-54.

Rothenbuhler, W. C. Behavior genetics of nest cleaning in honeybees. IV. Responses of F1 and backcross generations to disease-killed brood. *American Zoology*, 1964, *4*, 111-123.

Rule, B. G. & Leger, G. J. Pain cues and differing functions of aggression. *Canadian Journal of Behavioral Science*, 1976, *8*, 213-223.

Ruse, M. *Sociobiology: Sense or nonsense?* Dordrecht, Holland: D. Reidel, 1979.

Sahlins, M. *The use and abuse of biology*. Ann Arbor: University of Michigan, 1977.

Seligman, M. (ed.). On the generality of laws of learning. *Psychological Review*, 1970, *77*, 406-418.

Shapiro, E. G. Is seeking help from a friend like seeking help from a stranger? *Social Psychology Quarterly*, 1980, *43*, 259-263.

Sherif, M. A. *Intergroup conflict and cooperation: The robber's cave experiment*. Norman, Okla.: University Book Exchange, 1961.

Shettel-Neuber, J., Bryson, J. B., & Young, L. E. Physical attractiveness of the "other person" and jealousy. *Perconality and Social Psychology Bulletin*, 1978, *4*, 612-614.

Silverman, P. & Maxwell, R. J. How do I respect thee? Let me count the ways: Deference towards elderly men and women. *Behavioral Science Research*, 1978, *13*, 91-108.

Singh, B. K. Correlates of attitudes toward euthanasia. Social Biology, 1979, *26*, 247-254.

Slater, E. Birth order and maternal age of homosexuals. *Lancet*, 1962, *1*, 69-71.

Sorenson, R. C. *Adolescent sexuality in contemporary America.* New York: World Publishing, 1973.

Spanier, G. B. & Glick, P. C. Martal instability in the U.S.: Some correlates and recent changes. *Family Relations*, 1981, *30*.

Sternglanz, S. H., Graz, J. L., & Murakami, M. Adult preferences for infantile facial features: An ethological approach. *Animal Behavior*, 1972, *25*, 108-115.

Stouffer, S. A., Lumsdaine, A. A., Lumsdaine, M. M., Williams, R. M., Jr., Smith, M. B., Janis, I. L., Star, S. A., & Cottrell, L. S., Jr. *The American soldier: Combat and its aftermath* (Vol. 2). New York: John Wiley, 1949.

Suarez, B. K. & Przybeck, T. R. Sibling sex ratio and male homosexuality. *Archives of Sexual Behavior*, 1980, *9*, 1-12.

Symons, D. The evolution of human sexuality. New York: Oxford University Press, 1979.

Takooshian, H., Haber, S., & Lucido, D. J. Who wouldn't help a lost child? *Psychology Today*, 1977, *10*, 67-88.

Tessor, A., Gatewood, R., & Puver, M. Some determinants of gratitude. *Journal of Personality and Social Psychology*, 1968, *9*, 233-236.

Thakerar, J. M. & Iwawaki, S. Cross-cultural comparisons in interpersonal attraction of females toward males. *Journal of Social Psychology*, 1979, *108*, 121-122.

Thornstrum, S. *Harvard encyclopedia of American ethnic groups.* Cambridge, Mass.: Belknap Publishers, 1980.

Tiger, L. *Men in groups.* New York: Vintage Books, 1970.

Tilker, H. A. Socially responsible behavior as a function of observer and victim feedback. *Journal of Personality and Social Psychology*, 1970, *14*, 95-100.

Tinbergen, N. *The study of instinct.* Oxford, England: Clarendon Press, 1951.

Triandis, H. T. Some universals of social behavior. *Personality and Social Psychology Bulletin*, 1978, *4*, 1-16.

Trivers, R. L. The evolution of reciprocal altruism. *Quarterly Review of Biology*, 1971, *46*, 35-57.

Trivers, R. L. Parental investment and sexual selection. In B. Campbell (ed.), *Sexual selection and the descent of man.* Chicago: Aldine, 1972.

Trivers, R. L. Parent offspring conflict. *American Zoologist*, 1974, *14*, 249-264.

Trivers, R. L. Interview. *Time*, 1977, August 1, 54-63.

Trivers, R. L. & Hare, H. Haplodiploidy and the evolution of the social insects. *Science, 191*, 249-263.

Trivers, R. L. & Willard, D. E. Natural selection of parental ability to vary the sex ratio of offspring. *Science*, 1973, *179*, 90-92.

Udry, J. R. Differential fertility by intelligence. *Social Biology*, 1978, *25*, 10-14.

Unger, S. The effects of effort and stigma on helping. *Journal of Social Psychology*, 1979, *107*, 23-28.

Vayda, A. P. *War in ecological perspective.* New York: Plenum Press, 1976.

Wagatsuma, E. & Kleinke, C. L. Ratings of facial beauty by Asian-American and caucasian females. *Journal of Social Psychology*, 1979, *109*, 299-300.

Walster, E. & Walster, G. W. *A new look at love*. Reading, Mass.: Addison-Wesley, 1978.

West, S. G., Whitney, G., & Schnedler, R. Helping a motorist in distress: Effects of sex, race and neighborhood. *Journal of Personality and Social Psychology*, 1975, *31*, 691-698.

Weyant, J. M. The effects of mood states, costs and benefits on helping. *Journal of Personality and Social Psychology*, 1978, *3*, 1169-1176.

Wheeler, L. & Nezleck, J. Sex differences in social participation. *Journal of Personality and Social Psychology*, 1977, *35*, 742-754.

Whyte, M. K. *The status of women in preindustrial society*. Princeton, N.J.: Princeton University Press, 1978.

Wiggins, J. S., Wiggins, N., & Conger, J. C. Correlates of heterosexual somatic preference. *Journal of Personality and Social Psychology*, 1968, *10*, 82-90.

Williams, G. C. *Adaptation and natural selection. A critique of some current evolutionary thought*. Princeton, N.J.: Princeton University Press, 1966.

Williams, G. C. *Sex and evolution*. Princeton, N.J.: Princeton University Press, 1975.

Wilson, E. O. *Sociobiology: The new synthesis*. Cambridge, Mass.: Belknap Press, 1975.

Wilson, E. O. *On human nature*. Cambridge, Mass.: Harvard University Press, 1978.

Wilson, L. & Rogers, R. W. The fire this time: Effects of race on target, insult and potential retaliation of black aggression. *Journal of Personality and Social Psychology*, 1975, *32*, 857-864.

Wilson, P. R. Perceptual distortion of height as a function of ascribed academic status. *Journal of Social Psychology*, 1968, *74*, 97-102.

Wispe, L. G. & Thompson, J. W. The war between the words: Biological vs. social evolution and some related issues. *American Psychologist*, 1976, *31*, 341-384.

Wolfe, L. Sexual profile of that cosmopolitan girl. *Cosmopolitan*, 1980, *189*, 254-265.

Wyers, E. Y., Adler, H. E., Carpen, K., Chiszar, D., Demarest, J., Flanagan, O. J., Jr., Von Glasersfled, E., Glickman, S. E., Mason, W. A., Menzel, E. W., and Tobach, E. The sociobiological challenge to psychology: On the proposal to "cannibalize" comparative psychology. *American Psychology*, 1980, *35*, 955-979.

Zahn-Waxler, A. Radke-Yarrow, A. & King, A. Child rearing and children's prosocial initiators towards victims of distress. *Child Development*, 1979, *50*, 319-330.

Zastrow, C. H. *Outcome of black children-white parents transracial adoption*. San Francisco: R&E Research Associates, 1977.

4

A Control-Systems Approach to Behavioral Self-Regulation

CHARLES S. CARVER

MICHAEL F. SCHEIER

Charles S. Carver is Associate Professor at the University of Miami. The author (with Michael F. Scheier) of *Attention and Self-Regulation: A Control-Theory Approach to Human Behavior* (New York: Springer-Verlag, 1981), his research focuses on the behavioral consequences of self-directed attention.

Michael F. Scheier is Associate Professor of Psychology at Carnegie-Mellon University. His research examines the role that attentional factors play in the manner in which people regulate their actions. He is coauthor (with Charles S. Carver) of *Attention and Self-Regulation: A Control-Theory Approach to Human Behavior.*

T he concept of motivation was devised to account for the regulation of behavior, that is, the fact that behavior often displays direction or purpose, and the fact that behaviors vary across instances in their vigor, thoroughness, or singlemindedness. This chapter presents the argument

AUTHORS' NOTE: Our thanks to Clyde Hendrick, Shelley Taylor, Neill Watson, and particularly Dan Wegner for their comments on an earlier draft of this chapter. Preparation of this chapter was facilitated by National Science Foundation grants BNS 80-21859 and BNS 81-07236.

that a set of assumptions identified with the terms *cybernetic, information-processing,* and *control-theory* (terms that we will use interchangeably here) represents useful tools for the understanding of human motivation. More specifically, in the following pages we first discuss how cybernetic concepts account in principle for self-regulation and then consider how these concepts bear on self-regulation and goal-attainment in behavior. This is followed by an attempt to draw a connection between that general line of reasoning and recent theory and research findings in personality, social, and cognitive psychology.

We begin our discussion by examining the central ideas of cybernetics, or control theory. Cybernetics is the science of communication and control (Wiener, 1948). Its principles are self-regulatory principles, potentially applicable to virtually any kind of self-regulating system—electronic, electromechanical, or biological. The principles of control are usually illustrated by pointing to devices like thermostats or computer programs. But the same logic is also implicit in the functioning of the homeostatic systems that regulate body temperature, levels of nutrients in the blood, and so on (cf. Cannon, 1932). And we argue below that the same principles are applicable to *behavioral* self-regulation as well.

THE FEEDBACK LOOP

The basic unit of cybernetic control is the negative feedback loop (see Figure 1). It is called a "negative" or discrepancy-reducing loop because its overall function is to reduce or eliminate any perceptible discrepancy between a sensed value and some standard of comparison. The feedback system is made up of several component processes that form a closed loop of control. Saying where it "begins" is somewhat arbitrary, because successful self-regulation requires the proper functioning of each component. If the loop is disconnected at any point, effective self-regulation ceases. In describing this system, however, it is perhaps most intuitive to begin with the input function (the left box of Figure 1). This process is simply the sensing or perception of some existing state of affairs. (As we describe these component processes, we will concurrently provide a concrete illustration of how they occur in a simple control device: a thermostat. To begin, the input function of a thermostat is the sensing of present room temperature.)

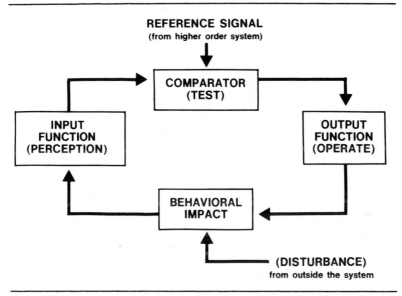

Figure 1. The component functions of a feedback loop, the basic unit of cybernetic control (from Carver & Scheier, 1981). Reprinted by permission of the publisher.

The value sensed through the input function is transferred to the next component of the loop, called a "comparator." At this point the sensed present state is compared against a reference signal or standard of comparison, provided from outside the loop. (For a thermostat, the reference value is the temperature at which the device has been set.) This comparison process (termed a "test" by Miller, Galanter, and Pribram, 1960) has two potential outcomes: Either the two values are the same or they are discriminably different. If they are the same, no further action is called for. If they are different, control is transferred to an output function (termed "operate" by Miller et al., 1960).

The output function is, in some sense or other, *behavior*.[1] A comparison that reveals a discrepancy between the sensed value and the reference value will authorize a change in present behavior, the purpose of which is to counter the sensed discrepancy. Thus the reference value can easily be conceptualized as providing a *goal* for behavior (cf. Powers, 1973a). (To continue with our example, if the thermostat's comparator finds that the room temperature has become discriminably higher than the reference value, it causes an air conditioning unit to be activated.)

The mere emission of the behavior does not in itself counter the discrepancy, however. It does so only by having an impact on the system's "environment" (i.e., anything external to the system itself). When the output function has an impact on the environment, the result is a different state of affairs than had previously existed. This different state of affairs, in turn, results in a change in the *perception* of the present situation (see Figure 1). This new perception goes to the comparator, which compares it with the reference value. If the action has countered the deviation, the action may be discontinued. (Thus when the room has cooled to the thermostat's set point, the air conditioner is deactivated.)

The only influence that we have not yet mentioned is what we have referred to categorically in Figure 1 as "disturbance." This variable reflects the fact that the system exists in what may be a continually changing environment. Unpredictable and often uncontrollable influences impinge on the system. These influences frequently act to create discrepancies between the present state and the reference value (e.g., a blazing midday sun raises the room's temperature). But sometimes they act to *reduce* discrepancies (e.g., a sudden thunderstorm may cool the room). The essence of the disturbance is not that it creates discrepancies, but simply that it *changes* the existing state and does so completely apart from the behavior of the system.

It is important to recognize, in this regard, that what is controlled— what is really at the heart of the concept of the feedback loop—is the *perceived discrepancy between the present state and the comparison value.* It does not matter how the discrepancy was created or how it is reduced (i.e., through the system's action or through an environmental distur- bance). The system has only one goal: keeping the discrepancy minimized. (This point has implications that go far beyond the scope of the present discussion; see Powers, 1973a, 1973b, 1979, for further detail.)

Two Illustrations in Behavior

The component functions that we have just described are observed as easily in human behavior as in a thermostat. Consider a very simple behavioral example. Most people have a mental representation of how they ought to look in the morning as they leave for work. This representation is a composite of cultural norms and people's memories of what they typically look like (i.e., most people do *not* expect to leave for work looking like Cary Grant or Sophia Loren). Further, it is not unusual for people to check on their appearances before leaving, by looking in a mirror. In so doing, one observes one's reflected image (input function) and compares it to the stored representation. If there is a discrepancy substantial enough to be noticed (e.g., one's shirt is buttoned crooked), the result is a rearrangement (output function) that counters the sensed deviation.

As another illustration, consider the behavior of a person who has written the first draft of a book chapter and is deciding how to revise it. The author reads the material through (perception and input function) and compares it to a vague mental image of whatever it is he or she wants to convey. Such comparisons could occur at many levels of analysis, of course. It could be, for example, at the semantic level—an assessment of whether the intended meaning is coming across. Or it could be at the level of style—a judgment as to whether the "tone" is right. In any case, the behavioral consequence depends upon the outcome of this comparison. If a discrepancy is perceived, the passage is rewritten or the section reorganized. If no discrepancy is perceived, no further action is taken.

Relationships Among Feedback Loops

Having established at least the plausibility of construing human behavior in terms of control processes, let us add some necessary elaboration. The single feedback loop, though of considerable interest in its own right, is not really a complete model of much of anything. In point of fact, it will not even suffice for a full understanding of the behavior of a room thermostat. It is quite easy to circumvent this apparent limitation, however, by virtue of the fact that control systems can be interconnected. There are two points to be made in this regard.

Branching chains. The first of these points is most easily illustrated by reference to Miller et al.'s (1960) TOTE sequence. The TOTE construct is a sequential description of the behavior of a feedback loop (see Figure 2). Because it is sequential, it may be said to have a beginning and an end. Though not all feedback systems are sequential in their functioning—see Powers (1973b)—some certainly are.

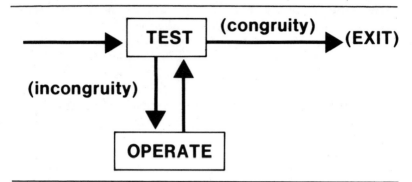

Figure 2. The TOTE unit (Miller, Galanter, Pribram, 1960), a description of the behavior of a feedback system (adapted from Miller et al., 1960). Reprinted
by permission of the publisher.

The "test" or comparison process in the TOTE sequence constitutes a
binary, yes-or-no decision. Control is transferred on the basis of this
decision, either to an "operate" function or to an "exit." Exit, in effect,
transfers control out of the loop altogether. But the TOTE unit typically
does not exist in isolation. Rather, systems often have a branching organization of control structures. In such systems exit transfers control *to
another loop,* which in turn makes another binary decision. Indeed, the
operate function of a given TOTE may also have subcomponents, each of
which involves separate tests and operates, all occurring as elements of the
initial operate. The result of having a large number of these loops linked
together is the creation of what can be a very complex, repeatedly
branching chain—a "decision tree."

We should also note that this process does not necessarily move to a
final end point, at which all decisions have been made. That is, it is
perfectly feasible for a TOTE unit that is very far into the chain to transfer
control back to a TOTE unit that initially appeared much *earlier* in the
chain. This possibility further compounds the potential complexity
offered by such an organization—an organization, it should be recalled,
that is wholly comprised of extremely simple elements.

This type of organization is the basis for the high-speed digital computers that we all take for granted. Their functioning consists of enormously complex chains of binary decisions. But this sort of organization
of activity is also implicit in a great many human behaviors. Consider the
use of "trouble-shooting" heuristics, the kind of thing that (for example)
amateur mechanics use in evaluating and resolving problems with their

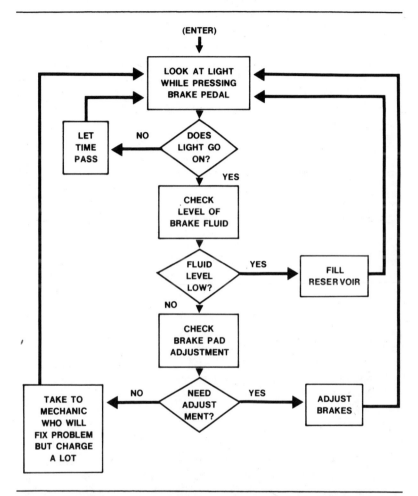

Figure 3. A trouble-shooting heuristic for an amateur mechanic. This flow diagram
describes the decision-making and behavioral sequence that occurs when a
person notices that the dashboard warning signal for the car's brake system
has begun to light up when the brake pedal is depressed (from Carver &
Scheier, 1981). Reprinted by permission of the publisher.

cars. An illustration of this sort of heuristic is shown as a flow diagram in
Figure 3. At several points in the behavioral sequence there are "tests."
The outcome of each test—a binary decision—determines the person's next
behavior. Furthermore, this particular chain constitutes a behavioral

sequence that never ends, as long as the person owns the car. That is, repairing the problem leads the person not to exit from the diagram altogether, but rather to return to a periodic monitoring of the warning light.

Hierarchies of feedback loops. A second important consideration is that feedback loops can be organized hierarchically (see, for example, Powers, 1973b, 1979). In such a case, the overall system would have both *super*-ordinate goals and *sub*ordinate goals. By introducing the notion of a hierarchical organization, we are now able to address a point that we glossed over earlier. Specifically, a given feedback loop regulates its activity with respect to some reference value, or standard. That standard comes from outside the loop. But where does it come from?

Part of the answer is that in a hierarchical organization, the standard for a subordinate feedback loop is specified by a superordinate feedback loop. Indeed, the *supplying* of that standard constitutes the *behavioral output* of the superordinate loop.

The meaning of this rather abstract assertion can be clarified quite easily by returning to an example that we used earlier: the behavior of the room thermostat. The thermostat regulates perceived room temperature with regard to a specific standard. Where does that specific standard come from? It is provided by the behavior of a superordinate feedback system: the person inhabiting the room. The standard of the superordinate system (the person) is to be comfortable. To achieve that goal, the person behaves by setting the thermostat higher (if the room seems too cold) or lower (if the room seems too warm).

This example illustrates in a concrete way two points that we have already made in abstract terms. First, the act of providing the reference value to the subordinate system (the termostat) is the behavioral *output* of the higher order system. Second, the higher order system does not attain its goals directly, that is, via its own behavior. The attainment of the superordinate goal is dependent upon the behavior of the lower order system, which acts to reduce discrepancies with regard to its new reference value.

This example also allows us to make an additional point that we have not yet addressed. Standards for a feedback loop (at any given level of analysis) can be set and reset repeatedly. The set point of a thermostat can be changed any number of times in the course of a week if (for example) the person who spends time in the room in question wears different types and amounts of clothing from day to day. Wearing a wool three-piece suit requires a lower ambient temperature for comfort than does wearing shorts and a T-shirt. But note that these changes in thermostat setting all occur in the service of attaining the same higher order goal: comfort. The fact that standards at a given level of control can be changed repeatedly by a higher order system gives a hierarchically organized control system a very high degree of flexibility in behavior.

Implicit in this discussion is an assumption concerning time, a dimension that we have ignored until now. The assumption is this: In a hierarchy of control structures, subordinate systems operate on a faster time scale than do superordinate systems. Because a low-level feedback loop executes its matching-to-standard activity as a *component* of the matching-to-standard sequence at a higher level, the lower level system may often match several different standards sequentially in the course of a single discrepancy reduction at a higher level. This line of argument derives from a consideration of the nature of control processes (see Carver & Scheier, 1981, or Powers, 1973b, for detail) rather than a consideration of behavior. But the argument does have important implications regarding behavior, which will become apparent in a moment.

HIERARCHICAL ORGANIZATION AND BEHAVIOR

The reasoning outlined in the preceding pages provides a basis for addressing a truth that is self-evident, but is usually ignored. Specifically, people have the capability of executing exceedingly abstract behavioral prescriptions (e.g., writing a book chapter) by means of activity so concrete as to appear to bear no resemblance whatever to the abstract goal (e.g., grasping a pen, holding it at an appropriate angle and with appropriate pressure, and moving it across paper to form patterns). The abundant evidence of this general capability—turning abstract goals into physical acts—makes it all the more remarkable how completely the capability is ignored in most theories of behavior.

It has not gone unnoticed by control theorists, however. Powers (1973b, 1979) has suggested what appears to be an eminently reasonable way of accounting for it. He has argued for the existence of a hierarchy of control in behavioral self-regulation, in which each successive superordinate level of feedback systems "behaves" by specifying reference

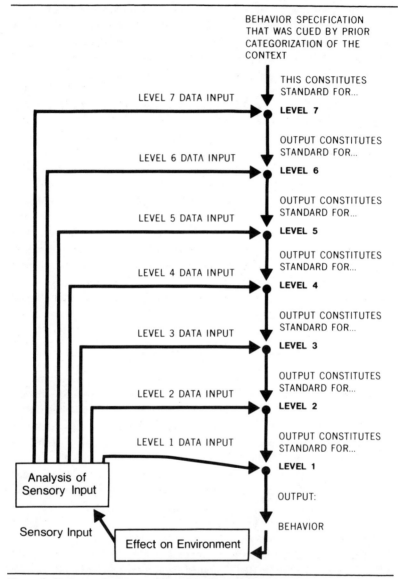

Figure 4. Diagram of a seven-level hierarchy of feedback systems. The behavioral output for each superordinate system consists of resetting the reference value for the next lower system. The output of the lowest level system is overt behavior. Goal attainment is monitored at each level by reference to perceptual input appropriate to that level (from Carver & Scheier, 1981). Reprinted by permission of the publisher.

values for the next lower level of control (see Figure 4). At the lowest level of control, the behavioral output is *literally* behavior, the only behavior there actually ever is: changes in muscle tensions.[2]

The levels of control in the Powers hierarchy that are of the greatest importance for personality and social psychologists are the relatively superordinate levels termed Program control, Principle control, and control of System Concepts (see Figure 5). Program control seems nearly identical to the control of what Schank and Abelson (1977) referred to as scripted behavior. That is, it involves courses of potential action, rather than simple sequences or lists of acts. Said differently, programs are characterized by the fact that their component acts are partially specified ahead of time—but *only partially*. What action is taken at any given point in the course of events depends upon what circumstance is encountered at that point. A simple example, adapted from Powers (1973b), is the behavior of a man looking for a missing object. If he does not find it the first place he looks, he looks elsewhere. When he does find it—wherever that happens to be—he stops looking for it. Programs thus have an "if, then" character, a character that is absent at lower levels of control.

The level of control immediately superordinate to the Program level is Principle control (Figure 5). This level in the hierarchy reflects the fact that people often make use of general guiding principles (equivalent to what Schank and Ableson termed meta-scripts) in making decisions in programs or in determining what programs to undertake. What characterizes this level of control is that a single principle (for example, the principle that a person should economize whenever possible) could be reflected in a great many programs. The programs may vary widely in their behavioral content (e.g., buying a new set of tires, going out to dinner, planning a vacation). But all may be guided in part by the attempt to satisfy the superordinate principle.

Control of System Concepts is a little harder to describe than the preceding two levels. But Powers (1973b) pointed out that there is a need to account for why a person adopts one set of principles rather than another. He suggested that such choices seem to be not arbitrary, but rather attempts to achieve the perception of a sort of systematic unity. The hazy goal behind such an attempt is what Powers termed a system concept. One important system concept (though there certainly are others) may be the sense of integration and coherence associated with a person's ideal self. The attempt to regulate behavior with regard to that

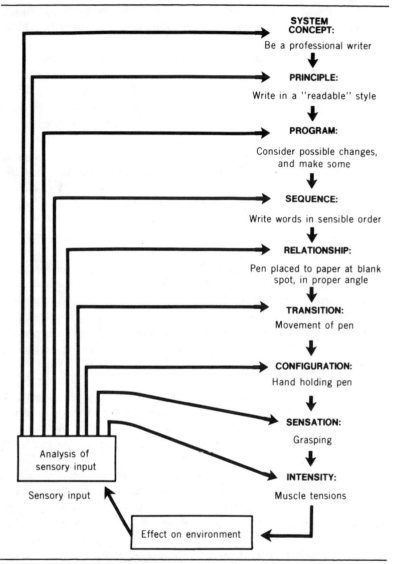

Figure 5. Diagram of the hierarchical organization implicit in the behavior of a professional writer who is revising the draft of a book chapter. This diagram provides a concrete illustration of the more abstract principles illustrated in Figure 4 (adapted from Carver & Scheier, 1981). Reprinted by permission of the publisher.

system concept, then, may be what is referred to by behavioral theorists as an attempt to maintain or enhance one's self-esteem (cf. Snyder, Stephan, & Rosenfield, 1978).

An Example

This description of the upper levels of the Powers hierarchy has been somewhat abstract. In order to illustrate how the hierarchical analysis can be applied to an activity with which we are all familiar—and in order to illustrate the value of the hierarchy in accounting for overt behavior—let us analyze an example. Consider the act of writing. More specifically, consider the behavior of the person to whom we alluded several pages earlier, who is trying to polish and smooth a manuscript that ultimately will become a book chapter. (Figure 5 illustrates this example graphically.)

The person in this example thinks of himself as a professional writer and a reasonably good one. Whenever he sits down to compose, he actively attempts to live up to that image of himself. How does he do that? Well, part of his effort to be a good writer entails adherence to certain *principles* of writing. For example, he holds a principle which says that good writing should be "readable," and in his writing he attempts to conform to that principle. (He also holds another principle, by the way, which says that good writing should be precise. Note that we often attempt to conform to several standards more or less simultaneously.)

But what does it mean to "make the manuscript readable?" In attempting to make his writing closely approximate the principle of readability, our writer proceeds through a program, a series of "if, then" decisions, in which some possibility for change is considered and evaluated. If the change seems to represent an improvement, an alteration is made in the manuscript. If not, he goes on to consider the next possibility. For example, if a section can be made more accessible to readers by adding a concrete illustration, the illustration is added. If not, perhaps the points are being made out of sequence and a rearrangement will help. If not, yet other possibilities are considered. Note that at this level of analysis what is done depends in part on decisions made along the way and on the specific circumstances encountered at any point in the chain. If adding a concrete illustration made the passage better, for example, the writer may be unlikely to consider reorganizing the section.

Suppose, now, that the writer *has* decided to make a change in the manuscript. What does this entail? Actually making such a change requires the execution of several actions in the correct sequence—taking up the pen and making marks on the page in a particular order to form words (Sequence control). Doing that requires in turn the creation of physical configurations, involving appropriate relationships between the writer's hand and the pen, and between the pen and the page. (All of these represent lower and lower levels of behavioral control.) At even more concrete levels, creating and maintaining the appropriate configurations and relationships (over the course of writing a sentence) requires the activation (and repeated readjustment and shifting of patterns of activation) of many different muscle groups. Control of muscle tensions is the most basic level of control in this hierarchy.

Now consider this: As we observe the writer in midword, what goal is he attaining? Is he creating muscle tensions? Maintaining the desired angle between the pen and paper? Forming a word? Adding an example to the manuscript? Making the chapter more readable? Attempting to enhance his self-image as a professional writer? The answer, in fact, is that he is doing all of these things simultaneously (see Figure 5).

In doing so, he is attaining goals faster at lower levels than at higher levels. That is, muscle tensions change faster than words are written; it takes many wording changes to make the manuscript readable; and it takes more than a single well-written manuscript to establish a sense of professional competence. But throughout the activity, feedback loops are matching reference values at all of the levels of the hierarchy. This account makes perfectly good sense in terms of control theory. It also accounts for the emission of physical behavior in the service of abstract goals. Furthermore, it even appears to fit well with intuition. That is, it is commonly accepted that the more abstract one's goal, the more involved the process of attaining it and (usually) the more gradual its attainment.

Two Additional Questions

Though this account of control theory has been somewhat sketchy, we feel that it provides a reasonable basis for examining research on behavioral self-regulation. There are, however, two additional questions that we should address briefly before we do so. The questions are these: What level of control is functionally superordinate at any given time? And where does the reference value at that superordinate level come from?

A partial answer to the first question is provided by the assumption that whatever level is being *attended to* is superordinate at that moment.

Levels lower than the one at which attention is focused presumably continue to self-regulate, because their activity is necessary for self-regulation at the higher level. We suggest, however (though this suggestion is clearly speculative), that self-regulation at any level *higher* than the one to which attention is directed ceases until attention is redirected to that higher level.

Considering the question in more concrete terms, we assume that for the most part the Program level is usually superordinate in adults, though occasionally something makes a reference value salient at the Principle level or (less frequently) even at the level of System Concepts. Attention can easily be drawn to lower levels, however, if there is a problem in creating a match between input and reference value (cf. Kimble & Perlmuter, 1970). Should this occur, the level at which the match is being prevented temporarily becomes superordinate. It is theoretically possible for any level of the hierarchy to be the focus of attention, and thus to be temporarily superordinate. We assume, however, that in most social behavior the Program and Principle levels of self-regulation are superordinate.

And where does the behavioral standard come from at whatever level is superordinate? It cannot be provided by the next higher level, because no higher level is *operating* at the moment. A partial answer to this question, however, comes from the following line of reasoning: that the act of perceiving and catergorizing one's behavioral context (social or nonsocial) involves the comparison of raw input to stored records of prior perceptions; that those records have been catalogued according to some organizational scheme (albeit a continually evolving one); and that information about behavior is stored along with some of those records of perceptions. When a category structure is activated in recognizing perceptual input, then, the behavioral information is also accessed. As this information is accessed, it becomes the superordinate reference value. Does this really happen? Theory and research bearing on the question are somewhat sparse. But they appear to be consistent with our position.

PERCEPTION OF PERSONS AND PLACES

Let us begin our examination of this question at a basic level, by considering the process of construing our behavioral contexts. Several different theories have been suggested by cognitive psychologists to account for the fact that perceptual experiences are organized (over time) into implicit or explicit categories (see, e.g., Anderson, 1980). These categories—knowledge structures—are typically referred to as perceptual or recognitory schemas. Some theorists have argued that a schema can best be characterized as comprised of two components: a representation of a hypothetical "best member" of the category (i.e., a prototype) and information about how far from that "best" member a given perception can deviate and still belong to the category (e.g., Posner, 1969; Posner & Keele, 1968; Franks & Bransford, 1971; Rosch, 1973). Others have argued that a schema can best be conceptualized in terms of the frequencies with which particular stimulus attributes have been encoded in the past as being relevant to the schema (Reitman & Bower, 1973; Neumann, 1977).

Despite these disagreements, there is a general consensus that such knowledge structures develop and that they are used to identify new perceptions. That is, salient attributes of the new perception apparently are used to access a schema or schemas in a preliminary way. The schema then suggests the presence of additional attributes which can be confirmed, resulting ultimately in a recognition or classification of the perception (cf. Neisser, 1976). Indeed, once the stimulus has been classified, one often assumes the presence of additional schema-consistent attributes even if they have not been verified.

Many social psychologists have come to view the process of person perception as involving much the same functions as outlined in the preceding paragraphs. First, knowledge about people—both perceptual and conceptual knowledge—appears to be organized schematically (see, e.g., Cantor & Mischel, 1977; Taylor & Crocker, 1979). Attributes of persons are not simply stored in memory in a disorganized fashion; information concerning cooccurrence of attributes is also stored, leading to an elaborate network of knowledge. Second, accessing a schema on the basis of one salient attribute of a new stimulus appears to evoke other aspects of the associated knowledge structure. Based on this preliminary accessing, the perceiver tends to assume the presence of attributes not yet observed. In personality-social psychology this tendency has been characterized as the use of an "implicit personality theory" (e.g., Hastorf, Schneider, & Polefka, 1970; Wegner & Vallacher, 1977).

Similar processes have also been postulated in the perception of behavior settings (e.g., Barker, 1968; Wicker, 1972; Stokols, 1978), though data bearing on this case come mostly from trained observers rather than naive subjects. And there is even evidence that knowledge structures exist which organize one's perceptual and conceptual knowledge about oneself (e.g., Markus, 1977; Rogers, 1977; Rogers, Rogers, & Kuiper, 1979). In each of these cases, as in the case of perceiving other persons, information appears to be stored in organized knowledge structures, and the information appears to be accessed when a current perception is being recognized by reference to one of those structures (see Carver & Scheier, 1981).

As suggested above, it seems reasonable to infer that many of the knowledge structures we have been describing incorporate *behavioral* information, as well as strictly perceptual or conceptual information. Accessing a schema that includes behavior-specifying information would evoke that information in the same manner as it evokes any other schema-related information. For example, just as accessing the category "cup" promotes the inference of a round top, accessing the category "church" evokes the behavioral specifications of walking softly and keeping one's voice low. Once evoked, such information would constitute a behavioral standard.

The assumption that behavioral information is incorporated in recognitory schemas is consistent with theoretical positions taken by many cognitive psychologists (see, e.g., Rosch, 1978). It is also consistent with findings from at least one investigation of environment perception and from a variety of studies of person perception. In the area of environment perception, Price (1974) asked subjects to rate the appropriateness of a list of behaviors (e.g., run, talk, write, eat) portrayed as taking place in a list of different settings (e.g., in class, in an elevator, in a dorm lounge). He found that classes of seetings did indeed "demand" or "pull for" classes of behaviors. This study must be regarded as preliminary, in that it involved only a limited range of behaviors and settings. But the results do suggest that behavior-specifying information is closely linked in people's minds with specifications of settings.

There is also evidence that categorizing a person has an important impact on how we subsequently *behave* toward that person. Relatively arbitrary group assignments (i.e., the target person either is or is not a member of the subject's group) have been found to lead to reliable biases in behaviors such as allocation of money (e.g., Allen & Wilder, 1975; Billig & Tajfel, 1973) and seeking information about the person (Wilder & Allen, 1978). Variations in racial categorization also lead to different behavioral tendencies (Rubovits & Maehr, 1973), as do variations in perceived physical attractiveness (Snyder, Tanke, & Berscheid, 1977). Note that these effects do not simply represent secondary inferences about what the person is *like*. They represent acts of *behavior* stemming from the categorization. Again, this evidence appears to indicate that behavioral specification is closely linked to certain kinds of category-membership judgments.

SELF-FOCUS AND BEHAVIORAL SELF-REGULATION

The evoking of a behavioral standard at the superordinate level of control is the first necessary process in a control-theory approach to human motivation. The second process is the operation of the feedback loop that promotes behavioral conformity to that standard. We have argued that when a standard has already become salient, the matching-to-standard sequence (at whatever level of control is superordinate) is partially governed by the person's attentional focus (Carver, 1979; Carver & Scheier, 1981). More specifically, behavioral conformity to the reference value is promoted by *self*-directed attention. We conceptualize self-focus in this context as leading to the "test" component of the feedback loop—the comparison between one's present state and the standard. The greater the frequency or the probability with which this test occurs, the closer the conformity to the standard.

Comparison with Standards

Does self-attention lead to an increase in the comparison between one's present state and the salient standard? Recent research suggests that it does. In these studies (Scheier & Carver, Note 2) situations were created in which covert, internal comparisons between self and standard would require (or at least would be facilitated by) the obtaining of external, standard-relevant information. It was reasoned that if self-focus leads to a tendency to compare one's present state to the salient standard, self-focus should also lead more reliably to seeking of the relevant information.

This reasoning was confirmed in a series of studies that utilized both experimental manipulations of self-attention and individual differences in the disposition to be self-attentive. In one paradigm, subjects were required to copy, as accurately as they could, complex geometric figures that were projected onto a screen. The figures were projected for only a few seconds at a time (during which the subject could not draw), but subjects could view each as often as they desired. In each of two studies, highly self-focused subjects consulted the figures more frequently than did less self-focused subjects.

Two additional studies were based on the assumption that test norms provide information that is relevant to the self-versus-standard comparison in performance settings (cf. Trope, 1975). Subjects in one study were allowed to choose from items for which norms either were or were not available. Subjects in another study were given an opportunity to examine norms for test items after working on the items. In both cases, high levels of self-focus were associated with enhanced norm-seeking behavior. Taken as a whole, these studies appear to indicate that self-focus results in a tendency to compare oneself with salient standards.

Discrepancy Reduction

Comparison with standards is only part of the process for which we are arguing, however. If the comparison between present state and standard in a feedback system reveals a discrepancy, the result is an attempt to reduce the discrepancy. Consistent with this picture of self-regulation, a wide variety of research has shown that self-focusing manipulations increase the degree to which subjects' behavior conforms to salient behavioral standards. For example, Wicklund and Duval (1971) told subjects to copy prose rapidly and found that they copied more when working in front of a mirror than when the mirror was absent. Similarly, a series of studies of instrumental aggression (Scheier, Fenigstein, & Buss, 1974; Carver, 1974, 1975) found that subjects utilized experimentally induced standards regarding how much aggression was suitable (standards that varied from study to study) to a greater degree when self-focus was high than when it was lower. Nor do these illustrations exhaust the range of matching-to-standard effects that have been found to be induced by manipulations of self-attention.

We should note that most of these effects implicitly involve self-regulation at either the Program or Principle level of control, which we suggested earlier are the levels that are normally superordinate in adult behavior. However, results of at least one research project suggest that self-directed attention can result in enhanced self-regulation even in systems usually thought to be inaccessible to conscious control. Specifically, Schwartz (1980) has reported that having subjects attend to perceptual feedback of their breathing and their heart rates resulted in decreased variability—greater "regulation"—of such behavior.

ABSENCE OF SELF-REGULATION

If increases in self-focus result in enhanced behavioral self-regulation, it follows that decreased self-focus leads to a relative absence of self-regulation. Recall that all components of a given feedback loop must be functioning in order for self-regulation to continue. There are several places where this loop could be disrupted. One place is the comparator. If no attention is directed to the self-versus-standard comparison at (for example) the Program level of control, regulation at that level is discontinued. The next lower level temporarily becomes superordinate.

It may be precisely this sort of situation that underlies the psychological and behavioral phenomena known as deindividuation. Diener (1980) has suggested that deindividuation involves a reduction in self-awareness, induced through involvement in group activities.[3] As a result, people fail to compare their behavior to the personal and social standards that usually govern it. Behavior then becomes more spontaneous, more impulsive, and more sensitive to cues of the moment (cues that suggest sequences of acts, but acts without the degree of organization that is implicit in a program). Support for this general line of reasoning has been obtained in studies conducted by Diener (1979) and by Prentice-Dunn and Rogers (1980).

The notion that all components of the feedback loop must be functioning in order for successful self-regulation to take place at a given level of analysis has a great many implications. Deindividuation, as characterized above, represents a state in which the comparator at the Program or Principle level has ceased to compare perceptual input with the standard that is available to it. But the loop can also be disrupted in other ways. For example, the relevant perceptual input is sometimes unavailable for one reason or another. If one is therefore unable to tell how one compares to the standard, there is no way to determine how to adjust one's behavior, and effective self-regulation ceases. (For an interesting account of how such processes influence health-related behavior, see Leventhal, Meyer, & Nerenz, 1980.)

Probably the most common cause of disruption of self-regulation, however, is in the output function, that is, the unavailability of a behavior that will reduce the sensed discrepancy or an inability to execute the behavior. If there is no behavior that can reduce the discrepancy, or if the appropriate behavior cannot be executed, self-regulation is interrupted. This state of affairs is common enough in behavior that it has received a good deal of attention in theory and research.

INTERRUPTION OF BEHAVIOR

Impediments encountered in the execution of some behavior may be external (i.e., some environmental, temporal, or social constraint is preventing the behavior) or they may be internal (i.e., some deficiency within the self makes the behavior difficult). The interruption to which such an impediment leads may be momentary, or it may be prolonged. We assume that such an interruption leads to an assessment of outcome expectancy: a subjective judgment of the likelihood of attaining the goal, given the situation and one's resources. If the behavior in question is directed toward attaining one component of a larger scale goal, the assessment process may apply to the component goal or it may apply to the larger scale goal. We believe that the outcome expectancy deriving from this assessment is reflected both in behavior and in affect, but we will focus here only on behavior.

Expectancy and the Approach-Withdrawal Decision

An assessment of outcome expectancy can be construed as a TOTE process, but one which is orthogonal to the hierarchy of feedback systems discussed earlier. Recall that the TOTE sequence involves a binary decision, based on a comparison between a present state and a standard. Similarly, the result of an expectancy judgment represents a binary decision, based on a comparison between one's present circumstances and the circumstances that one perceives as necessary for a favorable outcome. Said more concretely, we assume a rough dichotomy in expectancy judgments. Sometimes expectancy is sufficiently favorable to warrant further effort, sometimes it is not.

The result is a sort of psychological "watershed" in responses to the interruption. If expectancies are sufficiently favorable, the result is a return to the discrepancy-reduction attempt. If expectancies are unfavorable, the result is an impetus to withdraw from further attempts. Just where in the range of subjective probabilities these two possibilities diverge is difficult to say. Indeed, the turning point doubtlessly varies with the importance of the behavioral dimension in question. Yet all behavioral responses appear to fall ultimately into one or the other of these categories: renewed efforts or withdrawal (followed, perhaps, by the setting of a different goal). Both of these responses are presumed to be enhanced by subsequent self-focus.

These processes have now been investigated in several different behavioral domains. In one study (Carver, Blaney, & Scheier, 1979a), subjects were selected as being moderately fearful of snakes, but as varying in their chronic expectancies of being able to cope successfully with their fear. It was predicted that enhanced self-focus during the attempt to approach and hold a snake would lead uniformly to increased awareness of rising fear, resulting in interruption of behavior. Consistent with this reasoning, self-focus did cause the reporting of greater anxiety among both subject groups. How subjects would *respond* to this interruption, however, was expected to depend upon their chronic expectancies of being able to cope with the fear. This also proved to be the case. Self-focus led to earlier withdrawal among subjects who doubted their ability to cope, but tended to facilitate approach among more confident subjects.

Additional research applied this line of reasoning to persistence at an insoluble problem (Carver, Blaney, & Scheier, 1979b). A large within-self discrepancy was created among all subjects in this research by means of an initial failure. Some subjects then were led to have favorable expectancies of making up for that failure on a second task; others were led to have unfavorable expectancies. Once again enhanced self-focus interacted with expectancies, increasing persistence among subjects with favorable expectancies and decreasing persistence among subjects with unfavorable expectancies.

Physical withdrawal is sometimes prevented by social or other constraints. We have argued that in such cases the withdrawal impetus leads to a psychological or *mental* withdrawal from the dimension in question. This would be reflected in performance decrements, as the person ignored available goal-relevant information. Support for this reasoning comes from a study by Brockner (1979). Brockner was interested in the effects of low self-esteem upon performance, as mediated by self-directed attention. He predicted—and found—that self-focus impairs performance among persons low in self-esteem following an initial failure, but does not impair performance following an initial success. Furthermore, he presented evidence that this performance difference is mediated by differences in outcome expectancies.

Theoretical Implications

In addition to the three projects just discussed, this theoretical analysis fits well with the findings of several earlier studies conducted by other researchers in the self-awareness area (e.g., Duval, Wicklund, & Fine, 1972; Gibbons & Wicklund, 1976; Steenbarger & Aderman, 1979) and it has received direct support in several additional studies (Carver & Scheier, 1981). Moreover, it has some interesting similarities to lines of argument that have been advanced independently by theorists in other areas. In each case, however, our analysis appears to contribute elements that other theories do not, while simultaneously suggesting the potential of integrating diverse areas of work.

Consider, for example, the area of test anxiety. Wine (1971, 1980) has characterized the test anxious as being hampered by self-focus during evaluative test situations. Self-focus presumably gets in the way of their efforts, resulting in impaired performances. We would account for such effects by assuming that the test anxious have unfavorable expectancies when placed in evaluative settings. Self-focus then leads to an impetus to withdraw, which is expressed in impaired performances. Both Wine's analysis and our model thus can account for decrements associated with test anxiety. But only our model would allow the prediction that self-focus can *facilitate* performances *even among the test anxious,* provided the situation is nonevaluative and conducive to favorable expectancies. Such an effect has recently been demonstrated by Slapion and Carver (1981).

Another area of theory to which this aspect of our model bears a considerable resemblance is learned helplessness in humans. The basic findings of this area are that exposure to uncontrollable outcomes sometimes leads to giving-up responses, at other times to reassertion responses. Recent approaches to human helplessness have emphasized the role of cognitive variables in these effects, particularly subjects' expectancies (e.g., Abramson, Seligman, & Teasdale, 1978; Wortman & Brehm, 1975). That is, whether giving up or reassertion occurs appears to depend upon whether or not the subject expects to be able to produce the desired outcome when attempting the task that constitutes the dependent measure.

Our reasoning is quite consistent with this sort of model of helplessness. However, the fact that our ideas originated in a broader context suggests that helplessness effects are simply a *specific reflection of more general principles* of behavioral self-regulation. Moreover, our approach to such phenomena adds in at least two other respects. First, we have pointed out that both reassertion and giving-up behaviors are exaggerated by self-directed attention. Second, we suggest the possibility that the various performance impairments have their roots in a withdrawal impulse, which is often executed mentally rather than physically.

ADDITIONAL ISSUES

Let us now turn to two remaining issues concerning our attempt to apply the concepts of control theory to the analysis of behavioral self-regulation. Both issues are related to the fact that most recent theories in personality and social psychology have borne the stamp of the learning paradigm.

Alternative Models of Motivation

This characterization is certainly appropriate with regard to theories that concern motivation. Probably the most pervasive motivational assumption in social psychology today is that behavior (or even attitude change) is impelled by aversive drive states. This assumption is deeply ingrained in the field. It is part of social comparison theory and dissonance theory, and it provides the basis for the most commonly accepted interpretation of social facilitation effects. Indeed, the drive assumption is also part of the original analysis of self-awareness effects (Duval Wicklund, 1972; Wicklund, 1979). That is, Duval and Wicklund assume that the awareness of a discrepancy between one's present state and a salient standard creates an aversive drive state, which has the goal of eliminating one's awareness of the discrepancy.

We have implicitly taken the position in this chapter that a control-theory approach to motivation should be considered as a successor to drive models (among others). But how are we to determine whether one approach is more useful or more "correct" than the other? It will not help in this case to compare behavioral predictions, because the two classes of theory make similar predictions regarding overt behavior. Where they differ is in the assumptions that each makes about mediating states. Traditionally, motivational theories in social psychology incorporate a drive assumption. We have not.

Drive theory and social facilitation. Though the drive assumption is made in many behavioral domains, perhaps nowhere has it been more prominent than in the literature of social facilitation. Zajonc (1965, 1966) argued that the facilitating effect of coactors or observers could best be explained by assuming that such stimuli increased the subject's drive level. Other theorists have since raised questions about the *basis* for such a drive state (e.g., Cottrell, 1968, 1972; Henchy & Glass, 1968; Sanders & Baron, 1975; Sanders, Baron, & Moore, 1978), but they have almost invariably agreed about the existence of such a state.

Empirical evidence of the existence of such states has also been reported (Martens, 1969a, 1969b; see also Cohen & Davis, 1973). Making the assumption that drive would be reflected in arousal (cf. Geen & Gange, 1977; Malmo, 1958), Martens first demonstrated that the presence of an audience in a facilitation setting led to increases in a measure called the Palmar Sweat Index (PSI). Dabbs, Johnson, and Leventhal (1968) had previously characterized this pattern as reflecting arousal, based on a survey of earlier findings.

More recent research appears to demonstrate, however, that such a pattern is short-lived, occurring only when the subject confronts the audience, and *not* when the subject is actively attempting the task (Carver & Scheier, in press). Indeed, during task performances all subject groups in this research displayed an opposite pattern—a reduction in PSI compared to baseline values. Interestingly, Dabbs et al. (1968) had characterized the latter pattern as reflecting concentration and *inward focus* of attention. Thus the Carver and Scheier (in press) data seem to suggest that subjects' task attempts involved inward focus, but not "arousal."

These findings concerning physiological state do not appear to be compatible with existing drive theories. But what relevance do they have for cybernetic theory?

Response patterning. A tentative answer to this question is provided by an emerging approach to understanding physiological activity which emphasizes qualitative differences in the *patterning* of responses, rather than simply response magnitude. Deriving from positions taken by Sokolov (1963) and the Laceys (Lacey, 1967; Lacey & Lacey, 1970), this approach holds that specific patterns of physiological activity are associated with different modes of perceptual-cognitive functioning (e.g., Williams, Bittker, Buchsbaum, & Wynne, 1975; Williams, 1978). According to this viewpoint, what is observed in physiological activity is not simply "arousal." Instead, one pattern of change is seen as reflecting "sensory intake" as a processing mode, another pattern as reflecting "sensory rejection." Indeed, descriptions of these processing modes (see Williams et al., 1975) seem not too different from Dabbs et al.'s (1968) characterization of the psychological states associated with increases and decreases in PSI, respectively.

The response-patterning conceptualization of physiological activity is one that is perfectly compatible with cybernetic thinking. That is, it is obvious that changes in bodily state are required in order to do work (cf. Guilford, 1965). But such changes must necessarily be complex and subtle. Treating them all as "arousal" must ultimately be misleading. Examination of the possibility suggested above—that shifts in response patterns provide information about what sorts of information-processing events are momentarily dominating behavior—has really just begun. But it is an idea that clearly deserves further attention.

Changing Perspectives on Learning

A second issue that we wish to address briefly is the changing face that learning theory has presented to personality-social psychology over recent years. Most notably, there has been a pervasive movement to recast learning principles in much more cognitive terms, as the awareness has grown that cognitive variables play a major role in the regulation of behavior. It has been widely noted, for example, that the mental representation or construction of a situation (which varies considerably from person to person) may be a more important determinant of behavior than is the objective nature of the situation itself (cf. Bandura, 1978; Mischel, 1973). There is also an increasing acceptance of the notion that people do not always behave blindly, but monitor their activities and use mental representations as guides to the adequacy of their behavior.

An examination of the recent theoretical statements of three prominent adherents of social learning theory—Mischel, Bandura, and Kanfer—reveals that they hold a common core of assumptions about the structure of self-regulation. Consider, first, Mischel's position. Mischel (1973) has emphasized the importance of understanding how people categorize and encode events, the expectancies that they hold about the outcomes of their actions, and their use of goals and plans in self-regulation. "Persons set performance goals for themselves and react with self-criticism or self-satisfaction to their behavior depending on how well it matches their expectations and criteria" (Mischel, 1973: 273-274).

Similarly, Bandura (e.g., 1978) has assumed a set of cognitive functions that provide "reference mechanisms" for behavior. He has further specified that people observe their actions, compare those actions to personal standards, and ultimately respond evaluatively when the standards are met or not met. He has also emphasized the role of perceptions of personal efficacy in determining whether or not difficult behavior will be attempted (Bandura, 1977). It is of interest as well that Bandura (1978) has explicitly rejected the mechanistic perspective of environmental determinism, arguing that behavior and the context in which it occurs are an intertwined system of reciprocal influence.

Kanfer's (e.g., 1971, 1977) position is very similar to both of these. He, too, has discussed the process of self-regulation as involving the use of self-imposed behavioral standards and self-evaluation in terms of those standards. And Kanfer has explicitly noted the importance in the self-regulatory process of the person's expectancies of being able to execute the behavior in question (e.g., Kanfer & Hagerman, 1981).

These theoretical statements are not just similar to each other, however. They also bear considerable resemblance to the model of self-regulation that we have been discussing throughout this chapter. The emphasis on goal states, comparisons between one's behavior and those states, and the attempt to match the one with the other—all of these hypothetical processes are precisely the processes of a system of cybernetic control. We believe that the evolving ideas of theorists such as Mischel, Bandura, and Kanfer are plainly more assimilable to the cybernetic than to the learning paradigm (cf. Kanfer & Hagerman, 1981). And we suggest that the time is ripe for a more thorough consideration of the usefulness of control-theory assumptions as an underlying meta-theory for the analysis of behavioral self-regulation.

CONCLUDING COMMENT

We close this chapter by looking first backward in time and then forward. We look to the past by way of noting that we are not the first to see control theory as providing a useful meta-theory for behavioral self-regulation. Miller et al.'s (1960) discussion of the TOTE construct was greeted enthusiastically by a contingent of motivational theorists (see, e.g., Guilford, 1965; Hunt, 1965; Taylor, 1960). And a few years later a group of personality psychologists developed a somewhat independent interest in information processing ideas (e.g., Loehlin, 1968; Mancuso, 1970; Schroder & Suedfeld, 1970). Despite this, cybernetic principles of self-regulation never really caught on in personality and social psychology during that period.

There doubtlessly were many reasons for this. We suspect that two important reasons were (1) the fact that the learning paradigm was in full flower during these years and (2) the fact that a clear connection appears never to have been made between the components of cybernetic control (on the one hand) and psychological states or experimental manipulations (on the other). Thus the control-theory approach lacked an empirical base at the very time when the learning-theory approach was engendering a great deal of research.

As outlined in this chapter, we believe that the nature of each of these constraints has changed in recent years. First, the conceptualizations of social learning theorists have drifted inexorably in the direction of feedback models of behavior.[4] Second, an empirical literature has developed which seems easily interpreted in control-theory terms. Thus we now can examine control theory not merely in terms of general notions about the nature of self-regulatory systems but also in terms of research support for those notions. Certainly there is much work yet to be done. There is, for example, a need to develop a taxonomy of potential behavioral standards (cf. Wegner & Vallacher, Note 1) and a need to specify more completely how standards are encoded in memory. We feel, however, that a consideration of the issues raised in this chapter indicates that control theory represents a promising model for future development.

NOTES

1. Certainly many control systems exist in which the output function is not *overt* behavior. However, because our emphasis in this chapter is on the regulation of human action, we will restrict ourselves primarily to cases in which output functions have relatively immediate overt consequences.

2. We should perhaps interject at this point three brief remarks for the sake of clarity and completeness. First, Powers (1973b) has discussed at length the logical and empirical bases for postulating each of the levels in his hierarchy. Readers who are interested in the plausibility of the existence of such a hierarchy in the human nervous system should turn to his discussion.

Second, the following account of how Powers's hierarchy can be applied to behaviors that are of interest to personality and social psychologists is adapted from a more extensive treatment of the topic published elsewhere (Carver & Scheier, 1981) It has—of necessity— been abbreviated considerably, resulting in sketchy treatment of some rather complex issues. Readers desiring a more thorough discussion may find that volume to be of interest.

Finally, we should also note that we are not alone in being interested in this conceptual problem. Wegner and Vallacher (Note 1) have independently developed a theory of levels of action identification, which has some conceptual similarity to the model presently under discussion. For the sake of simplicity, however, we will stay within the framework of the Powers model in the paragraphs that follow.

3. We should note that there is some difference of opinion as to whether deindividuated behavior is guided at a more primitive level than normal or whether it instead involves the giving over of oneself to the group in which one is immersed. The latter could reflect a sort of "group regulation," which might be construed as superordinate to normal self-regulation (cf. Wegner, 1981). Though evidence on the precise nature of deindividuation is in fact open to multiple interpretations, Diener's reasoning provides a useful vehicle for us to illustrate our more general point.

4. Though somewhat tangential to this point, it is also of interest that recent statements in the area of philosophy of mind also appear to be particularly compatible with control-theory assumptions (cf. Dennett, 1978; Fodor, 1981).

REFERENCE NOTES

1. Wegner, D. M. & Vallacher, R. R. Action identification and self-regulation. Presented at the meeting of the American Psychological Association, Montreal, 1980.

2. Scheier, M. F. and Carver, C. S. Self-directed attention and the comparison of self with standards. Manuscript submitted for publication, 1981.

REFERENCES

Abramson, L. Y., Seligman, M.E.P., and Teasdale, J. D. Learned helplessness in humans: Critique and reformulation. *Journal of Abnormal Psychology*, 1978, *87*, 49-74.

Allen, V. L. & Wilder, D. A. Categorization, belief similarity, and intergroup discrimination. *Journal of Personality and Social Psychology*, 1975, *32*, 971-977.

Anderson, J. R. *Cognitive psychology and its implications*. San Francisco: Freeman, 1980.

Bandura, A. Self-efficacy: Toward a unifying theory of behavioral change. *Psychological Review*, 1977, *84*, 191-215.

Bandura, A. The self system in reciprocal determinism. *American Psychologist*, 1978, *33*, 344-358.

Barker, R. G. *Ecological psychology: Concepts and methods for studying the environment of human behavior*. Stanford, Calif.: Stanford University Press, 1968.

Billig, M. & Tajfel, H. Social categorization and similarity in intergroup behavior. *European Journal of Social Psychology*, 1973, *3*, 27-52.

Brockner, J. The effects of self-esteem, success-failure, and self-consciousness on task performance. *Journal of Personality and Social Psychology*, 1979, *37*, 1732-1741.

Cannon, W. B. *The wisdom of the body*. New York: W. W. Norton, 1932.

Cantor, N. & Mischel, W. Traits as prototypes: Effects on recognition memory. *Journal of Personality and Social Psychology*, 1977, *35*, 38-48.

Carver, C. S. Facilitation of physical aggression through objective self-awareness. *Journal of Experimental Social Psychology*, 1974, *10*, 365-370.

Carver, C. S. Physical aggression as a function of objective self-awareness and attitudes toward punishment. *Journal of Experimental Social Psychology*, 1975, *11*, 510-519.

Carver, C. S. A cybernetic model of self-attention processes. *Journal of Personality and Social Psychology*, 1979, *37*, 1251-1281.

Carver, C. S., Blaney, P. H., & Scheier, M. F. Focus of attention, chronic expectancy, and responses to a feared stimulus. *Journal of Personality and Social Psychology*, 1979, *37*, 1186-1195. (a)

Carver, C. S., Blaney, P. H., & Scheier, M. F. Reassertion and giving up: The interactive role of self-directed attention and outcome expectancy. *Journal of Personality and Social Psychology*, 1979, *37*, 1859-1870. (b)

Carver, C. S. & Scheier, M. F. *Attention and self-regulation: A control-theory approach to human behavior*. New York: Springer-Verlag, 1981.

Carver, C. S. & Scheier, M. F. The self-attention-induced feedback loop and social facilitation. *Journal of Experimental Social Psychology*, in press.

Cohen, J. L. & Davis, J. H. Effects of audience status, evaluation, and time of action on performance with hidden word problems. *Journal of Personality and Social Psychology*, 1973, *27*, 74-85.

Cottrell, N. B. Performance in the presence of other human beings: Mere presence, audience, and affiliation effects. In E. C. Simmel, R. A. Hoppe, & G. A. Milton (eds.), *Social facilitation and imitative behavior.* Boston: Allyn and Bacon, 1968.

Cottrell, N. B. Social facilitation. In C. G. McClintock (ed.), *Experimental social psychology.* New York: Holt, Rinehart, & Winston, 1972.

Dabbs, J. M., Jr., Johnson, J. E., & Leventhal, H. Palmar sweating: A quick and simple measure. *Journal of Experimental Psychology,* 1968, *78,* 347-350.

Dennett, D. C. *Brainstorms: Philosophical essays on mind and psychology.* Montgomery, Vt.: Bradford, 1978.

Diener, E. Deindividuation, self-awareness, and disinhibition. *Journal of Personality and Social Psychology,* 1979, *37,* 1160-1171.

Diener, E. Deindividuation: The absence of self-awareness and self-regulation in group members. In P. B. Paulus (ed.), *The psychology of group influence.* Hillsdale, N.J.: Erlbaum, 1980.

Duval, S. & Wicklund, R. A. *A theory of objective self-awareness.* New York: Academic Press, 1972.

Duval, S., Wicklund, R. A., & Fine, R. L. Avoidance of objective self-awareness under conditions of high and low intra-self discrepancy. In S. Duval & R. A. Wicklund (eds.), *A theory of objective self-awareness.* New York: Academic Press, 1972.

Fodor, J. A. The mind-body problem. *Scientific American,* 1981, *244,* 114-123.

Franks, J. J. & Bransford, J. D. Abstraction of visual patterns. *Journal of Experimental Psychology,* 1971, *90,* 65-74.

Geen, R. G. & Gange, J. J. Drive theory of social facilitation: Twelve years of theory and research. *Psychological Bulletin,* 1977, *84,* 1267-1288.

Gibbons, F. X. & Wicklund, R. A. Selective exposure to the self. *Journal of Research in Personality,* 1976, *10,* 98-106.

Guilford, J. P. Motivation in an informational psychology. In D. Levine (ed.), *Nebraska symposium on motivation* (Vol. 20). Lincoln: University of Nebraska Press, 1965.

Hastorf, A. H., Schneider, D., & Polefka, J. *Person perception.* Reading, Mass.: Addison-Wesley, 1970.

Henchy, T. & Glass, D. C. Evaluation apprehension and the social facilitation of dominant and subordinate responses. *Journal of Personality and Social Psychology,* 1968, *10,* 446-454.

Hunt, J. McV. Intrinsic motivation and its role in psychological development. In D. Levine (ed.), *Nebraska symposium on motivation* (Vol. 20). Lincoln: University of Nebraska Press, 1965.

Kanfer, F. H. The maintenance of behavior by self-generated stimuli and reinforcement. In A. Jacobs & L. B. Sachs (eds.), *The psychology of private events.* New York: Academic Press, 1971.

Kanfer, F. H. The many faces of self-control, or behavior modification changes its focus. In R. B. Stuart (ed.), *Behavioral self-management: Strategies, techniques, and outcomes.* New York: Brunner/Mazel, 1977.

Kanfer, F. H. & Hagerman, S. The role of self-regulation. In L. P. Rehm (ed.), *Behavior therapy for depression: Present status and future directions.* New York: Academic Press, 1981.

Kimble, G. A. & Perlmuter, L. C. The problem of volition. *Psychological Review,* 1970, *77,* 361-384.

Lacey, J. I. Somatic response patterning and stress: Some revisions of activation theory. In M. H. Appley & R. Trumbull (eds.), *Psychological stress.* Englewood Cliffs, N.J.: Prentice-Hall, 1967.

Lacey, J. I. & Lacey, B. C. Some autonomic-central nervous system relationships. In P. Black (ed.), *Physiological correlates of emotion.* New York: Academic Press, 1970.

Leventhal, H., Meyer, D., & Nerenz, D. The common sense representation of illness danger. In S. Rachman (ed.), *Medical psychology* (Vol. 2). New York: Pergamon, 1980.

Loehlin, J. C. *Computer models of personality.* New York: Random House, 1968.

Malmo, R. B. Measurement of drive: An unsolved problem in psychology. In M. R. Jones (ed.), *Nebraska symposium on motivation* (Vol. 6). Lincoln: University of Nebraska Press, 1958.

Mancuso, J. C. (ed.). *Readings for a cognitive theory of personality.* New York: Holt, Rinehart & Winston, 1970.

Markus, H. Self-schemata and processing information about the self. *Journal of Personality and Social Psychology,* 1977, *35,* 63-78.

Martens, R. Palmar sweating and the presence of an audience. *Journal of Experimental Social Psychology,* 1969, *5,* 371-374. (a)

Martens, R. Audience effects on learning and performance. *Journal of Personality and Social Psychology,* 1969, *12,* 252-260. (b)

Miller, G. A., Galanter, E., & Pribram, K. H. *Plans and the structure of behavior.* New York: Holt, Rinehart & Winston, 1960.

Mischel, W. Toward a cognitive social learning reconceptualization of personality. *Psychological Review,* 1973, *80,* 252-283.

Neisser, U. *Cognition and reality.* San Francisco: Freeman, 1976.

Neumann, P. G. Visual prototype formation with discontinuous representation of dimensions of variability. *Memory and Cognition,* 1977, *5,* 187-197.

Posner, M. I. Abstraction and the process of recognition. In G. H. Bower & J. T. Spence (eds.), *The psychology of learning and motivation* (Vol. 3). New York: Academic Press, 1969.

Posner, M. I. & Keele, S. W. On the genesis of abstract ideas. *Journal of Experimental Psychology,* 1968, *77,* 353-363.

Powers, W. T. Feedback: Beyond behaviorism. *Science,* 1973, *179,* 351-356. (a)

Powers, W. T. *Behavior: The control of perception.* Chicago: Aldine, 1973. (b)

Powers, W. T. A cybernetic model for research in human development. In M. Ozer (ed.), *A cybernetic approach to the assessment of children.* Boulder, Colo.: Westview Press, 1979.

Prentice-Dunn, S. & Rogers, R. W. Effects of deindividuating situational cues and aggressive models on subjective deindividuation and aggression. *Journal of Personality and Social Psychology,* 1980, *39,* 104-113.

Price, R. H. The taxonomic classification of behaviors and situations and the problem of behavior-environment congruence. *Human Relations,* 1974, *27,* 567-585.

Reitman, J. S. & Bower, G. H. Storage and later recognition of exemplars of concepts. *Cognitive Psychology,* 1973, *4,* 194-206.

Rogers, T. B. Self-reference in memory: Recognition of personality items. *Journal of Research in Personality,* 1977, *11,* 295-305.

Rogers, T. B., Rogers, P. J., & Kuiper, N. A. Evidence for the self as a cognitive prototype: The "false alarms effect." *Personality and Social Psychology Bulletin,* 1979, *5,* 53-56.

Rosch, E. On the internal structure of perceptual and semantic categories. In T. E. Moore (ed.), *Cognitive development and the acquisition of language.* New York: Academic Press, 1973.

Rosch, E. Principles of categorization. In E. Rosch & B. B. Lloyd (eds.), *Cognition and categorization.* Hillsdale, N.J.: Erlbaum, 1978.

Rubovits, P. C. and Maehr, M. L. Pygmalion black and white. *Journal of Personality and Social Psychology,* 1973, *25,* 210-218.

Sanders, G. S. & Baron, R. S. The motivating effects of distraction on task performance. *Journal of Personality and Social Psychology,* 1975, *32,* 956-963.

Sanders, G. S., Baron, R. S., & Moore, D. L. Distraction and social comparison as mediators of social facilitation effects. *Journal of Experimental Social Psychology,* 1978, *14,* 291-303.

Schank, R. C. & Abelson, R. P. *Scripts, plans, goals, and understanding.* Hillsdale, N.J.: Erlbaum, 1977.

Scheier, M. F., Fenigstein, A., & Buss, A. H. Self-awareness and physical agression. *Journal of Experimental Social Psychology,* 1974, *10,* 264-273.

Schroder, H. M. & Suedfeld, P. (eds.), *Personality theory and information processing.* New York: Ronald Press, 1970.

Schwartz, G. E. The brain as a health care system. In G. C. Stone, F. Cohen, & N. E. Adler (eds.), *Health psychology—a handbook.* San Francisco: Jossey-Bass, 1979.

Schwartz, G. E. Self-attention and automatic psychophysiological self-regulation: A cybernetic analysis. Presented at the meeting of the American Psychological Association, Montreal, 1980.

Slapion, M. J. & Carver, C. S. Self-directed attention and facilitation of intellectual performance among persons high in test anxiety. *Cognitive Therapy and Research,* 1981, *5,* 115-121.

Snyder, M., Tanke, E. D., & Berscheid, E. Social perception and interpersonal behavior: On the self-fulfilling nature of social stereotypes. *Journal of Personality and Social Psychology,* 1977, *35,* 656-666.

Snyder, M. L., Stephan, W. G., & Rosenfield, D. Attributional egotism. In J. H. Harvey, W. Ickes, & R. F. Kidd (eds.), *New directions in attribution research* (Vol. 2). Hillsdale, N.J.: Erlbaum, 1978.

Sokolov, Y. N. *Perception and the conditioned reflex.* New York: Macmillan, 1963.

Steenbarger, B. N. & Aderman, D. Objective self-awareness as a nonaversive state: Effect of anticipating discrepancy reduction. *Journal of Personality,* 1979, *47,* 330-339.

Stokols, D. Environmental psychology. In M. R. Rosenzweig & L. W. Porter (eds.), *Annual review of psychology* (Vol. 29). Palo Alto, Calif.: Annual Reviews, 1978.

Taylor, D. W. Toward an information-processing theory of motivation. In M. R. Jones (ed.), *Nebraska symposium on motivation* (Vol. 8). Lincoln: University of Nebraska Press, 1960.

Taylor, S. E. & Crocker, J. Schematic bases of social information processing. In E. T. Higgins, P. Herman, & M. P. Zanna (eds.), *The Ontario symposium on personality and social psychology* (Vol. 1). Hillsdale, N.J.: Erlbaum, 1979.

Trope, Y. Seeking information about one's own ability as a determinant of choice among tasks. *Journal of Personality and Social Psychology, 1975, 32,* 1004-1013.

Wegner, D. M. Justice and the awareness of social entities. In J. Greenberg & R. L. Cohen (eds.), *Equity and justice in social behavior.* New York: Academic Press, 1981.

Wegner, D. M. & Vallacher, R. R. *Implicit psychology.* New York: Oxford University Press, 1977.

Wicker, A. W. Processes which mediate behavior-environment congruence. *Behavioral Science, 1972, 17,* 265-277.

Wicklund, R. A. The influence of self on human behavior. *American Scientist, 1979, 67,* 187-193.

Wicklund, R. A. & Duval, S. Opinion change and performance facilitation as a result of objective self-awareness. *Journal of Experimental Social Psychology, 1971, 7,* 319-342.

Wiener, N. *Cybernetics: Control and communication in the animal and the machine.* Cambridge, Mass.: MIT Press, 1948.

Wilder, D. A. & Allen, V. L. Group membership and preference for information about others. *Personality and Social Psychology Bulletin, 1978, 4,* 106-110.

Williams, R. B., Jr. Psychophysiological processes, the coronary-prone behavior pattern, and coronary heart disease. In T. M. Dembroski et al. (eds.), *Coronary-prone behavior.* New York: Springer-Verlag, 1978.

Williams, R. B., Jr., Bittker, T. E., Buchsbaum, M. S., & Wynne, L. C. Cardiovascular and neurophysiologic correlates of sensory intake and rejection. I. Effect of cognitive tasks. *Psychophysiology, 1975, 12,* 427-433.

Wine, J. D. Test anxiety and direction of attention. *Psychological Bulletin, 1971, 76,* 92-104.

Wine, J. D. Cognitive-attentional theory of test anxiety. In I. G. Sarason (ed.), *Test anxiety: Theory, research, and application.* Hillsdale, N.J.: Erlbaum, 1980.

Wortman, C. B. & Brehm, J. W. Responses to uncontrollable outcomes: An integration of reactance theory and the learned helplessness model. In L. Berkowitz (ed.), *Advances in experimental social psychology* (Vol. 8). New York: Academic Press, 1975.

Zajonc, R. B. Social facilitation. *Science, 1965, 149,* 269-274.

Zajonc, R. B. *Social psychology: An experimental approach.* Belmont, Calif.: Wadsworth, 1966.

5

Language and Individual Differences:
THE SEARCH FOR UNIVERSALS IN PERSONALITY LEXICONS

LEWIS R. GOLDBERG

Lewis R. Goldberg is Professor of Psychology at the University of Oregon and Director of the Institute for the Measurement of Personality. He has written on clinical judgment and decision making, the comparative validity of different strategies of test construction, the properties of personality items, response sets and styles, college instructional and grading practices, and situational versus dispositional attributions in self and peer descriptions.

Virtually every scientist who has worked in the field of personality—certainly everyone who has tried to develop a personality theory—has had to grapple with one fundamental problem: Of the enormous variety of individual differences that we observe around us, which are the most important? For, we can look at a theory of personality as a specification of the *most important* individual differences and then as a model of how they come about.

The most promising of the empirical approaches to systematizing personality differences have been based on one critical assumption: *Those*

AUTHOR'S NOTE: Support for writing this article has been provided by Grant MH-32585 from the National Institute of Mental Health, U.S. Public Health Service. This article has profited enormously from the critiques of earlier versions

individual differences that are of the most significance in the daily transactions of persons with each other will eventually become encoded into their language. The more important is such a difference, the more will people notice it and wish to talk of it, with the result that eventually they will invent a word for it. One can see this process exemplified in the introduction of other concepts into languages; for example, snow, of more importance to the Eskimo than to the English, has led to more terms in Eskimo dialects than in English. Presumably, the same process must occur for those nouns (e.g., *bigot, bully, fool, grouch, hick, loafer, miser, sucker*) and adjectives (e.g., *assertive, brave, energetic, honest, intelligent, responsible, sociable, sophisticated*) that are used to describe persons.

Moreover, this fundamental axiom has a highly significant corollary: *The more important is an individual difference in human transactions, the more languages will have a term for it.* In the strongest form of this corollary, we should find a *universal order of emergence* of the individual differences encoded into the set of all the world's languages.

LEXICAL UNIVERSALS

The search for cross-language regularities has recently been reviewed by Witkowski and Brown, who argued that "contemporary linguistics has focused upon language universals with the idea that these uniformities reflect the underlying nature of human cognition" (1978: 427). Indeed, the discovery of some lexical universals may be one of the most important developments in the social sciences in the past few decades. Since this exciting research is at the interface of cognitive psychology, linguistics, and anthropology, much of it has not yet been assimilated into the secondary literature of each discipline. Consequently, I will briefly review some of these recent findings; for more extensive discussions, see Clark and Clark (1978), Greenberg (1975, 1978), Lonner (1980), and Witkowski and Brown (1978).

provided by Michael H. Bond, William F. Chaplin, Roy G. D'Andrade, Robyn M. Dawes, John M. Digman, Baruch Fischhoff, Donald W. Fiske, Lita M. Furby, Douglas L. Hintzman, Willem K.B. Hofstee, Robert Hogan, James Kelly, Adrienne Lehrer, Richard Littman, Walter J. Lonner, Ulric Neisser, Warren T. Norman, Charles E. Osgood, Dean Peabody, Leonard G. Rorer, Seymour Rosenberg, Norman D. Sundberg, Harry C. Triandis, Geoffrey White, Wayne A. Wickelgren, and Jerry S. Wiggins.

By far the most famous of these discoveries was that of a uniform order of emergence of color terms in the set of natural languages (Kay & McDaniel, 1978). For example, if a language has a term for the color *yellow,* it will also have a term for *red,* whereas some languages have a term for *red* and not (yet) for *yellow.* The original demonstration of these color regularities was provided by Berlin and Kay (1969), whose work led to the significant theoretical extensions of Rosch (e.g., Heider, 1972; Rosch, 1975a, 1975b, 1975c). Figure 1 presents a recent model for the temporal-evolutionary ordering of color terms in the natural languages (Witkowski & Brown, 1977).

One of the most active arenas for seeking lexical universals is that of "folk biology," or common terms for botanical (e.g., *tree, grass, vine*) and zoological (e.g., *fish, bird, snake*) life forms. Using data from 105 languages, Brown (1977) demonstrated that five important botanical life forms are encoded in a highly regular manner. Similarly, there may be a universal lexical order of emergence of zoological life forms as well (Brown, 1979). While one could view the ordering of color terms in the natural languages as a direct consequence of the physics and physiology of the processes involved in human color vision, the discovery of such orders for biological life forms can hardly be explained in the same manner. As a result, these findings provide a compelling motive for the continued search for lexical universals in other domains. For an extensive discussion of the implications of the research in folk biology, see Berlin, Breedlove, and Raven (1973); for extensions to a number of nonbiological domains, see Brown et al. (1976), Clark and Clark (1978), and Lehrer (1974).

One such domain provides a logical bridge between the discovery of universal orders for such natural categories as colors, plants, and animals and the search for a universal order within the domain of personality-descriptive terms. Williams (1976) has argued that there may be a universal law governing the metaphorical transfer of adjectives from one sensory domain to another, and he has tested his model in an Indo-European language (English) and a non-Indo-European one (Japanese). Figure 2, an adaptation of Williams's model, indicates the few possible directions that adjectives do transfer out of the many directions that are possible. For example, if a Touch-modifier transfers, it may transfer to Tastes (e.g., *sharp* tastes), to Colors (e.g., *dull* colors), or to Sounds (e.g., *soft* sounds), but not to Dimensions or Smells. Taste-modifiers may transfer to Smells (e.g., *sour* smells) or to Sounds (e.g., *sweet* sounds), but not to Touch,

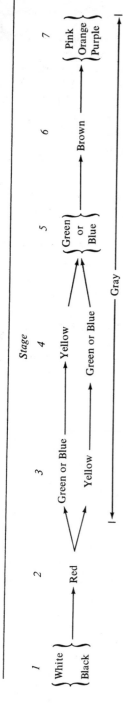

Note: This figure (adapted from Witkowski & Brown, 1977) is to be read as follows: (1) Most languages contain terms for white and black; (2) if a language contains three (or more) color terms, then it contains a term for red; (3) if a language contains four (or more) color terms, then it either contains a term for yellow or it contains one for green or blue; (4) if a language contains five (or more) color terms, then it contains a term for yellow, plus one for either green or blue; (5) if a language contains six (or more) color terms, then it contains terms for white, black, red, yellow, green, and blue; (6) if a language contains seven (or more) color terms, then it contains a term for brown; etc.

FIGURE 1   The Temporal Order in Which Languages Encode the Color Categories

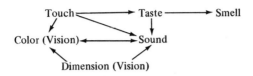

Note: This figure (adapted from Williams, 1976) is to be read as follows: If an adjective metaphorically transfers from its earliest sensory meaning to another sensory modality, it will transfer only in the direction indicated by the arrows.

FIGURE 2   A Possible Universal Ordering for the Transfer of Synaesthetic Adjectives from One Modality to Another

Dimensions, or Colors. Dimension-modifiers may transfer to Colors (e.g., *flat* colors) or to Sounds (e.g., *deep* sounds), but not to Touch, Tastes, or Smells. Color-modifiers may transfer only to Sounds (e.g., *bright* sounds), and Sound-modifiers may transfer only to Colors (e.g., *quiet* colors). As Williams noted:

> Sensory words in English have systematically transferred from the physiologically least differentiating, most evolutionary primitive sensory modalities to the most differentiating, most advanced, but not vice versa. It should be emphasized that there is no intrinsic reason why this order should be observed. In a forced-choice test, 25 undergraduates displayed a high level of agreement (90%+) on the meaning of metaphors such as *loud heights* (high or low?), *sour blades* (sharp or dull?), and *quiet angles* (acute or obtuse?). Since such metaphors can be understood, there seems to be no principled reason for them not to develop. But except in poetry, they do not [1976: 464-465].

A more general theory of metaphorical transfer for adjectives has been proposed by Lehrer (1978). She has argued that for any set of words that are semantically related (by synonymy, antonymy, hyponymy, or whatever; Lyons, 1977), if one term transfers to another sematic field, then the other terms in the set are all available for extension to the second semantic field, regardless of their perceived similarity:

> This hypothesis allows us to state what semantic transfers we can expect to occur. It also shows that an adequate semantic analysis must not only describe meanings of individual lexical items, but

must also show the structure of each word to other words in a semantic domain. For example, *cook, bake, boil, roast, fry,* and *grill* are cooking words, but *fry* and *grill* also have meanings in the domain of inflicting pain, punishment, or discomfort (e.g., The police *grilled* the suspect. The criminal will *fry* for his crime). The hypothesis predicts that other cooking words could also be used in this domain, and indeed, have been, as exemplified in the television series in which Dean Martin *roasts* various celebrities [1978: 96].

Lehrer (1978) tested this hypothesis with a large set of English terms for taste, smell, and feel, all of which are used by wine writers, oenologists, and/or ordinary wine drinkers to describe wines, although this use of each word is typically only a peripheral meaning. Lehrer concluded that:

> In examining semantic transfer—the transfer of words with a mean-ing in one domain to another—it is a mistake to look at all transfers taking place in the same way. Most likely, the first transfer will be the result of perceived similarity, association, or even synaesthesia. However, once this has happened, other words from the first domain can transfer, even though there is no similarity. This is probably why *cold* and *flat* acquired the meaning of *bland.* Only one member of an antonymous pair need have any perceived similarity, and only one member of a synonymous set need transfer. Other members of the lexical set are available for transfer and often do transfer [1978: 122].

Clearly, one of the most important types of semantic transfer is one to which both Williams and Lehrer alluded but did not study, namely, the transfer from a sensory modality (more concrete) to a personality descrip-tion (more abstract). At least in English, if not in all large languages, the lexicon is filled with terms that have been transferred to personality from such modalities as Touch (e.g., *coarse, cold, cool, dull, hard, harsh, rough, sharp, smooth, soft, warm*), Taste (e.g., *bitter, bland, sour, sweet*), Color (e.g., *bright, brilliant, clear*), Dimension (e.g., *deep, shallow*), and Sound (e.g., *loud, quiet*). It is probable that the first terms to enter any persona-lity-descriptive lexicon are those originally used for other purposes (see Asch, 1955, 1958). But, are there any regularities, any cross-language universals, in the manner in which such words transfer into the personality domain?

By far the most famous of the recent attempts to discover lexical universals is the 20-year program of research conducted by Osgood and his associates (Osgood, May, & Miron, 1975). Osgood has hypothesized that most of the "affective" meaning—the emotional aspects of the meaning—of all concepts can be viewed as an amalgamation of three basic dimensions: Evaluation, Potency, and Activity. Osgood's major technique for studying affective meaning is called the Semantic Differential: One takes a representative set of concepts, including common objects (e.g., *house, girl, meat, book, star,* and *cup*) as well as abstract concepts (e.g., *trust, success, danger, sympathy, progress, courage,* and *love*), and has native speakers rate the meaning of each of them on a set of seven-step scales, each anchored by bipolar adjectives (e.g., *warm* versus *cold, light* versus *dark*). Then, one correlates the adjectival scales across the set of concepts and factor analyzes that matrix of intercorrelations. Whenever a reasonably large and heterogeneous set of concepts (nouns) has been rated on a reasonably diverse set of adjectival scales, Osgood has found much the same three major factors: Evaluation (*bad-good*), Potency (*weak-strong*), and Activity (*passive-active*).

To test whether this structure might be a universal one, Osgood and an international team of colleagues have now studied over 20 different languages, including some that are quite distant linguistically. As subjects, the Osgood team has used 14 to 18-year-old males in urban high school settings. A common set of 100 simple English nouns are first translated into the language under study, and each is used by native subjects to elicit the first adjective that comes to mind. From the large number initially so elicited, a subset of 100 terms is selected on the grounds of frequency, diversity, and independence. For each of these, native subjects are asked to produce antonyms, from which a final set of 50 seven-step rating scales are constructed. Native subjects are then asked to rate each of the original set of 100 nouns on each of the 50 scales, and the correlations among the 50 scales across the 100 nouns are factor analyzed. From their extensive analyses, Osgood, May, and Miron concluded: "We feel that the theoretical purpose of this research has been achieved. We have been able to demonstrate conclusively that the three affective factors of meaning are truly pancultural—at least to the extent that our sample of some 21 language/culture communities is representative of all human societies" (1975: 190).

In the quest for the discovery of lexical universals, an important contribution has been provided indirectly by Dixon, a linguist. In an analysis of a variety of small languages, Dixon (1977) inquired whether all languages contain the major grammatical classes of Noun, Verb, and Adjective, concluded that the Noun and Verb classes are universal whereas the Adjective class is not, and then analyzed the manner in which adjective-impoverished languages use nouns and/or verbs for adjectival functions. Dixon classified adjectives on semantic, syntactic, and morphological criteria into seven major types: (1) Dimension (e.g., *big, large, little, small; long, short; wide, narrow; thick, fat, thin*); (2) Color; (3) Other Physical Properties (a large class, including *hard, soft; heavy, light; rough, smooth; hot, cold; sweet* and *sour*); (4) Human Propensities (by far the largest class, including *jealous, happy, kind, clever, generous, cruel, rude,* and *proud*); (5) Age (e.g., *new, young, old*); (6) Value (e.g., *good, bad, proper, perfect, excellent, fine, delicious, atrocious, poor*); and (7) Speed (a small class, including *fast, quick,* and *slow*). Table 1 lists those adjectives from 20 languages with extremely small adjective classes (range 7 to 24) that are included in two or more lexicons.

One must be wary of interpreting the terms listed in Table 1 as those describing the most primitive or basic types of physical and/or individual differences, since each of these 20 languages includes a host of nouns and verbs that serve the same function as do adjectives in English. Moreover, one should not infer from this table that terms for which antonyms are not listed (e.g., *strong, female, beautiful, generous*) are not capable of being negated in those languages by some expression similar in function to the English word *not.* As far as we know, no one has ever investigated the Human Propensity class of adjectives, nouns, and verbs in a wide variety of languages, and until this is done we will not know which types of individual differences are most basic, and/or if there is a universal order for encoding these differences. In the words of Dixon:

A lot can be learnt concerning the speakers of a language and the kind of life they lead from a study of the language's semantic structure. Members of the (deep) class Noun indicate the kinds of objects occurring in the speakers' environments. . . . Areas of concentration of vocabulary indicate objects or phenomena that are focal points of the community's life—well-known examples concern the Arabs' superfluity of terms for parts of the camel, Eskimos' terms for different kinds of snow, and so on. . . .

All languages have words belonging to the main semantic types associated with the (deep) class Verb—MOTION, ACTION, GIVING,

TABLE 1   The Most Universal Adjectives? The English Translations of
Adjectives from 20 Languages with *Very* Small Adjective
Classes

Term	Number of Languages	Adjectival Type
large	20	Dimension
small	19	
short	15	Dimension
long	14	
new	15	Age
old	14	
bad	14	Value
good	13	
white	14	Color
black	13	
red	8	Color
raw (unripe)	7	Other Physical Property
heavy	5	Other Physical Property
light	5	
sharp	4	Other Physical Property
blunt	2	
thin	3	Dimension
thick	2	
hot	3	Other Physical Property
cold	2	
fierce/angry/wild	3	Human Propensity
strong	3	Human Propensity
female	3	Human Propensity
beautiful	3	Value
generous	2	Human Propensity
soft	2	Other Physical Property
wet	2	Other Physical Property
sour	2	Other Physical Property
whole	2	Other Physical Property

Note: This table, which has been prepared from Dixon (1977), lists all of the adjectives that are included in two or more of the 20 languages. In this set of languages, the number of adjectives included in each lexicon ranges from 7 to 24,
with a mean of 13.

SAYING, LIKING, and so on. Areas of vocabulary concentration here indicate types of actions that are important in the community. . . .

Just as the nouns in a language give some idea of the relevant objects in the speaker's environment, and the verbs the important cultural actions, so the HUMAN PROPENSITY words give an idea of the mental attitudes of speakers of the language.

HUMAN PROPENSITY would certainly be the most difficult semantic type to investigate in depth and to make detailed generalisations about; but it would also be one of the most revealing [1977: 66-67; emphasis added].

LANGUAGE AND PERSONALITY

Given the enormous importance of comparative research on the expression of individual differences in diverse languages, it is startling to realize how few systematic studies have yet been conducted. Indeed, only a few investigators have analyzed data from as many as a half dozen or more languages. Yet, those few who have panned this cross-cultural stream have found gold. For example, Murphy (1976) drew on the ethnographic literature, supplemented by her own field studies of Eskimos in northwest Alaska and the Yoruba tribes of rural tropical Nigeria, to ask whether one important type of individual difference, namely, mental illness, is universally recognized in the languages of diverse peoples. Murphy concluded that (1) the phenomenal processes of disturbed thought and behavior similar to schizophrenia are found in most (if not all) cultures and (2) they are sufficiently distinctive and noticeable that almost everywhere a name has been created for them. Moreover, Murphy concluded that:

If one defines intolerance of mental illness as the use of confinement, restraint, or exclusion from the community (or allowing people to confine or exclude themselves), there does not appear to be a great deal of difference between Western and non-Western groups in intolerance of the mentally ill. Furthermore, there seems to be little that is distinctively cultural in the attitudes and actions directed toward the mentally ill, except in such matters as that an abandoned anthill could not be used as an asylum in the arctic or a barred igloo in the tropics. There is apparently a common range of possible responses to the mentally ill person, and the portion of the range brought to bear regarding a particular person is determined more by the nature of his behavior than by a preexisting cultural set to respond in a uniform way to whatever is labeled mental illness [1976: 1025].

While Murphy (1976) was hesitant about concluding that terms for anxiety and depression were also universal (see also Marsella, 1980), Morice (1978) has recently argued that they probably are. In an intensive analysis of the language of the Pintupi Aborigines of Central Australia, until recently palaeolithic hunter-gatherers, Morice found lexical categories for both anxiety and depression:

The degree of verbal differentiation in the Pintupi language for the affects of anxiety and depression shows that Pintupi Aborigines experience a range of subjective feelings, from mild anxiety and depression to severe affective disorders. . . . This same degree of differentiation in the Pintupi verbal repertoire means that they also possess the ability to express and communicate their emotions, a fact questioned in the past by many transcultural psychiatrists [1978: 93].

Seemingly, then, one quite basic, if not universal, set of individual differences encoded into the natural languages involve distinctions between the normal and the insane (Draguns, 1980). Other candidates include the highly abstract dimensions of affective meaning (Evaluation, Potency, and Activity) transferred to the personality domain (see Kuusinen, 1969; Mehrabian, 1980; Tzeng, 1975; Warr & Haycock, 1970). And, finally, some additional candidates stem from those systematic analyses of self and peer ratings carried out initially in English (e.g., Cattell, 1947, 1957; Eysenck & Eysenck, 1969; Guilford, 1959, 1975; Norman, 1963; Wiggins, 1979), and now beginning to be extended to other languages as well (e.g., Bond, 1979; Bond et al., 1975; White, 1978, 1980). To these efforts we now must turn.

MODELS OF PERSONALITY STRUCTURE:
SOME GENERAL CONSIDERATIONS

It is clear that languages differ from each other not so much in what they *can* convey, but rather in what they can *easily* convey. While it is naive to expect to find one-to-one translations for any single personality descriptive term across all languages, there may be some individual differences of such critical import in human transactions that all languages permit speakers to convey that characteristic relatively easily. But, how should we look for such individual differences? To even begin this quest, we need to first consider some possible models of personality structure.

Discrete (Categorical) Versus Dimensional (Ordered)

In English, if not in most contemporary languages, persons can be described both by nouns (e.g., *cynic*) and by adjectives (e.g., *cynical*). The former involves a discrete or categorical classification, while the latter more easily permits the expression of degree or extent (e.g., James is (a) slightly, (b) somewhat, (c) quite, (d) very, or (e) extremely *cynical*). Languages differ in their ratios of personality nouns to adjectives, as well as in the types of individual differences encoded by each linguistic class. For example, in English there are far more personality adjectives than personality nouns; the distribution of personality nouns on the Evaluation continuum is markedly different than that for personality adjectives (a higher proportion of nouns than adjectives carry negative implications); and a far greater proportion of personality nouns than personality adjectives are colloquial or slang terms, perhaps because personality nouns are used most typically in oral communication and personality adjectives are used most typically in written communication (Goldberg, 1981).

When looking at the ways in which individual differences are encoded in different languages, we have to decide whether to use a typological model or a dimensional one. Are people to be fitted into types or categories, or are they to be ordered along continuous dimensions? In all probability a dimensional approach will prove more useful. Indeed, if one thinks of personality types—that is, discrete categories of people—there may be only one genuine typology in nature, namely, biological sex. Sex comes packaged in two brands—a male one and a female one—and while there is a tiny bit of overlap, nonetheless by and large people are well-differentiated. But, even when one considers other *physical* characteristics (e.g., eye or hair color), we observe orderly progressions rather than genuine types. Whatever kind of a structure we are going to use, it has to at least *permit* some ordering. Many languages contain terms which vary in their placement on the same dimension; in English, for example, the four terms *stupid, dull, smart,* and *brilliant* certainly imply a continuum of intellect. That is, considering any potential model for individual differences, a dimensional approach will probably prove to be more tractable, as long as it permits categories or types as special cases.

Unipolarity Versus Bipolarity

Another general issue we must consider: Should the dimensions of individual differences be considered as if they were unipolar or bipolar? Is it more reasonable to view intelligence and stupidity as two separate dimensions or as a single bipolar one? In English at least, most adjectives can be negated by the addition of a prefix (e.g., *un-, non-, in-*) or a suffix (e.g., *-less*); indeed, in a variety of languages, the single most common response to an adjective in a word association task is an antonym (e.g., *sweet* → *sour, dry* → *wet*; Deese, 1965). Linguists as well as psychologists generally assume that the capacity to make bipolar contrasts is a fundamental aspect of linguistic competence. Two examples:

> The encoding priority . . . is due in part to the general human tendency to classify by means of *binary opposition*. This tendency is particularly apparent in the adjectival component of vocabularies. The oppositional characteristics of dimensional concepts such as height, width, depth, etc., are usually encoded by two terms, and only rarely are finer lexical distinctions carved out. This results in such familiar adjectival oppositions as *wide/narrow, deep/shallow, hard/soft, rough/smooth, sharp/blunt,* and so on [Witkowski & Brown, 1978: 435].

> A productivity-ranked and pruned list of 60-70 qualifiers was sent back to each community, where a small group of native speakers was asked to produce *opposites* for each term—again, with appropriately adapted instructions. . . . What is interesting here is that in *none* of the 28 language/culture communities where this stage has been reached—and this now includes several non-urban and/or non-literate groups—has any difficulty been experienced in eliciting qualifier-opposites. It would appear that the tendency to organize models of qualification in terms of polar opposition is yet another universal of human languages [Osgood, 1976: 77].

On the other hand, Dixon has argued that the Human Propensity class of adjectives differs from most other adjectival classes in their lack of clear bipolarity. In his words:

HUMAN PROPENSITY adjectives—such as *jealous, loyal, merry*—do not appear to have clear (monomorphemic) complements or antonyms. . . . Yet they behave somewhat like members of antonym pairs, depending on milieu—a certain person could be described as relatively loyal, or as rather lacking in loyalty, according to the company he is in—and forming semantically proper comparatives. It is as if these adjectives specified an antonym dimension of which only one pole is named. A term like *jealous* describes certain human proclivities and is used relative to the human norm, the norm implying lack of the proclivities; it is not clear what the opposite of *jealous,* on the opposite side of the norm, could be. . . .

A number of HUMAN PROPENSITY adjectives appear to be in almost antonymous relation: *happy/sad, cruel/kind, clever/stupid, generous/mean, proud/humble, rude/polite* and a few more; however speakers agree far less when asked to give the opposite of one of these terms, than they do in the case of . . . other terms. In fact each HUMAN PROPENSITY adjective is best considered as a singleton, individually specifying an antonym-like parameter. Some of the parameters—as in the pairs just mentioned—are *almost* opposites of each other. The lack of exact opposition is apparent from the triples *kind/unkind/cruel, polite/impolite/rude, happy/unhappy/sad. Unkind,* the antonym of *kind,* is not perfectly synonymous with *cruel* (and still less *unhappy* with *sad*) implying that *cruel* cannot be considered the antonym of *kind* (nor *sad* of *happy,* and so on) [1977: 34-35].

Seemingly, the implication of these arguments is that any model of individual differences must have the facility for handling antonymlike bipolarity, as well as the facility for permitting unipolar dimensions (see Bentler, 1969).

Orthogonal (Uncorrelated) Versus Oblique (Correlated)

Should those personality dimensions be orthogonal or oblique? That is, should the dimensions be construed as correlating with each other or should each be independent of all the others? Dimensions which are mutually orthogonal are very lovely. While they are the nicest possible kind for prediction purposes, they are grossly unrealistic. For, in any natural language, there are terms to describe individual differences that are at varying levels of abstraction and/or at varying degrees of generality. An example from English: The terms *prompt* and *punctual* are far more specific than is the general term *conscientious,* which includes punctuality as well as a number of other characteristics. Moreover, the term *conscientious* is itself more specific than, say, a term like *reliable,* which may include conscientiousness, honesty, and perhaps intelligence. That is, within the English language there are differences in the kinds of words that we can apply to people, differences in their concreteness versus abstractness. This makes it look as if an optimal structure must be capable of unfolding in some kind of a hierarchical fashion, with very specific attributes being combined into ones which are more general, which in turn are combined into others which are yet more general, and so on up the branches of the inverted tree. This kind of structure implies oblique dimensions of personality.

Concrete (Specific) Versus Abstract (Global)

At what level of this molar-molecular hierarchy of individual differences can we expect to find lexical universals? Should we search for lexical counterparts to the English term *punctual*? Or *conscientious*? Or *reliable*? It seems unreasonable to assume that all the fine-grained details of individual differences are universally encoded in the natural languages. Rather, modern scientific work on cognitive processing (e.g., Rosch, 1975a, 1975b, 1975c) would suggest that a search for individual differences as expressed at some basic level (e.g., *chair/conscientiousness*)—a level that is neither too abstract (e.g., *furniture/reliability*) nor too specific (e.g., *rocking chair/punctuality*)—would be most likely to uncover universal characteristics (see Wiggins, 1980). Seemingly, then, if we are to find a universal order of emergence of individual differences into diverse lexicons, we must search at the right level of abstraction. Two dimensions (e.g., Wiggins, 1979, 1980) are probably too few (general); 20 to 30 dimensions (e.g., Cattell, 1957) are probably too many (specific). What is clear is that we must have some structure in mind before we can dare to test its cross-language robustness.

TOWARD A SYNTHESIS OF PERSONALITY DIMENSIONS

When we consider how individual differences are encoded in different natural languages, we are talking about semantics, the *meanings* of the words that we use to describe ourselves and other people. And so a logical place to begin our search for the universals of personality is to consider what is known about the meaning of words in general. As already noted, Osgood has argued that the "affective" meaning of all concepts can be viewed as an amalgamation of three basic dimensions—Evaluation, Potency, and Activity—and thus these three dimensions are logical places to start when we look at the meanings of the words used to describe people. But, when real people are rated on a representative set of bipolar adjectival scales, Potency and Activity turn out to be quite highly correlated (e.g., Kim & Rosenberg, 1980).

Figure 3 lists some of the bipolar adjectival scales which mark the three major dimensions of affective meaning, both for concepts in general and for people in particular. One can see why the Potency dimension would be correlated with both Activity and Evaluation when individuals are rated: *Brave, forceful,* and *independent* people are likely to be seen as more Active than are *cowardly, meek,* and *dependent* ones. If we combine Potency and Activity, we have a more general construct called "Dynamism" by Osgood and "Surgency" by Norman (following Cattell). The *surgent* individual is both *active* and *brave.* (The direct psychometric analog to Potency is an old concept in individual differences—namely, Dominance versus Submissiveness.)

The first person in psychology to take seriously the scientific task of constructing a personality taxonomy was Cattell, who began with a perusal of English personality-descriptive terms. Allport and Odbert (1936) catalogued about 18,000 such terms and divided them into four alphabetical lists, the first of which were those that in their judgment reflected stable "biophysical" traits. Of the approximately 4,500 trait terms, Cattell (1943) selected 171, which were then used by people to rate others whom they knew. On the basis of the correlations among those ratings, Cattell developed a set of 35 to 40 clusters of related terms and used those clusters as the basis for constructing rating scales for factor analyses of people's ratings of themselves and others.

The number of primary personality factors in Cattell's system is in the 20-to-30 range, of which the 16 most famous are included in his Sixteen

Factor	Concepts in General	People
Evaluation (E)	Bad - Good Dirty - Clean Worthless - Valuable	Insincere - Sincere Dishonest - Honest Unreliable - Reliable
Potency (P)	Weak - Strong Small - Large Light - Heavy	Cowardly - Brave Meek - Forceful Dependent - Independent
Activity (A)	Passive - Active Slow - Fast Cold - Hot	Passive - Active Apathetic - Energetic Sluggish - Rambunctious

FIGURE 3 Rating Scales Marking the Three Primary Factors in Osgood's Semantic Differential

I. Surgency

    Talkative -Silent
    Sociable - Reclusive
    Adventurous - Cautious
    Open - Secretive

II. Agreeableness

    Good-natured - Irritable
    Cooperative - Negativistic
    Mild/Gentle - Headstrong
    Not Jealous - Jealous

III. Conscientiousness

    Responsible - Undependable
    Scrupulous - Unscrupulous
    Persevering - Quitting
    Fussy/Tidy - Careless

IV. Emotional Stability

    Calm - Anxious
    Composed - Excitable
    Not hypochondriacal - Hypochondriacal
    Poised - Nervous/Tense

V. Culture

    Intellectual - Unreflective/Narrow
    Artistic - Nonartistic
    Imaginative - Simple/Direct
    Polished/Refined - Crude/Boorish

FIGURE 4 The Big Five: Norman (1963)

	0	I	II	III	IV	V
Osgood	Evaluation	Potency / Activity				
Kuusinen	Evaluation	Potency / Activity	[Tolerance]	[Conscientiousness]	[Self-confidence]	[Rationality]
Peabody	Evaluation	Assertiveness		Impulse Control (Tight-Loose)		
Leary	["Intensity"]	Dominance	Affiliation			
Wiggins		Dominance	Affiliation			
Cattell (2nd order)		Exvia	Cortertia	Superego Strength	Anxiety	Intelligence
Norman		Surgency	Agreeableness (Warmth)	Conscientiousness	Emotional Stability	Culture
Guilford		Social Activity	Paranoid Disposition	Introversion	Emotional Stability	
Eysenck		Psychoticism / Extroversion-Introversion			Neuroticism	
Buss &		Activity	Sociability	Impulsivity	Emotionality	
Block				Ego Control	Ego Resiliency	

FIGURE 5   Decoding Babel: Alternative Varieties of Structures for Personality Characteristics

Personality Factors Questionnaire (16PF). When his data were made available to others, however, virtually everyone who factored those data found only 5. The investigators who discovered these 5 factors were first Fiske (1949) and later Tupes and Christal (1961). However, since the most systematic work was subsequently done by Norman (1963), it is common now to refer to these factors as the Norman Five: Surgency (the fusion of Potency and Activity), Agreeableness (or Coldness versus Warmth), Conscientiousness, Emotional Stability, and Culture (a mixture of intellectual or cognitive aspects of individual differences, such as cultural sophistication, knowledge, and various aptitudes). Figure 4 lists abbreviated versions of the scales that loaded most highly on these five major factors, which by now have appeared repeatedly in analyses of both peer ratings and self ratings in a large number of different studies (see Borgatta, 1964; Digman & Takemoto-Chock, 1981).

Figure 5 includes the structural dimensions from a variety of personality theorists, aligned in a single framework. The "big five" factors provide the background for placing the major dimensions provided by Cattell and Guilford, both at the second-order level, and for a number of other investigators who have restricted their work to only a few dimensions (e.g., Eysenck, Peabody, Leary, Wiggins,[1] Block). For example, in the most recent version of Guilford's (1975) hierarchical structure of personality, at the second-order level, there are four concepts, which Guilford calls Social Activity, Paranoid Disposition, Introversion-Extroversion, and Emotional Stability. While the names obviously differ, these factors appear to be the direct equivalents of the first four of the five Norman factors.

THE ROBUSTNESS OF THE FIVE-FACTOR REPRESENTATION

While it is not possible at this early stage to provide compelling evidence for the correct positioning of each theorist on each dimension, it should be possible to argue the case that *any* model for structuring individual differences will have to encompass—at some level of abstraction—something like these "big five" dimensions. That is, this part of the model is not all will-of-the-wisp; we have here something reasonably solid and method resilient. For example, Norman sorted 1,431 English trait-descriptive adjectives into 75 categories, based solely on their similarity of meaning. One can think of these as bins into which he tossed similar terms: For example, in one bin he tossed words like *companionable, sociable,* and *outgoing*—in all, nine such terms. If one asks people to describe themselves or to describe other people using those 1,431 terms, and one treats each bin as a scale, one can intercorrelate these scales across the subjects and factor the matrix of correlations.

How robust are these factors to procedural variations? Goldberg (1980) showed that it hardly matters what number of factors are extracted, since the loadings on the first five factors are always nearly the same. For example, in a five-factor solution, the Sociability scale had a factor loading on the first factor of .75; for six, it had a factor loading of .78; for seven, it was .79; for eight, it was .78 (the intermediate numbers are omitted here to save space); in a 13-factor solution, that loading was .82. Indeed, for 70 of the 75 scales, the factor on which that scale had its highest loading remained invariant across all solutions.

What is the best algorithm for use in factor analysis? Goldberg (1980) showed what happens when one uses every kind available in a popular computer program, two varieties of component analysis and three varieties of factor analysis. Once again, the procedure does not seem to affect the results. For example, using component analysis with a Varimax rotation, Sociability had a loading on the first factor of .79; it was .78 with a Quartimin (oblique) rotation; with traditional factor analysis (communalities in the main diagonal) it was .78 for a Varimax rotation, .77 for a Quartimin rotation, and .84 for Little Jiffy Mark-II (Kaiser's new orthoblique rotation). Clearly, there is something *to* this structure. It is not simply a matter of extracting a particular number of factors or using a particular type of rotational algorithm. These are data speaking for themselves.

As another example, 475 very common trait-descriptive adjectives were sorted into 131 tight synonym clusters. The terms in a cluster mean virtually the same thing and have much the same social desirability values. The results from factor analyses of the correlations among the scales, in two samples of peer ratings and two samples of self ratings, are presented in Goldberg (1980). Once again there were five very clear factors. For both peer ratings and self ratings, in two separate samples of each, analyzed in many different ways, the factors were virtually identical. The object of this demonstration is to prove that, at least at the level of those five dimensions, the results are remarkably method-resilient. Whether the data come from self reports or from descriptions of other people, whether based on one kind of rating scale or another, no matter what the method for factor extraction or rotation, the results are much the same. Clearly, these five individual differences are compelling candidates for extensions into other languages.

TOWARD A UNIVERSAL REPRESENTATION OF INDIVIDUAL DIFFERENCES

Do I really believe that these five factors will turn out to be universally encoded in the natural languages? The most I would be willing to argue is that they are logical places to start our search for a universal order of emergence of personality terms. Clearly, a more complete structure must be hierarchical, encoding individual differences at various levels of generality versus specificity. The "big five" factors are highly general. Indeed, some scientists (e.g., Cattell) have argued that they are too general for most predictive purposes.

Nonetheless, even at this stage, they provide a framework for organizing the English personality lexicon, a framework that can now be tested with other languages. Seemingly, these dimensions focus on individual differences of enormous import in persons' transactions with each other. They suggest that those who have contributed to the English lexicon as it has evolved over time wished to know the answers to at least five types of questions about a stranger they were soon to meet: (1) Is X *active and dominant* or passive and submissive (Can I bully X or will X try to bully me)? (2) Is X *agreeable* (warm and pleasant) or disagreeable (cold and distant)? (3) Can I count on X (Is X *responsible and conscientious* or undependable and negligent)? (4) Is X *crazy* (unpredictable) or sane (stable)? (5) Is X *smart* or dumb (How easy will it be for me to teach X)?

Are these universal questions?

NOTE

1. In a brilliantly articulated article in the first volume of this series, Wiggins (1980) has argued for the utility of a circumplex model of personality structure. It is important for the reader to realize that such a circular structure will result from the combination of *any* two orthogonal bipolar factors. While Wiggins (1979, 1980) has

stressed the interpersonal primacy of two particular factors (Affiliation [e.g., *Cold-Warm*] and Power [e.g., *Submissive-Dominant*]), these are only the first two (Agree-ableness and Surgency) of a more complete five-factor representation.

REFERENCES

Allport, G. W. & Odbert, H. S. Trait-names: A psycho-lexical study. *Psychological Monographs,* 1936, *47* (1, Whole No. 211).

Asch, S. E. On the use of metaphor in the description of persons. In H. Werner (ed.), *On expressive language.* Worcester, Mass.: Clark University Press, 1955.

Asch, S. E. The metaphor: A psychological inquiry. In R. Tagiuri & L. Petrullo (eds.), *Person perception and interpersonal behavior.* Stanford, Calif.: Stanford University Press, 1958. (Also in M. Henle [Ed.], *Documents of gestalt psychology.* Berkeley: University of California Press, 1961.)

Bentler, P. M. Semantic space is (approximately) bipolar. *Journal of Psychology,* 1969, *71,* 33-40.

Berlin, B., Breedlove, D. E., & Raven, P. H. General principles of classification and nomenclature in folk biology. *American Anthropologist,* 1973, *75,* 214-242.

Berlin, B. & Kay, P. *Basic color terms: Their universality and evolution.* Berkeley: University of California Press, 1969.

Bond, M. H. Dimensions used in perceiving peers: Cross-cultural comparisons of Hong Kong, Japanese, American and Filipino university students. *International Journal of Psychology,* 1979, *14,* 47-56.

Bond, M. H., Nakazato, H., & Shiraishi, D. Universality and distinctiveness in dimensions of Japanese person perception. *Journal of Cross-Cultural Psychology,* 1975, *6,* 346-357.

Borgatta, E. G. The structure of personality characteristics. *Behavioral Science,* 1964, *9,* 8-17.

Brown, C. H. Folk botanical life-forms: Their universality and growth. *American Anthropologist,* 1977, *79,* 317-342.

Brown, C. H. Folk zoological life-forms: Their universality and growth. *American Anthropologist,* 1979, *81,* 791-817.

Brown, C. H., Kolar, J., Torrey, B. J., Truong-Tuang, G., & Volkman, P. Some general principles of biological and non-biological folk classification. *American Ethnologist,* 1976, *3,* 73-85.

Cattell, R. B. The description of personality: Basic traits resolved into clusters. *Journal of Abnormal and Social Psychology,* 1943, *38,* 476-506.

Cattell, R. B. Confirmation and clarification of primary personality factors. *Psychometrika,* 1947, *12,* 197-220.

Cattell, R. B. *Personality and motivation structure and measurement.* New York: World Books, 1957.

Clark, E. V. & Clark, H. H. Universals, relativity, and language processing. In J. H. Greenberg (ed.), *Universals of human language: Vol. 1. Method and theory.* Stanford, Calif.: Stanford University Press, 1978.

Deese, J. *The structure of association in language and thought.* Baltimore: Johns Hopkins University Press, 1965.

Digman, J. M. & Takemoto-Chock, N. K. Factors in the natural language of personality: Re-analysis, comparison, and interpretation of six major studies. *Multivariate Behavioral Research,* 1981, *16,* 149-170.

Dixon, R.M.W. Where have all the adjectives gone? *Studies in Language,* 1977, *1,* 19-80.

Draguns, J. G. Psychological disorders of clinical severity. In H. C. Triandis & J. G. Draguns (eds.), *Handbook of cross-cultural psychology: Vol. 6. Psychopathology.* Boston: Allyn & Bacon, 1980.

Eysenck, H. J. & Eysenck, S.B.G. *Personality structure and measurement.* San Diego, Calif.: Knapp, 1969.

Fiske, D. W. Consistency of the factorial structures of personality ratings from different sources. *Journal of Abnormal and Social Psychology,* 1949, *44,* 329-344.

Goldberg, L. R. Some ruminations about the structure of individual differences: Developing a common lexicon for the major characteristics of human personality. Presented at the meeting of the Western Psychological Association, Honolulu, May 1980.

Goldberg, L. R. From Ace to Zombie: Some explorations in the language of personality. In C. D. Spielberger & J. N. Butcher (eds.), *Advances in personality assessment* (Vol. 1). Hillsdale, N.J.: Erlbaum, 1981.

Greenberg, J. H. Research on language universals. In B. J. Siegel, A. R. Beals, & S. A. Tyler (eds.), *Annual review of anthropology* (Vol. 4). Palo Alto, Calif.: Annual Reviews, Inc., 1975.

Greenberg, J. H. (ed.). *Universals of human language* (Vols. 1-4). Stanford, Calif.: Stanford University Press, 1978.

Guilford, J. P. *Personality.* New York: McGraw-Hill, 1959.

Guilford, J. P. Factors and factors of personality. *Psychological Bulletin,* 1974, *82,* 802-814.

Heider, E. R. Universals in color naming and memory. *Journal of Experimental Psychology,* 1972, *93,* 10-20.

Kay, P. & McDaniel, C. K. The linguistic significance of the meanings of basic color terms. *Language,* 1978, *54,* 610-646.

Kim, M. P. & Rosenberg, S. Comparison of two structural models of implicit personality theory. *Journal of Personality and Social Psychology,* 1980, *38,* 375-389.

Kuusinen, J. Affective and denotative structures of personality ratings. *Journal of Personality and Social Psychology,* 1969, *12,* 181-188.

Lehrer, A. Universals in a culture-bound domain. In L. Heilmann (ed.), *Proceedings of the Eleventh International Congress of Linguists.* Bologna, Italy: Societa editrice il Mulino Bologna, 1974.

Lehrer, A. Structures of the lexicon and transfer of meaning. *Lingua*, 1978, *45*, 95-123.

Lonner, W. F. The search for psychological universals. In H. C. Triandis & W. W. Lambert (eds.), *Handbook of cross-cultural psychology: Vol. I. Perspectives.* Boston: Allyn & Bacon, 1980.

Lyons, J. *Semantics.* London: Cambridge University Press, 1977.

Marsella, A. J. Depressive experience and disorder across cultures. In H. C. Triandis & J. G. Draguns (eds.), *Handbook of cross-cultural psychology: Vol. 6. Psychopathology.* Boston: Allyn & Bacon, 1980.

Mehrabian, A. *Basic dimensions for a general psychological theory: Implications for personality, social, environmental, and developmental studies.* Cambridge, Mass.: Oelgeschlager, Gunn & Hain, 1980.

Morice, R. Psychiatric diagnosis in a transcultural setting: The importance of lexical categories. *British Journal of Psychiatry*, 1978, *132*, 87-95.

Murphy, J. M. Psychiatric labeling in cross-cultural perspective. *Science*, 1976, *191*, 1019-1028.

Norman, W. T. Toward an adequate taxonomy of personality attributes: Replicated factor structure in peer nomination personality ratings. *Journal of Abnormal and Social Psychology*, 1963, *66*, 574-583.

Osgood, C. E. *Focus on meaning: Vol. 1. Explorations in semantic space.* The Hague, The Netherlands: Mouton, 1976.

Osgood, C. E., May, W. H., & Miron, M. S. *Cross-cultural universals of affective meaning.* Urbana: University of Illinois Press, 1975.

Rosch, E. Cognitive representations of semantic categories. *Journal of Experimental Psychology: General*, 1975, *104*, 192-233. (a)

Rosch, E. The nature of mental codes for color categories. *Journal of Experimental Psychology: Human Perception and Performance*, 1975, *1*, 303-322. (b)

Rosch, E. Universals and cultural specifics in human categorization. In R. W. Brislin, S. Bochner, & W. J. Lonner (eds.), *Cross-cultural perspectives on learning.* New York: Wiley, 1975. (c)

Tupes, E. C. & Christal, R. E. Recurrent personality factors based on trait ratings. Aeronautical Systems Division Technical Report ASD-TR-61-97, Lackland Air Force Base, Texas, May 1961.

Tzeng, O.C.S. Differentiation of affective and denotative meaning systems and their influence on personality ratings. *Journal of Personality and Social Psychology*, 1975, *32*, 978-988.

Warr, P. B. & Haycock, V. Scales for a British personality differential. *British Journal of Social and Clinical Psychology*, 1970, *9*, 328-337.

White, G. Ambiguity and ambivalence in A'ara personality descriptors. *American Ethnologist*, 1978, *5*, 344-360.

White, G. M. Conceptual universals in interpersonal language. *American Anthropologist*, 1980, *82*, 759-781.

Wiggins, J. S. A psychological taxonomy of trait-descriptive terms: The interpersonal domain. *Journal of Personality and Social Psychology*, 1979, *37*, 395-412.

Wiggins, J. S. Circumplex models of interpersonal behavior. In L. Wheeler (ed.), *Review of personality and social psychology* (Vol. 1). Beverly Hills, Calif.: Sage, 1980.

Williams, J. M. Synaesthetic adjectives: A possible law of semantic change. *Language,* 1976, *52,* 461-478.

Witkowski, S. R. & Brown, C. H. An explanation of color nomenclature universals. *American Anthropologist,* 1977, *79,* 50-57.

Witkowski, S. R. & Brown, C. H. Lexical universals. *Annual Review of Anthropology* (Vol. 7). Palo Alto, Calif.: Annual Reviews, Inc., 1978.

6

Political Creativity

HENRY A. ALKER

Henry A. Alker is on the faculty of the Humanistic Psychology Institute in San
Francisco and also lecturing in the Psychology Department of the University of
California, Berkeley. His interests are in personality, philosophical, and political
psychology. He currently chairs the task force on training of the International
Society of Political Psychology.

The concern here is to develop an empirically plausible model of
creativity in politicians. Little systematic, relevant data on this subject are
available. Except for recent work by Barber and Burns, explicit theoretical
attention is also infrequent. Reviewing and integrating this material will
lead to several propositions on political creativity later in this article—
certainly not a complete theoretical model, but a start. More serious
empirical attention probably has been paid to studying creativity in
severely retarded individuals than in politicians. Rothenberg's (1976) massive bibliography of 6,823 studies on creativity from 1566 to 1974 lists no
study explicitly featuring this topic in its title. The index to this com-

AUTHOR'S NOTE: Numerous friends have provided helpful comments on
earlier versions of the manuscript. The richly detailed, constructive comments of Ken
Craik and Brewster Smith deserve special mention.

pendium lists neither political creativity nor creativity in politicians among its more than 600 specific topics. There is obvious need for change here.

The criterion problem—what would a creative politician look like?—is not and need not become a stumbling block, preventing research attention to this topic. Using a broad, inclusive definition seems appropriate given the paucity of well-articulated theory and research. Following the model used by MacKinnon and co-workers (1962) in their studies of creativity in numerous occupational groups, I would emphasize realized rather than merely potential creativity. Creative political accomplishment (1) must be original and novel and (2) must solve some substantial political problem effectively and intentionally. Paradigm cases of politically creative persons would include individuals such as Ghandi, Franklin Roosevelt, Mao, and Lenin. One does not need to endorse the political views or goals of any of these individuals in order to appreciate the massive, original, and effective way they reorganized the lives of millions, resolving numerous political conflicts in the process and producing new political order.

These exemplars would presumably elicit consensual validation from both academic scholars of political leadership and practicing politicians. There are more controversial and debatable nominees, for example, Hitler, Stalin, Castro, Jimmy Carter. One test of the theoretical propositions articulated later will be whether or not they help adjudicate such debates in a nonarbitrary manner. Here it is noteworthy that Hitler's problem-solving political innovations were self-defeating, at least in the long run. Peace brought Germany more prosperity than war. And Germany has subdivided itself into two entities that politically tend to cancel each other out.

Furthermore, one does not need to espouse what used to be called the great man theory of political history in order to assert that there is room for substantial individual impact in certain political situations. Greenstein (1975) has effectively countered the assumption of actor dispensability advocated by some critics of a political psychology. Political creativity, of course, involves significant causal responsibility for the political actor(s) in the manner outlined by Greenstein. Predilections for historical, cultural, or even a situational determinism have not prevented constructive study of creative architects, engineers, writers, and even graduate students.

Studies that do contribute to this area sometimes come under the heading of creative leadership or simply leadership. These two topics should be distinguished from each other. Effective leadership in a political context can embody virtually nothing by way of tactics or rationale that is particularly novel or creative. Politics as usual, as a phrase, does not connote leaderless behavior. Two systematic approaches reviewed here, those of Barber and of Burns, both focus on political leadership. But both approaches have the virtue, from the perspective of political creativity, that they distinguish creative leadership from less creative though perhaps equally influential impact. Before turning to that work, one first needs to consider briefly what, if anything, the available psychological literature on creative leadership contributes to the study of political creativity.

STUDIES OF CREATIVE LEADERSHIP IN NONPOLITICAL SAMPLES

The first generalization that this meager literature suggests is that creativity and leadership are not typically related. Both Taylor (1978) and Inmire (1968) report this finding using diverse inventory measures of creativity. Curtis (1972) found no significant relation between an inventory measure of creative *disposition* and military rank in an interesting sample of senior Army officers ranging in rank from Colonel to four star General, including 20 of the latter. Note here that disposition and creative accomplishment are not identical. In fact, compared with a sample of business executives and educational researchers, the military officer sample was relatively least creative on the inventory measure. Curtis, however, does not accept the conclusion that persons in the army lack creative *accomplishment*. He documents this case with short biographical vignettes and concludes that the inventory measure (taken from the Omnibus Personality Inventory) is imperfect.

Taylor goes beyond asserting the null hypothesis that leadership and creativity are uncorrelated. He compares persons scoring high on both an inventory measure of leadership and the Torrance Tests of Creative Thinking with individuals scoring high on only one of these measures. "Creative leaders" compared with either "creatives" or "leaders" appear more motivationally mature or self-actualizing on Shostrom's POI inventory measure of Maslow's needs. This finding anticipates a theme Burns addresses below. All of thest studies leave much to be desired for familiar methodological reasons. Besides having numerous doubts about the validity and comparability of the diverse paper-and-pencil measures, one wants some behavioral demonstration of creative political accomplishment and generally does not receive it. Holding office in high school, as in the Inmire study (1968), may be at best a step in this direction but what one did while in office would be much more to the point. For that reason one might turn to a more promising line of research that deals with a carefully validated assessment procedure, a well-articulated theoretical construct, and demonstrable, behavioral correlates in the exercise of interpersonal influence or power.

Machiavellianism Research

Consider the research on Machiavellianism (Christie and Geis, 1970). This term is used here in the technical sense developed by Christie with explicit reference to Machiavelli's writings. Machiavellians combine tactics that *may* violate conventional morality with a cynical view of human nature in their pursuit of competitive success. Consider, for example, an experiment in which high and low scorers on the Mach V measure of Machiavellianism are given the opportunity to manipulate others (Geis, Christie, and Nelson, 1970). In this experiment the actual subject is supposedly a confederate of the experimenter who wishes to study the effects of distraction on cognitive problem solving. High-scoring Machiavellians (Machs) attempted more manipulative interventions and exhibited a greater variety of manipulations than lows. They also told more lies and introduced more verbal distractions. High Machs also reported enjoying carrying out the manipulation more than low Machs. However, the feature of their manipulative interventions that differentiated them from low Mach experimental confederates most sharply was a set of behaviors coded by the researchers as innovative manipulations. These were distractive interventions not included among those suggested by the experimenter as techniques available to the "confederates" in their assigned job.

Some of these innovations performed by the (male) "confederates," while they were administering the cognitive discrimination tasks to the supposed subjects, were remarkably imaginative. One high Mach confederate, for instance, would rub his hands together in a stereotyped gesture of anticipation. Another would bend over double, untie his shoe, shake his foot, and then, retie his shoe. Other tactics used by the high Machs included reaching around the divider separating the "experimenter" from the person performing the cognitive discrimination tasks, carefully knocking it over. This apparent accident produced a loud crash and sent the problem solver's papers flying in all directions. This high Mach then waited for 10 seconds saying nothing. Following this period he would apologize profusely for distracting the subject. Another highly innovative experimental confederate dismantled his ballpoint pen, used the spring to shoot it, parts flying apart, across the room. He then would rush across the room to retrieve those parts. He explained his behavior to the subject by saying, "Sorry, I'm a little nervous." Certainly, though the space-time scale is smaller than usually considered in political studies, these activities are a creative use of power. Nobody has developed an explicit test for measuring this domain, with one possible exception.

Guilford, Hendricks, and Hoepfner (1968) have not studied political creativity as such, though one study addresses some of the divergent thinking abilities that might be involved. I submit, however, that if one were to develop a behavioral test of creativity in exercising interpersonal power, the Machiavellian would do remarkably well. Both the number of different solutions and their originality are customarily scored in Guilford's studies of creative products. And on both these grounds, Machiavellians get high marks.

One may well question whether the exercise of creative skills in interpersonal manipulation is political creativity rather than simple creative human engineering. The context is not distinctively political. Certainly Machiavellians display their skills in educational and economic contexts, as Christie and Gies (1970) demonstrate, with no apparent preference for political arenas over any other. Contexts that have face-to-face interaction, ambiguous norms, and sufficient latitude for improvisation offer Machiavellians a competitive advantage that they are not reluctant to exploit, whether they are political or not.

The Machiavellian does perform in arenas of political power. But in order to study that context and the links, if any, that Machiavellianism has with political creativity, we must turn to a different class of research, less familiar to most psychologists. This research is conducted on active political leaders. In the first instance—the work of Barber—relatively familiar assessment procedures such as questionnaires and interviews are employed. But both Barber and Burns give substantial weight to detailed biographical investigations that psychologists rarely use for either systematic theory construction or testing. While concern here is with theory rather than advocating a research method, it should be noted that both Barber and Burns take their research methods very seriously. Barber (1977) reports checking on the reliability of his reading of political biographies and typically employed multiple biographies to protect against perspectival selectivity. Burn's careful, well-documented political biographies have won at least four national awards.

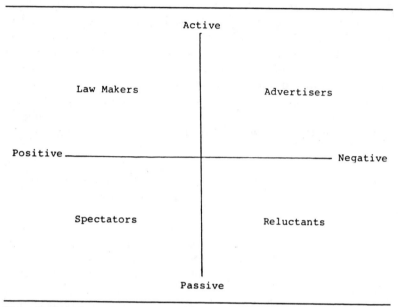

Figure 1. Barber's typology.

Barber's Model: The Active Positive Lawmaker

Barber has developed a theory of leadership based on extensive study of a sample of first-term Connecticut state legislators (1965) and twentieth-century presidents (1977). The former study, which involved standardized questionnaires followed up by detailed structured interviews, is more rigorous by normal psychological standards. Barber also monitored the legislators' actual legislative behavior, counting the number of bills introduced and speeches made in the legislature. From this analysis, Barber constructed a typology for organizing the wealth of information obtained. Figure 1 summarizes Barber's model. The lawmaker group in the upper left-hand quadrant are, according to Barber's account, the most creative group, particularly in contrast to the equally influential active negatives.

Barber constructs this typology with two independent dimensions, one representing activity and the other prevailing affective disposition toward one's work (positive or negative). The operational procedure for assigning a legislator to a given category is apparently very simple. Barber counted the amount of legislation introduced and the speaking done on the floor of the legislature. A person was considered high on activity if his or her scores were above the median for the sample and low if the same scores were below the median. Operationally this procedure is clear, though the underlying theoretical dimension is rather vague. Barber classified prevailing affective orientation by noting the politician's answer to an innocuous and somewhat unobtrusive question. The question concerned whether or not the politician would like to serve in the legislature three terms hence. An affirmative answer indicated, according to Barber, a positive disposition to one's current political activity. A negative answer suggested a predominantly negative disposition toward one's political participation.

A possible reason why this seemingly innocuous question achieved empirical differentation between other indicators is that politicians, one would expect, might be unwilling to answer such a question in the negative if it referred to the next term in the legislature. So doing might create in others the impression that they were lame ducks. Consequently their opportunities for successful influence might be seriously weakened if such a disposition were made known. Asking the question in a more indirect and unobtrusive form would not have such a bearing on the impression management taking place within or beyond the assessment situation. In any case it is obvious that this question in its exact form would not be a very promising operationalization of the positive-negative concept for occupants of other political offices. A president, for instance, is constitutionally prohibited from serving more than two terms so that virtually no such individual could reasonably be expected to answer the same literal question in the affirmative. Presidents might, however, vary considerably, as we shall see, on this dimension. The crucial question, of course, is what this basic dimension means.

The meaning of the positive-negative dimension and, for that matter, the active-passive dimension comes through more clearly when we consider Barber's detailed portrait of the lawmakers. These active positives, according to Barber, are no more effective in getting legislation adopted than the advertisers. But their motives differ. Advertisers see the passing of legislation as a test of either their power or righteousness. Lawmakers, as behooves exemplars of a criterion for political creativity, focus more simply on whether the legislation will work. More than other members of their cohort, lawmakers devote extraordinary time and energy to the task of developing and writing legislation. In their interviews they continually turn the conversation to detailed discussion of specific legislation. After such legislation is passed, the lawmaker remembers while the advertiser tends to forget. The lawmaker wants to know whether his or her bill is working. The advertiser, being preoccupied with passing the bill, is less interested, according to Barber, in follow-up. Complementing this focus, lawmakers' involvement in politics *is* issue oriented. They *enjoy* debate and the opportunity legislative activity provides for rational persuasion.

In this sample, lawmakers' personal and political backgrounds also set them apart from the other legislators classified as either advertisers, spectators, or reluctants. Lawmakers tend more often to be under 40 than over 40 and are much more likely to be educated beyond high school and come from towns with populations over 5000. Parents and relatives of individuals in this category compared with all other categories are more likely to be active and interested in politics. Even though the job of state legislator in Connecticut is only part time, lawmakers more often identify themselves as politicians. One is reminded of John F. Kennedy's favorite anecdote that 70% of the mothers of America want their sons to grow up to be President while the majority of the same group do not want their offspring to be politicians.

The activities involved in political life seem more enjoyable to lawmakers. They like campaigning more than their fellows and report attending more meetings during their campaigns than the other legislators. In the legislature they, along with the advertisers, are more often involved in major negotiations and, though in their first term, have already achieved some leadership role or important committee post. Interview and questionnaire data lead Barber to offer some more inferential, but suggestive psychological assessments of lawmakers, going beyond simple elements in their political biographies.

The lawmakers find others who are different and perhaps inferior easier to accept. This acceptance stems from understanding that even though people may approach problems differently, they may still have the same goals. Barber also reports that lawmakers indicate in their questionnaires that they have taken "much interest in the psychology of other legislators." Only 38% of the remaining legislators are so disposed, while 61% of those classified as lawmakers give this indication of their budding interest in political psychology. Further evidence for the interpretation that lawmakers nondogmatically tolerate and even welcome different perspectives comes from their responses to a questionnaire item concerning whether they would seek advice from "the best expert on the bill regardless of whether I know or like him." Lawmakers respond affirmatively 70% of the time to this question; others (advertisers, spectators, and reluctants combined) do likewise in 50% of the cases. Perhaps this nondogmatic element is a key to their creativity.

All of these results at best are suggestive. As with any typology, most individuals do not fit perfectly into the proposed categories. Barber's typology including only four cells certainly omits potential refinements that could easily change it into a more complicated scheme. Nonetheless, Barber's discussion of the typology, even in the early form it takes prior to his work on American presidents, covers considerable range. Important substantive criticism has been addressed to Barber's theory (e.g., by George, 1974). Others (Qualls, 1972; Barber, 1977) have questioned the slippery quality of its basic dimensions.

For our purpose of developing an understanding of political creativity, an essential weakness of this approach is its theoretical underarticulation. Suppose, for example, one interpreted the activity dimension as Machiavellianism. That interpretation fits Barber's data rather well. Active positives (lawmakers) *enjoy* their manipulative activity as do Machiavellians. And they have an interesting weakness Barber mentions in that their very eagerness to solve problems makes them tend to "cut corners." Procedural rules are sometimes broken. Active negatives (advertisers), Barber acknowledges, are quite prone to making Machiavellian moves. They skillfully manipulate public opinion, profiting personally and politically from group antagonisms among their constituents. The negative affect prevailing in the active negatives apparently makes it easier for them to manipulate others through anger, anxiety, envy, and fear. The fit is not perfect here because Barber reports these legislators sometimes worry about their unethical tactics, something a pure and simple Machiavellian would not do.

Passive positives (spectators) and passive negatives (reluctants) are both clearly non-Machiavellian. The former are controlled by strong group loyalties while the latter are driven by a stern and even painful sense of duty. Further support for this interpretation comes from Barber's extension of the typology to the American presidency. Consider the way Barber develops his model for explaining (and predicting) performance in the American presidency. Figure 2 presents his identifications (based typically upon reading multiple biographies) with question marks following Ford and Carter because Barber was more tentative on these identifications (as of 1976).

The activities of both a negative and positive character seem to display Machiavellian inclinations more than passives do. The active positives in their eagerness for results tend to violate some of the procedural rules

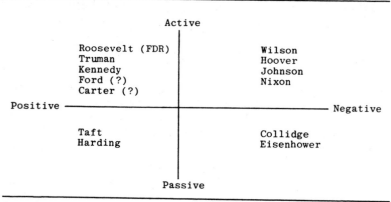

Figure 2. Presidential character of twentieth-century American leaders.

conventionally expected to apply to defenders of the Constitution. Roosevelt, for example, not only tried in vain to stack the Supreme Court but also, prior to the Congress passing any authorization remotely resembling a declaration of war, plotted with Churchill to delay Hitler's invasion of Russia by encouraging German's destructive involvement in the Balkans. Roosevelt himself recognized this action as a potentially impeachable offense. In 1940 Roosevelt, much like Lyndon Johnson on a later occasion and Wilson earlier, ran for reelection as a "peace" candidate but turned out to be otherwise. And the active negatives such as Nixon with their cynical views of their fellow human beings and conflicted but ready adoption of expedient tactics to enhance their own political careers seem high in Machiavellianism, even for politicians. Passives, on the other hand, are much more likely to follow the rules, hold noncynical views of their fellows, and be genuinely bound by duty and/or loyalty. So are low Machiavellians. Taft, for example, was happier as a Supreme Court Justice than as president.

What about the positive/negative contrasts? Machiavellianism has an interesting link with creativity mentioned above. Is there a more theoretically explicit interpretation of the other key dimension in Barber's model that can help, too?

Dogmatism comes to mind as a most plausible interpretation for the positive/negative contrast, especially as applied to activities. Dognatism (Rokeach, 1960) can involve a decision maker in the self-defeating unflexibility that Barber claims make active negatives failures as presidents.

Hoover, Nixon, and to a lesser degree Lyndon Johnson and Wilson all had basic premises they would not question. And active negatives are more intolerant of others than active positives. This description fits the legislative sample too, as described above.

Given this plausible though by no means necessary interpretation of Barber's underarticulated perspective, some important answers to questions about the political creativity emerge. First, psychological variables such as dogmatism can exercise constraints on the fecund, creative political imagination of the high Machiavellian. Active negatives, in Barber's terms, are not likely to be politically creative, though they may be adroit and successful in manipulating antagonisms for reasons of political interest—for example, Nixon's playing of the China card. Technically, this proposed relation makes dogmatism a "moderator variable" intervening between Machiavellianism and an effect of political creativity.

This interpretation of Barber's fascinating but slippery dimensions illuminates other facets of his analysis. Consider, for example, the brilliant characterization by Wills (1970) of Nixon as a "pious Machiavellian." This apparent self-contradiction now makes sense. Barber mentions and approves of this description but does not explain it. Barber certainly displays the adherence by Nixon to what I call the Vince Lombardi ethic—"success isn't everything; it's the only thing." And Barber shows how Nixon was preoccupied with his power and righteousness as all active negatives are supposed to be. But the concept of dogmatism (Rokeach, 1960) captures the contradiction in a belief system that a "pious Machiavellian" exemplifies. Only a dogmatic commitment to a success ethic could rationalize Machiavellian tactics as virtues. Within a value system that emphasizes that one proves one's value by competing with others successfully, only limited creativity is possible. Insofar as political problems are cooperative and not just competitive in nature, Machiavellian dognatists have a handicap. They are constrained in the definition of the political problem that requires creative solution. Woodrow Wilson's well-known problems (Barber, 1977) in cooperating with others within a context of legitimately shared authority exemplify this point further.

This analysis leaves open how one would give theoretical meaning to the positive end of the positive-negative dimension. Alker and Poppen (1973) demonstrated a pervasive bipolar dimension that organizes the interrelations between well-known measures of ideology such a dogmatism, fate control, Machiavellianism, and Kohlberg's notion of moral maturity. This dimension is Tomkin's (1963, 1965) contrast between an external and an internal locus of value. External locus of value characterizes belief systems, such as those of dogmatists, in which external authority determines what is right and wrong, good or bad. Tomkins calls this orientation "normative." The bipolar contrast he makes with normative ideology is humanistic ideology. This latter view maintains that value is discovered within and created from a person's own experience. Also contained in Tomkin's notion is a central contrast between prevailing positive affects and negative affects. This element maps very nicely onto Barber's positive-negative dimension.

It may appear that a Machiavellian humanist (in place of an active positive) is another contradiction in terms. Consider a typical item from the Machiavellian scale (Christie and Geis, 1970). No humanist would easily assert that "P.T. Barnum was right in saying that a sucker is born every minute." This contradiction can be resolved at least partially at this point by distinguishing, as Christie and Geis do (1970), between Machiavellian tactics and Machiavellian views of human nature (see also Gold, Christie, and Friedman, 1976). These two factors in the Mach V scale correlate +.40. So, empirically there are persons who share Machiavelli's rejection of conventional morality concerning tactics without holding cynical views about human nature. They are rare. Such individuals, I propose, are in political contexts the creative and effective politicians whom Barber calls active positives.

This analysis, extended one step further, leads to a final supporting argument. Given the marked communality between normative ideology and dogmatism reported earlier (Tomkin's Normative Scale and Rokeach's Dogmatism Scale have identical coordinates in a small space analysis; Alker and Poppen, 1973), it should be no surprise that the Machiavellian facility for imaginative human engineering does not always translate into realized political creativity. Dogmatism, no matter how intelligent, is the antithesis of creative thinking. Humanism is not. With Tomkins's bipolar dimension serving as a moderator variable, a plausible explanation how Machiavellianism may be importantly involved in political creativity is emerging.

Even if this point is granted, a good deal more theoretical specification is needed concerning how political creativity does occur. Situational and historical constraints come into play (Barber, 1980). At best this account opens up the possibility that Machiavellian imagination might be politically creative. Additional perspective on this matter fortunately comes in a more recent study of political leadership by Burns.

Burns's Theory

Burns (1978) has developed a theory of political leadership that embodies claims clearly relevant to creativity. Central to this theory is a distinction between transactional and transformational leadership. The former essentially involves the exchange of valued goods, be they material or psychological. Initiating contact with another for the purpose of promoting such an exchange is an act of transactional leadership. In response, for example, to a candidate's promise to support certain legislation, a voter may give that candidate political support. The bargainers in this transaction have no other purpose binding them together other than their mutual interest in concluding the bargaining process satisfactorily.

Transforming leadership, on the other hand, "occurs when one or more persons engage with others in such a way that leaders and followers raise one another to higher levels of motivation and morality" (1978: 20). Here Burns refers to developmental theory in psychology developed for motivation by Maslow (1954) and for morality by Kohlberg (1976). Very briefly, in motivation one purportedly moves from physiological and safety needs through love and belong needs. As these needs are met and satisfied, self-esteem and finally self-actualization become prepotent. In morality levels one moves from premoral, hedonistic thinking through conventional, moral reasoning involving duty and responsibility to principled, postconventional moral thought.

The test of successful transformational leadership is not, as it may be in transactional leadership, whether people's opinions and behaviors change in the manipulated direction. Transforming leadership, instead, must achieve real and intended social change grounded in the needs and values of those who are led. Such leadership in its ultimate form is intentionally obsolescent. People will change so that different leadership becomes desirable.

A good example Burns provides of this process comes from the political career of Chairman Mao. Following the stabilization and secure dominion Mao achieved in China, a large centralized bureaucracy developed that separated the people from their leaders and government. Mao's cultural revolution was designed by him to challenge and renew the very institutions that he had helped establish. The point of Mao's much ridiculed "record breaking" swim among thousands of his people in the Yangtze River was that leaders must be among the people and vice versa. Given that a degree of political stability and security had been established, Mao recognized that his people's needs were changing and turning to other matters. In encouraging and guiding this change, Mao, as Burns puts it, realized with Jefferson that the tree of liberty must be watered by revolution every 20 years. While institutional change was not forthcoming in exactly the way that Mao had hoped, his cultural revolution apparently did succeed in "raising" people's consciousness (developmentally), mobilizing their aspirations, and transforming their personal and political values. Note that by virtue of this contrast between transactional and transformational leadership, Burns has made the latter concept resemble the conception of political creativity presented here. Such action is anchored in an effective, collective outcome that cannot be a mere reintroduction of the status quo. This leadership is essentially innovative. His numerous examples of transforming leadership all appear to be relevant examples of political creativity. The intellectual leadership that manifested itself in shaping the American Revolution and subsequently developing a new system of government is a case in point. So are his numerous examples of reform leadership and nonidolatrous heroic leadership, for example, Churchill. One need not conclude, however, that Burns has exhausted the domain of political creativity with his concept. Occasionally transactional leadership, for example, can embody innovative and effective solutions to problems in political communication. Black political language, for example, may not actually leave transformed either black or white peoples' lives but it has created a context within which black protest can be heard and (by statute) must be listened to.

Turning to the substance of Burns's theory one is struck by its explicit psychological content appearing as Burns elaborates the notion of transformational leadership. Maslow's theory of motivational maturity and Kohlberg's theory of moral development both explicty guide Burns's thought. He uses Kohlberg's work not as a universally valid theory, acknowledging criticisms by Simpson (1974) and Loevinger (1976), but as a theory allowing Burns to specify strong probabilities "that most leaders in interacting with followers will behave in similar ways most of the time" (1978: 30). In this vein the transforming leader, particularly as a reforming leader, raises the level of moral concerns among his or her followers in line with a process described by Kohlberg (1976). Persons at lower levels of moral reasoning can be "moved" by appeals couched in somewhat higher levels. Appeals way beyond one's moral and developmental level are usually ineffective.

Some recent work in moral development theory (Gilligan, 1978; Basseches, 1978, 1980; Turiel, 1977) has refined and qualified the sense in which moral development is hierarchically organized. These developments to a degree strengthen rather than diminish the support a neo-Kohlbergian framework can lead to the concept of transforming moral leadership.

Basseches develops a notion of organization and change in moral reasoning that is dialectical. The confrontation of moral beliefs and actions with contrary positions leads to emerging, more complex views. In dialectical terms, thesis meets antithesis producing conflict that is resolved by synthesis. This cycle then repeats. Basseches (1978, 1980), for example, argues that dialectical reasoning can provide the form for a postconventional moral reasoner. Dialectical reasoning, while not antithetical to principled reasoning, is more directly involved with conflict in a way that anticipates and guides change. For example, from a dialectical perspective one would not categorically assert a moral principle as universally valid and conclude simply that the highest level of moral reasoning had been attained. Others might also assert moral principles with apparently contrary implications. Morally articulated conflict allows for a creative resolution, or at least a creative rearticulation in dialectical form. Consider, for example, a clash between the values of freedom and equality. For a morally principled thesis that human freedom is absolute, and its apparent antithesis, for example, equality of all humans is paramount rather than freedom for a few, some synthesis is possible. One could, for example, require that no increases in equality be adopted that decrease freedom and vice versa. This dispute could gradually and dialectically evolve into a moral *and political* theory about justice and fairness. Such a modification of postconventional moral reasoning in terms of dialectics, if accepted, broadens the scope of contexts and systems within which political creativity may be systematically studied.

Maslovian theory (Maslow, 1954) complements Kohlberg's account because of its focus on motivational concerns that are peripheral to Kohlberg's focus on cognitive structure. Though not cited by Burns, Green and Haymes (1977) show empirically that Maslovian motivational maturity and Kohlberg's moral maturity do covary. Simpson (1976) has elaborated the theoretical links between these complementary perspectives and incidentally served as one of Burns's major advisors on psychology.

Movement from safety and security concerns through belongingness and esteem needs toward self-actualization provides a systematic context for evaluating realtions between leader and followers. And, as Burns notes explicitly, leadership is a relational concept. The transformational leader, according to Burns, intuitively grasps the sequential organization in motive gratification and subsequent motive arousal. First things are first. Without food and safety, concern with civil liberties is a luxury. Thus that leader can effectively anticipate and guide change that both meets people's needs and helps change those needs in the process. Mao's and for the matter Roosevelt's actions vis-à-vis the Supreme Court are cases in point.

While Maslow's theory is well-known to psychologists, the degree of empirical support that it enjoys is not widely recognized. Notably, Aronoff and collaborators (Aronoff, 1967; Aronoff and Messe, 1971) have demonstrated that prior sustained gratification of security needs serves as a prerequisite for subsequent preoccupation with esteem needs. Aronoff also shows how preferred leadership style (authoritarian versus democratic) varies as a function of those needs. More mature (esteem) needs motivate a preference for more democratic leadership. Simpson (1974) also supports this view with her data. Sniderman (1975) offers a dissenting voice that neglects Aronoff's research.

As a theory of political creativity, Burns places strong emphasis on the cognitive complexity involved in principled moral reasoning. Speaking of postconventional moral reasoning, he claims that this stage sets the opportunity for rare and creative leadership. When the leader is at a higher level than his or her constituents, effective leadership in the service of values such as equality, freedom, empathy, and justice becomes more likely. The complexity so engendered might resemble that found by Suedfeld and Rank (1976) in their study comparing revolutionary leaders who successfully consolidated their initial overthrow of an existing government as compared with revolutionary leaders who did not. Their measure of cognitive complexity derives from a theoretical framework (Harvey, Hunt, and Schroeder, 1961) that is explicitly dialectical involving theses, antitheses, and developmental syntheses.

Burns explicitly rejects Machiavellianism as sufficient to produce transforming leadership. While perhaps well-suited for transactional leadership, the Machiavellian purportedly lacks both empathy and morality and thus cannot be a transformational leader. The extensive cognitive ability to take another point of view characterizing Kolhberg's conception of optimal moral maturity apparently makes empathy more likely. Adding in the motivational maturity to Burns's account rounds out the capacity for empathy. According to Maslow (1954), motivationally mature people are more complexly determined in their actions. Safety, security, love, and esteem needs all may be involved. Awareness of this complexity in oneself allows one to discern both actual and potential complexity in others. As the Machiavellian purportedly is unqualified on both accounts for transforming leadership, Burns's reasoning appears valid. But is it true?

Burns's theory is consistent with the data provided in Taylor's (1978) study, which found, as mentioned above, that creative leaders were more mature in Maslovian terms. But Burns's own examples call the assumption about Machiavellianism into question. Certainly Roosevelt and Lenin, two examples of transforming leaders that Burns discusses in considerable detail, are a lot more Machiavellian in tactics than Burns's own formulation would appear to comprehend. Burns acknowledges Roosevelt's exquisite tactical skills and his occasional overinvolvement in the tasks of transactional leadership. His portrait of Lenin urging terrorist tactics in 1905 and systematically spreading contempt for parliamentary democracy would appear at least as congenial with Machiavelli as with Maslow.

Although more hard evidence is needed, one study using a humdrum sample of college students (Alker and Poppen, 1973) did find that Machiavellianism and moral maturity were not empirically as antagonistic as a purely conceptual expectation might lead one to suppose. For males the negative correlation was a mere −.20 and for females being a principled moralist was uncorrelated with Machiavellianism. Indeed, certain similarities between Machiavellianism and principled morality emerged in this study. Both orientations enjoy the cognitive complexity that allows them to recognize the arbitrary nature of conventional morality.

And, to carry this argument forward another step, Berlin (1971) has suggested that Machiavelli himself was much like the transforming politically creative leader Burns admires. In the Italy of his day, factional strife in a country yet to be unified made virtually all citizens uncertain as to their physical survival as well as lacking in psychological security. Following the emergence of a strong leader, however, ruthless in tactics, a unified country would permit the citizenry to turn to more elevated needs and concerns. Without such a political structure, anarchy would continue and inhibit motivational and moral development. Because Christie used Machiavelli's writings so closely in developing his scale, Machiavelli the person may be an ideal type helping define what the research construct Machiavellianism means.

Burns's theory supplements the contribution to the theory of political creativity made by Barber's work. It specifies cognitive and motivational capabilities that help one become politically creative. The similarity with the reformulation given Barber's notion of the creative Lawmaker is worth of note. Principled moralists creative morals for themselves rather than taking it from external sources and are likely to favor humanistic ideology. In Alker and Poppen's (1973) sample of college students, in fact, principled morality does correlate significantly with endorsing Tomkins's (1963, 1965) humanistic ideology.

It must be recognized, however, that Burns would not agree with the claim made here that Machiavellianism is a necessary ingredient of effective political creativity. With the distinction developed earlier between Machiavellian tactics and views, some but not all of this disagreement may be resolved. For Burns, moral transforming leadership must involve moral means. I submit that his own biographies, for example, Burns (1956, 1970, 1978) show otherwise if moral means are merely those consistent with conventional morality. Machiavellianism, in the view advanced here, of course, is not sufficient to generate political creativity. Its substantial contribution must be moderated by the moral and motivational maturity Burns emphasizes as well as by a humanistic as opposed to dogmatic belief system. Efficacy is essential in a creative political leader. The Machiavellian has much to contribute toward this end.

As the theory recognized (Christie and Geis, 1970), some contexts invite and reward Machiavellian manipulation more than others. In contexts that do not require face-to-face interaction, do enjoy unambiguous norms, and permit no latitude for improvisation, Machiavellianism may not be a necessary ingredient for political creativity. Such contexts undoubtedly do exist, for example, a computer chess match, but are not very prevalent or typical in the contemporary political arena.

These claims also speak to the criterion question: What is political creativity? As a descriptive matter there may be room for disagreement whether Stalin, Hitler, and others produced original, effective solutions to substantial, collective political concerns. As a theoretical matter, the claim here is that they fail to qualify. Machiavellian, to be sure, neither Hitler nor Stalin eschewed dogmatism, exemplified principled morality, or advocated essential reliance on internal experience as a basis for discovering value. Killing off all one's adversaries, or trying to, does not provide for a dialectical synthesis of opposing views and values either. Machiavellianism is insufficient for political creativity without these further ingredients.

CONCLUSIONS AND IMPLICATIONS

The politically creative persons identified by the several approaches studied here are relatively rare and complex personalitites. Developing a training program for them or, for that matter, for highly creative persons in the arts and sciences is at the limit of our current capabilities if not beyond them. Consequently, reforming political organizations so that they are more likely to encourage creativity would be a worthy objective. Scholarly work to date on this subject is almost as meager as work on the political creativity, for example, Steiner (1966) and Thompson (1968).

It should be clear from the arguments advanced above that personal characteristics interact with environmental features in generating and implementing creative solutions to political problems. Introducing Machiavellianism *theory* makes this matter explicit. That theory and research specifies situational parameters dealing with latitude for improvisation, ambiguous norms, irrelevant affect, and face-to-face interaction. These, unfortunately, have never been operationalized—with one exception (Tessler and Alker, 1978)—at a more aggregate or national level appropriate for the political creatives discussed here. A much richer form of person-sitaution interaction is involved in the dialectical formulation as Basseches (1980) makes clear. Dialectical thinking involves reciprocal interaction with environmental challenges (antitheses to the theses one is asserting). This conflict develops with syntheses and then reformulated theses and antitheses. It is sequentially organized in a fashion that might be called transsituational.

Encouraging further attention to the use of dialectical concepts for representing political creativity are the several apparently contradictory variables that have reappeared in the several multivariate models of political creativity developed in this article. Machiavellians who are principled moralists would appear, on semantic grounds, to be impossible though empirically they occur. Likewise, Machiavellians sharing some features of a humanistic orientation is an empirical actuality (Alker and Poppen, 1973) that semantically seemed absurd. Semantic contstraints cloud our vision of reality here as elsewhere. It may be that dialectical concepts offer a general way out of the semantic constraints incorporated in our implicit theories and limiting our perception and understanding of social conflicts.

Here, only a much more limited claim is made. A dialectical conception of postconventional reasoning helps us understand political creativity. Some added, if unexpected support on this matter comes from MacKinnon (1964). The best theory he found to summarize the enormous amount of empirical data obtained in the research on architects, a profession specifically selected with the hope that it would yield generalizable results, can be summarized as follows. The creative type represents an integration of three "powers, the will, the counter will and the ideal formation born from a conflict between them which itself has become a goal-setting, goal-seeking force" (1964: 177).

Here is the essential structure of dialectically organized conflict. The will is the original attempt to change the environment. The counter will is the social reaction at least partially in opposition. A true synthesis in this context is what Burns's concept of transformational leadership is about. When this synthesis itself becomes a goal-setting and goal-seeking force, it must be pleasureful. Barber's active positives, in any case, enjoy this experience.

REFERENCES

Alker, H. A. and Poppen, P. Personality and ideology in university students. *Journal of Personality,* 1973, *41,* 653-671.

Aronoff, J. *Psychological needs and cultural systems.* Princeton, N. J.: Van Nostrand, 1967.

Aronoff, J. and Messe, L. A. Motivational determinants of small group structure. *Journal of Personality and Social Psychology,* 1971, *17,* 319-324.

Barber, J. D. *The lawmakers: Recruitment and adaptation to legislative life.* New Haven, Conn.: Yale University Press, 1965.

Barber, J. D. *Presidential Character: Predicting performances in the White House.* Englewood Cliffs, N. J.: Printice Hall, 1977.

Barber, J. D. Comment: Qualls nonsensical analysis of nonexistent works. *American Political Science Review,* 1977, *71,* 212-222.

Basseches, M. Dialectical schemata: A framework for the empirical study of the development of dialectical thinking. *Human Development,* in press.

Basseches, M. Beyond closed systems problem solving: A study of metasystematic aspects of mature thought. Ph.D. dissertation, Harvard University, 1978. (Available from University Microfilms International, 1979).

Berlin, I. The question of Machiavelli. *New York Review of Books,* 1971, *17,* 20-31.

Burns, J. M. *Roosevelt: The lion and the fox.* New York: Harcourt Brace Jovanovich, 1956.

Burns, J. M. *Roosevelt: The soldier of freedom.* New York: Harcourt Brace Jovanovich, 1970.

Burns, J. M. *Leadership.* New York: Harper & Row, 1978.

Christie, R. and Geis, F. (eds.) *Studies in Machiavellianism.* New York: Academic Press, 1970.

Curtis, J. O., Jr. An exploratory study of leadership. Ph.D. dissertation, University of California, Berkeley, 1972. Order No, 72-20, 399.

Geis, F., Christie, R., and Nelson, C. In search of the Machiavelli in R. Christie and F. Geiss (eds.), *Studies in Machiavellianism*. New York: Academic Press, 1970.

George, A. L. Assessing presidential character. *World Politics*, 1974, *26*, 234-282.

Gilligan, C. In a different voice: Women's conception of self and morality. *Harvard Education Review*, 1977, *47*, 481-517.

Gold, A. R., Christie, R., and Fredman, L. N. *Facts and flowers*. New York: Academic Press, 1976.

Green, L. and Haymes, M. Moral anecedents to maturity of moral judgment. *Motivation and Emotion*, 1977, *1*, 165-178.

Greenstein, F. *Personality and politics*. New York: Norton, 1975.

Guilford, J. P., Hendricks, M., and Hoepfner, R. Solving social problems creatively. *Journal of Creative Behavior*, 1968, *2*, 155-164.

Harvey, O. J., Hunt, D. E., and Schroder, H. M. *Conceptual systems and personality organization*. New York: Wiley, 1961.

Ingmire, B. D. Relationship between creativity scores and leadership behaviors in a group of high school seniors. Ed.D. dissertation, Arizona State University, 1968. Order No. 68-15, 003.

Kohlberg, L. Moral stages and moralization: The cognitive-developmental approach. In T. Lickona (ed.) *Moral development and behavior*. New York: Holt, Rinehart & Winston, 1976.

Loevinger, J. *Ego development*. San Francisco: Jossey-Bass, 1976.

MacKinnon, D. W. Personality and the realization of creative potential. *American Psychologist*, 1965, *20*, 273-281.

MacKinnon, D. W. The nature and nurture of creative talent. *American Psychologist*, 1962, *17*, 484=495.

Maslow, A. H. *Motivation and personality*. New York: Harper & Row, 1954.

Qualls, J. M. Barber's typological analysis of political leaders. *American Political Science Review*, 1972, *71*, 184-211.

Rokeach, M. *The open and closed mind*. 1960.

Rothenberg, A. *The index of scientific writings on creativity: 1566-1974*. Garden City, N. Y.: Doubleday, 1976.

Simpson, E. L. *Democracy's step children*. San Francisco: Jossey-Bass, 1971.

Simpson, E. L. A holistic approach to moral development and behavior. In T. Lickona (ed.), *Moral development and behavior*, New York: Holt, Rinehart and Winston, 1976.

Sniderman, P. M. *Personality and democratic politics*. Unversity of California, 1975.

Steiner, G. (ed.), *Creativity and organizations*. Chicago: University of Chicago Press, 1965.

Suedfeld, P. & Rank, A. D. Revolutionary leaders: Long term success as a function of changes in conceptual complexity. *Journal of Personality and Social Psychology*, 1976, *34*, 169-178.

Taylor, I. A. Characteristics of "creative leaders." *Journal of Creative Behavior*, 1978, *12*, 221-222.

Tessler, B. & Alker, H. A. Machiavellianism at a societal level. Presented at the meeting of the American Psychological Association, Toronto, 1978.

Thompson, V. A. *Bureaucracy and innovation.* University: Unversity of Alabama Press, 1968.

Tomkins, S. S. Left and right. In R. W. While (ed.), *The study of lives.* New York: Atherton, 1963. Tomkins, S. S. Affect and the psychology of knowledge. In S. S. Tomkins and C. E. Osgood (eds.), *Affect, cognition and personality.* New York: Springer, 1965.

Turiel, E. Distinct conceptual and developmental domains: Social convention and morality. In C. B. Keasey (ed.), *Nebraska symposium on motivation.* Lincoln: University of Nebraska Press,) 1977.

Wills, G. *Nixon agonistes.* Boston: Houghton Mifflin, 1970.

7

Private and Public Aspects of Self

MICHAEL F. SCHEIER

CHARLES S. CARVER

Michael F. Scheier is Associate Professor of Psychology at Carnegie-Mellon University. His reasearch examines the role that attentional factors play in the manner in which people regulate their actions. He is coauthor (with Charles S. Carver) of *Attention and Self-Regulation: A Control-Theory Approach to Human Behavior.*

Charles S. Carver is Associate Professor at the University of Miami. The author (with Michael F. Scheier) of *Attention and Self-Regulation: A Control-Theory Approach to Human Behavior* (New York: Springer-Verlag, 1981), his research focuses on the behavioral consequences of self-directed attention.

A group of workers are discussing the state of the world economy during a coffee break. One remarks that the heads of the major oil companies are all extortionists, and three others are quick to agree. One listener privately thinks otherwise. Someone turns to him and asks for his opinion. What will he say? How will he present himself?

AUTHORS' NOTE: Preparation of this chapter was facilitated by grants BNS 80-21859 and BNS 81-07236 from the National Science Foundation.

THE ISSUE: SELF-COMPLETION VERSUS SELF-PRESENTATION

In attempting to predict this person's response, one confronts a controversy regarding human behavior which underlies many areas of theory and research in social and personality psychology. Put simply, the issue is this: Does it make more sense to construe human behavior as guided and motivated by personal concerns and private needs or as motivated by the desire to manage successfully the external and public display of self? Our field has harbored a disagreement over this question for many years. It often lies hidden deep beneath the surface, but more recently it has emerged as a focal issue and a subject of much debate.

Clearly, both points of view have had their share of advocates (see Greenwald, in press). At least as far back as Freud (e.g., 1920, 1949) theoretical statements have been made that emphasize the importance of internal and hidden pressures on people's actions. Freud saw behavior as being undertaken to satisfy such pressures, even if only momentarily and incompletely, and even if we are not aware that those pressures are determining our actions. While external considerations were not exactly trivial in Freud's theory, there is an important sense in which they were clearly secondary as determinants of behavior (for additional discussion of this point, see Watzlawick, Beavin, & Jackson, 1967).

Freud's position on motivation was surely unique in other respects, but of greatest importance in the present context is the stress it placed on the assumption that people are largely motivated by internal—implicitly private—concerns. Though other theorists would differ from Freud in important ways, many theories were subsequently advanced which retained the perspective that behavior is determined by internal, private needs. For example, many later writers emphasized the need to maintain internal consistency within the self (e.g., Allport, 1961; Lecky, 1945; Rogers, 1947; Maslow, 1970).

Not everyone has assumed that private considerations predominate in directing behavior, however. Two of the best known early proponents of an alternative approach were Cooley (1902) and Mead (1934). Both conceptualized the self as being a social product that develops over time, as the person takes the perspective of others and views himself or herself from that viewpoint. Although their approaches made some provision for personal needs, the overriding orientation clearly focused on the self as a social entity. To the extent that the self guided behavior, in their analysis, it did so by considering how behavior would be viewed and reacted to by others (see also Shibutani, 1961, and Blumer, 1969).

A similar orientation is reflected in the writings of Goffman (e.g., 1959, 1967). Goffman has argued that encounters between people are essentially theatrical performances. Each person has "lines" to speak, and each tries to create a particular image of himself or herself in the minds of other performers and observers. The context of the interaction presumably dictates what image is chosen for portrayal.

Other theorists have also echoed this general perspective, while varying in their specific emphases. For example, Crowne and Marlowe (1964) argued that people often choose their actions in order to gain social approval and social rewards. Tedeschi and his colleagues have more recently taken a similar position. They hold that people are very much interested in "managing" the impressions of them that are being created in the minds of onlookers. One chooses one's actions, then, in order to portray oneself as rational and consistent or whatever else the situation calls for (see, e.g., Schlenker, 1980; Tedeschi, 1980; Tedeschi, Schlenker, & Bonoma, 1971).

Reflections of the Issue in Research

This division of opinion over whether people are responsive primarily to internal motivations or to self-presentational concerns is reflected in many substantive areas in social psychology (cf. Greenwald, in press). Consider, for example, the variables that influence responses to requests for help. It has been argued that guilt causes subjects to be more likely to accede to such requests (Carlsmith & Gross, 1969). Guilt is a private emotion, reflecting a personal sense of transgression against internalized standards. Presumably being helpful makes people feel more acceptable to themselves, thereby diminishing the guilt. This is not the whole story, however. Other research (e.g., Apsler, 1975; Wallace & Sadalla, 1966) indicates that embarrassment, an emotion associated with inadequacies in one's public display, may be just as important as guilt in such situations.

Another illustration comes from the literature of attribution theory. There is currently a good deal of discussion among attribution theorists concerning the nature of possible self-serving biases in causal attribution (e.g., Bradley, 1978; Miller, 1978; Miller & Ross, 1975). Bradley (1978), for example, has noted that there are two separate classes of esteem-enhancing attributions: namely, those that protect our *own* images of ourselves and those that create favorable images of us in *other* people's eyes. Once again the question revolves around the issue of whether the behavior is calculated to satisfy covert personal needs or self-presentational needs.

SELF OR SELVES: A RECONCILIATION

As these examples illustrate, both classes of motivational concerns have been implicated in behaviors of many different types (see also Carver & Scheier, 1981; Greenwald, in press). It seems clear that the resolution of the issue with which we began is not that one approach is correct and the other incorrect. Rather, there is truth to each portrayal. Our task, then, is to identify factors that contribute to the separate influences on behavior that are exerted by the two motivational classes.

There are doubtlessly many different ways to approach this task. We will focus here, however, on one specific approach, an approach that we have used in our own work. This approach incorporates two rather straightforward assumptions. The first is that the self as a psychological entity is multifaceted. Stated more colloquially, the self has a number of different faces and sides. A particularly important distinction, in this regard, is between what has been called the *private* and the *public* aspects of the self (Fenigstein, Scheier, & Buss, 1975; see also Buss, 1980). The private self consists of the person's own feelings, attitudes, covert thoughts, and other self-aspects that are hidden from others—that is, those elements of the self that one would expect to be involved in motivational phenomena reflecting internal, egocentric needs. The public self, in contrast, is the observed self, the facets of the person that are exposed to public scrutiny—that is, those elements of the self that are most relevant to motives involving self-presentation or self-portrayal.

The second assumption we make is that any given aspect of the self can be expected to influence the person's behavior *only* if that self-aspect is taken, at least temporarily, as the object of the person's own attention (see also Duval & Wicklund, 1972; Wicklund, 1979). Our ideas about the manner in which the self exerts its influence are described in detail elsewhere (Carver, 1979; Carver & Scheier, 1981; see also Carver & Scheier, this volume). For the present, however, what is important is simply this: Attention to a specific self-aspect is believed to be a necessary precondition for that self-aspect to have an impact on overt behavior.

These two assumptions are very simple. But taken together, they have pervasive implications for behavior. Before describing several recent tests of these implications, however, let us indicate how attention to these two aspects of the self is varied in the laboratory.

Varying Self-Attention in Research

Two rather disparate techniques are available for this purpose. One technique involves the use of a self-report instrument to identify and select persons who differ from each other in their chronic tendencies to be self-attentive. The second technique relies on experimental manipulations to alter persons' momentary levels of self-attention. These are discussed, in turn, in the following paragraphs.

Individual Differences. It was apparent very early in the development of this research area that people differ in the degree to which they habitually attend to themselves. The disposition to be self-attentive has been labelled self-*consciousness,* to distinguish it from the manipulated state of self-*awareness,* a convention that we will follow throughout this chapter. Self-consciousness is measured by the Self-Consciousness Scale (Fenigstein et al., 1975), an instrument that has three separate subscales. The *private* self-consciousness subscale, comprised of items such as "I'm generally attentive to my inner feelings" and "I'm constantly examining my motives," was designed to measure the tendency to be aware of the covert and hidden aspects of the self. People who are high on this dimension are presumed to be particularly attentive to their thoughts, feelings, attitudes, and other private self-aspects. Consistent with this conceptualization, persons high in private self-consciousness have been found to be more responsive to their transient affective states (Scheier, 1976; Scheier & Carver, 1977) and to make more accurate self-reports regarding both bodily sensations (Scheier, Carver, & Gibbons, 1979) and behavioral dispositions (Scheier, Buss, & Buss, 1978; Turner, 1978).

The *public* self-consciousness subscale, comprised of items such as "I'm concerned about what other people think of me" and "I'm concerned about my style of doing things," was intended to measure the tendency to be aware of the publicly displayed aspects of the self, the self as a social object that has an impact on others. People high on this dimension are thought to be especially cognizant of how they are being viewed by others in their social contexts and how those others are reacting to them.

Consistent with this conceptualization, Fenigstein (1979) has shown that high public self-conscious women are more sensitive to rejection by others. After being shunned by a group, they were less willing to affiliate with the group, and more likely to express dislike for the group members, than were women lower in public self-consciousness.[1]

Both subscales possess adequate reliability (Fenigstein et al., 1975), and a substantial amount of evidence has now been gathered establishing both convergent and discriminant validity (Carver & Glass, 1976; Turner, Scheier, Carver, & Ickes, 1978; see Carver & Scheier, 1981, for a review). Finally, factor analyses have confirmed that the private and public self-consciousness dimensions are factorially distinct. The correlations between the two subscales, though invariably positive, are generally quite low—typically falling in the high .20s and low .30s (see, e.g., Fenigstein et al., 1975; Carver & Glass, 1976; Turner et al., 1978). Thus, not only are private and public self-consciousness distinct theoretically, they are also relatively independent empirically.

This finding—that private and public self-consciousness are separable dimensions—has important implications. Specifically, being low in one aspect of self-consciousness does *not* automatically imply that the person is simultaneously high on the other aspect. That is, they are not simply two ends of the same continuum, but are rather two distinct dispositional tendencies. Use of the Self-Consciousness Scale thus makes it possible to isolate four different groups of persons. One group is quite aware of their private self-aspects, but relatively oblivious to their public selves. Another set of persons is quite attentive to the public aspects of themselves, but not very conscious of their private self-aspects. A third group is highly cognizant of both facets of self. And the final group is not particularly attentive to either self-aspect.

This is probably a good context in which to mention an alternative approach to the subject matter of this chapter, which in some respects is quite similar to the approach we have taken. Specifically, Snyder (1974, 1979) has argued that in choosing their actions some people are especially attuned to the social contingencies surrounding their behavior and that other people are responsive instead to their own views of themselves. The former are termed high self-monitors, the latter low self-monitors. There are obviously strong parallels between this general perspective and the approach that we are outlining. That is, high self-monitors appear to be somewhat akin to persons who are high in public self-consciousness and low in private self-consciousness. Low self-monitors seem not too different from persons who are high in private self-consciousness and low in public self-consciousness.

It is important to note, however, that Snyder's conceptualization appears to incorporate the assumption that an awareness of the public self is always inversely related to an awareness of the private self. It is clear that the structure of the Self-Monitoring Scale forces this dichotomy upon respondents. What is less apparent, however, is that this dichotomy is artificial. That is, recall that the public and private subscales of the Self-Consciousness Scale—which separately bear at least a superficial resemblance to the opposite poles of the Self-Monitoring Scale—tend to be only weakly correlated. And the correlations that are obtained are invariably *positive*. This leads to the following question: Where on the self-monitoring dimension would a person fall who is high in both private and public self-consciousness? Being high in private self-consciousness seems to suggest low self-monitoring; but being high in public self-consciousness suggests high self-monitoring. Indeed, the same ambiguity arises in trying to decide where on the self-monitoring dimension *any* person would fall whose levels of private and public self-consciousness were roughly equivalent.

Thus, although the self-monitoring construct has certainly led to important research in recent years (for a review, see Snyder, 1979), the ambiguity inherent in the Self-Monitoring Scale would seem to render it a less desirable instrument than the Self-Consciousness Scale for investigating the research problem that we are addressing in this chapter (see also Briggs, Cheek, & Buss, 1980). That is, knowing only that persons high and low in self-monitoring differ in some behavioral way does not allow one to infer whether the effect was attributable to variations in subjects' sensitivity to the social context, variations in sensitivity to personal self-images, or both. With the Self Consciousness Scale, in contrast, these variables can be separated from each other and their independent influences assessed.[2]

Manipulations of Self-Focus. In addition to dispositional tendencies, there are also situational cues that either raise or lower the level of a person's self-attention. Wicklund and Duval (1971) were the first to attempt to manipulate self-attention in the laboratory. They argued that any stimulus that reminded people of themselves should serve to heighten self-focus. They operationalized this reasoning with manipulations that seemed intuitively to serve as reminders of the self—for example, cameras, mirrors, and tape-recordings of subjects' voices.

Later studies provided evidence that such manipulations do seem to heighten self-attention. For example, Geller and Shaver (1976) obtained indirect support for the position that a camera and a mirror (together) selectively activated subjects' self-relevant memory content. Using a modified version of the Stroop color-word test, they found that color-naming latencies for self-relevant words were increased by the manipulations, but latencies for other words were not. Additional research by Davis and Brock (1975) and by Carver and Scheier (1978) determined that either manipulation by itself resulted in an increased tendency to use self-related language. There is also evidence that a salient audience increases self-focus (Carver & Scheier, 1978).

When researchers first used these various manipulations, little thought was given to the public-private distinction. The manipulations were used more or less interchangeably. It was implicitly assumed that attention would gravitate toward whatever self-aspect was made salient by the behavioral context. We now believe, however, that these manipulations may differ dramatically from each other in terms of the aspects of the self to which they direct attention. Specifically, we now believe that some manipulations (such as cameras and audiences) serve primarily to heighten the subject's cognizance of public self-aspects, whereas other manipulations (such as mirrors) serve mainly to heighten awareness of private self-aspects (see also Buss, 1980). This belief derives from the results of several of the studies that have been conducted to test the conceptual approach we are outlining. These studies are discussed later in the chapter.

EFFECTS OF ATTENDING TO THE PUBLIC AND PRIVATE SELVES

Let us now turn to an explicit consideration of the behavioral consequences of focusing either on the public self or on the private self. As we said earlier, the conceptualization that we have outlined has testable implications. Creating a clear test of those implications, however, is not as simple as it might appear. In some behavioral contexts, attention to the private self and attention to the public self might be expected to exert similar influences. For example, Scheier, Fenigstein, and Buss (1974) found that the intensity of electric shocks delivered by men to women (under the guise of the learning experiment) decreased when the men were exposed to either a small mirror or an audience. Was this because they privately held the attitude that they should be "chivalrous" and nonaggressive toward women and were more responsive to this private belief when attention was self-directed? Was it because they were more conscious of the fact that the socially defined norm is to be nonaggressive toward women and were responsive to that norm when attention was self-directed? Or was there one effect in the mirror condition and another in the audience condition? We cannot tell.

In order to separate the influences that public and private aspects of the self have on behavior, it is necessary to examine situations in which the influences of these two self-aspects ought to differ from each other. At a minimum, this means that situations must be created in which one aspect of self would be expected to have an impact on behavior, but the other aspect of self would not. In such a case, heightened attention to the *relevant* self-aspect should influence behavior, but attention to the *irrelevant* self-aspect should have no effect.

Even more compelling, however, would be cases in which both the public and private aspects of self would be expected to influence behavior, but would be expected to do so *in opposing ways*. Under these circumstances, increased focus on the private self should have one impact, compared to conditions of low self-focus. And, compared to the same control condition, increased focus on the public self should have a discriminably different impact.

In the sections that follow, we describe several studies that have examined such situations. Each appears to offer support for the usefulness of the public-private distinction. Taken as a group, they also suggest two conclusions. First, *both internal, private motivations and self-presentational concerns are potentially operative in many behavioral contexts* (e.g., in all of those under examination here). Second, *each of these sets of motivational concerns has a greater impact on behavior when attention is directed to the aspect of self that is relevant to it.* We begin with several studies of the effects of dispositional self-consciousness.

Private and Public Self-Consciousness and Compliance

One of these studies (Froming & Carver, 1981) represents an experimental analog of the example with which we opened the chapter. In this study, subjects were exposed to simulated group pressure to make incorrect responses on a perceptual task (cf. Asch, 1951, 1956; Crutchfield, 1955). Recall that private self-consciousness is associated with an awareness of responsivity to one's own feelings and opinions. Indeed, persons high in private self-consciousness are so responsive to their own reactions that they are even resistant to external "suggestibility" influences (Scheier et al., 1979). It therefore seems reasonable that private self-consciousness would be positively associated with a tendency to rely on one's own opinions and to disregard the misleading opinions of other group members.

In contrast, public self-consciousness is an awareness of and a responsivity to the impressions that are being made on others. This does not necessarily imply a desire to *please* others. Rather, it may be that public self-consciousness reflects a pragmatic orientation to self-presentation. High public self-conscious persons may simply calculate their self-portrayals so as to facilitate social exchange, instead of attempting to seek out favorable personal evaluations. Consistent with this characterization is the finding that public self-consciousness does not correlate reliably with the Crowne-Marlowe (1964) index of social desirability (Turner et al., 1978).

Nevertheless, we know that persons high in public self-consciousness are more sensitive to interpersonal rejection than are persons lower in public self-consciousness (Fenigstein, 1979). Inasmuch as compliance is often viewed as motivated by a desire to avoid rejection (cf. Gerard & Rotter, 1961), it seems reasonable to expect that high degrees of public self-consciousness would be associated with a tendency to go along with the incorrect majority. Thus, the independent effect of public self-consciousness was predicted to be opposite to that of private self-consciousness.

Subjects in this study participated in groups of four in what was portrayed as an investigation of auditory perception. An experimental apparatus allowed each subject to hear (via headphones) experimental instructions, the task stimuli, and the responses of three persons, whom the subject assumed were the other group members. In reality, all of this was prerecorded. Subjects were separated from each other by barriers, so that they would not become aware of this deception. The subjects were told that their task was to count, as accurately as they could, several sets of metronome clicks. After each set they were to report, one person at a time, how many clicks there had been. The sequence of responding was to be controlled by signal lights.

The tape-recorded voices of the ostensible cosubjects were always unanimous. Sometimes they were correct and sometimes not, the latter being the compliance trials. On these trials the cosubjects were wrong either by one click or by two. A set of 12 trials on which the subject responded before any of the presumed cosubjects was used as a control to assess subjects' ability to perform the task accurately. More specifically, subjects' error rates on these trials were used as an estimate of perceptual error.

Compliance was analyzed by means of partial correlations, partialing out perceptual error first (and thus controlling for "informational" conformity). This procedure revealed that private self-consciousness correlated significantly with overall compliance, in the expected (inverse) direction, and this relationship proved to hold true for both levels of group error (i.e., one or two clicks). After controlling for this strong influence of private self-consciousness, a significant—and opposite—correlation was obtained between public self-consciousness and compliance, but only on trials involving the larger degree of error (see Froming & Carver, 1981, or Carver & Scheier, 1981, for greater detail).

In summary, private and public self-consciousness had independent and opposite influences on compliance. Our confidence in these findings is additionally strengthened by the fact that they have since been conceptually replicated by other researchers (Santee & Maslach, Note 1).

Implications. The results for private self-consciousness were exactly as predicted. The findings for public self-consciousness, though somewhat weaker, were also supportive of the analysis underlying the study. Why was the public dimension related to compliance only on trials involving larger error, however? While this result was unanticipated, it seems consistent with the assumption (made earlier) that the public self-consciousness subscale taps an orientation toward "getting along," rather than a desire to please others. Such an orientation would presumably be relevant to behavior primarily when the potential exists to be seen by others as being relatively extreme in one's deviance. This would have been more clearly the case on the trials involving greater error. And it was those trials in which public self-consciousness was related to compliance.

This study also raises an additional issue. Duval and Wicklund (1972, Chapter 5) reported two studies of conformity in which self-focus was experimentally manipulated, either by showing subjects their live television images or by playing recordings of subjects' voices. Those studies both differed from the one just described in a number of ways. What is most relevant at the moment, however, is that Duval and Wicklund found that self-focus *increased* conformity to the opinions of others. In their view this indicated that focus on the self promotes conformity. They argued that these findings were consistent with a long history of research indicating that conformity to a bogus consensus is greater when the behavior occurs in public rather than in private circumstances. They concluded, in effect, that the public display of one's actions promotes self-attention.

We do not dispute this conclusion, but we suggest that it requires an important qualification. When one's actions are publicly displayed, attention is focused not only upon oneself but also upon the *public aspects* of oneself. As the Froming and Carver (1981) study shows, focus on the private aspects of the self has very different consequences. It is worth noting that both of the manipulations used by Duval and Wicklund (1972) caused subjects to view publicly displayed aspects of themselves that are normally not directly open to self-observation. Thus their findings may have depended upon their having induced a public self-awareness. This assumption--that different manipulations of self-focus may direct attention to different aspects of the self—is an important one. We introduced it earlier, and we will devote greater attention to it before the chapter is concluded.

Public and Private Self-Consciousness and Reactions to Coercion

Froming and Carver examined the effects of implicit conformity pressure. Private self-consciousness was associated with a tendency to ignore such pressure; public self-consciousness was associated with a tendency to accede to it (though perhaps grudgingly). But what happens when the pressure is increased? What happens when the influence attempt becomes coercive?

We have recently conducted a study that bears on these questions. In it we examined the effects of self-consciousness on the experience of reactance (Carver & Scheier, 1981). The research was guided primarily by a consideration of the nature of the private dimension. But public self-consciousness also proved to play an important—and independent—role.

Although the finding that the public dimension had an influence on the reactance effect was serendipitous, the nature of the finding lends further credence to the picture of public self-consciousness that we have sketched above. That is, this disposition appears to function less in the service of gaining social approval than in the service of avoiding disapproval.

Subjects in this study were told that the experiment concerned impression formation. They were led to expect a series of communications about a candidate for an appointive public office. After receiving a biographical description of the candidate (portraying him favorably), subjects made an initial rating of his suitability for the office. Subjects then received a printed persuasive message, either a straightforward recommendation of the candidate or a recommendation with decidedly coercive overtones. Subjects then completed a second rating of the candidate. The measure of interest was the shift in opinions between the two ratings.

On the basis of previous research and theory (Carver, 1977), we had expected private self-consciousness to be associated with enhanced resistance to the coercive communication. This expectation was confirmed. But there was also a significant influence of public self-consciousness, an effect that was opposite to that obtained from private self-consciousness. That is, persons low in public self-consciousness were persuaded by the straightforward message and reversed their opinions in response to the coercive message. Persons high in public self-consciousness were unresponsive to either message.

How are we to account for this pattern of results involving public self-consciousness? Recall that subjects had been told to expect a *series* of communications concerning the candidate. When the opinion postmeasure was collected, no indication had yet been given that the series had ended. Thus, the behavior of persons high in public self-consciousness may reflect caution in an ambiguous social situation. For all they knew, several more messages would be coming from several types of sources. People concerned with their position in the social matrix might be disinclined to overreact to one particular source of influence. People who are less conscious of this aspect of self, on the other hand, would be much less concerned about overreacting.

This reasoning is supported by evidence that the impact of public self-consciousness on reactance depends upon the "social" nature of the reactance-inducing stimulus (e.g., a coercive *interpersonal* communication). That is, in a subsequent study (Carver & Scheier, 1981: Experiment 2) in which reactance was induced in a nonsocial fashion, public self-consciousness had no effect whatever.

In sum, consciousness of the self clearly plays a role in reactance phenomena. But when the reactance is socially induced, a great deal depends upon what aspect of self is the object of that consciousness. Awareness of the private self may exacerbate the reactance response; awareness of the public self may inhibit it.

Public Expression of Privately Held Opinions

The Carver and Scheier study concerned ways in which people's expression of their opinions changes after a persuasion attempt. But people vary the expression of their opinions for other reasons, as well. In fact, we sometimes temper our statements of our beliefs *before* interacting with people, rather than afterward (cf. Cialdini, Levy, Herman, Kozlowski, & Petty, 1976; Newtson & Czerlinsky, 1974). Such "moderation" of opinions is usually conceptualized as a self-presentational tactic, used to influence the impressions that are conveyed to others. By stating a more moderate opinion to others, we lessen the likelihood of being viewed as extremely deviant by any one particular person.

These processes sound very much like ones that should be mediated by attending to the public aspects of oneself. If moderating opinions has the goal of creating a particular public image, one would expect people who are especially aware of their public selves to be most likely to engage in such a tactic. People who are primarily conscious of their private self-aspects, in contrast, should be very unlikely to moderate their opinions for public expression. These are people who are attuned to their inner selves. They are conscious of their real feelings about issues, but not necessarily conscious of the public contingencies surrounding their statements.

This hypothesis has been tested (Scheier, 1980) in a study in which subjects first reported their attitudes on a self-report questionnaire, and later in a social context where moderation of attitude might represent a useful impression-management strategy. The opinions in question were attitudes toward the use of physical punishment as a training technique. Several months after the questionnaires had been completed, subjects participated in group experimental sessions (ranging in size from two to four). They were told that they would be taking part in a social opinion

TABLE 1   Expressed Attitude as a Function of Pretest Attitude and
Public Self-Consciounsness (data from Scheier, 1980)

Self-consciousness	Pro punishment	Con punishment
High public	9.2	9.5
n	26	24
low public	11.0	8.2
n	39	24

Note: The higher the number, the stronger the attitude in favor of punishment.

survey. The experimenter indicated that the survey would assess attitudes in two quite different ways. First, the subjects would express their opinions by writing a brief essay. Later, they would discuss their views with another student participating in the study. This discussion would be tape-recorded and evaluated by the research team.

The subjects then were taken to separate cubicles, where they were left alone for a brief period. When the experimenter returned, the subject was handed a booklet to complete. In addition to reiterating the introductory remarks, the booklet informed the subject what attitude topic he or she was to write about and later discuss: specifically, the use of physical punishment as a child-rearing technique by parents.[3]

The dependent measure was the attitude toward punishment that was expressed in each subject's essay. Judges rated each essay in terms of the extremity of the attitude position it conveyed. Analysis of these ratings indicated that the positions taken in the essays were an interactive function of subjects' initial opinions and their levels of public self-consciousness (see Table 1). As predicted, among low public self-conscious subjects, those who were initially in favor of punishment wrote essays that were judged more favorable toward punishment than those who were initially against punishment. The essays written by subjects high in public self-consciousness, however, did not differ as a function of initial attitude position. That is, the attitudes they expressed were more moderate.

It is commonly observed that measures of opinions taken at one time, in one context, often differ from measures taken at other times, in

TABLE 2   Covariation Between Pretested Attitudes and Attitudes
           Expressed in the Experimental Session as a Function of
           Private and Public Self-Consciousness (data from Scheier,
           1980)

Dispositional tendency	High public	Low public
High private	.12	.68*
n	24	24
Low private	.00	.27
n	26	39

*p<.01.

different contexts. Consistent with this observation, the opinion premeasures of subjects in this study were only weakly related to the opinions expressed in their essays. When the various combinations of public and private self-consciousness were taken into account, however, the picture became quite different (see Table 2). As expected, consistency between premeasure and essay was highest for persons who were low in public self-consciousness and high in private self-consciousness. Indeed, it was stronger than for any other combination of public and private dispositions. Stated simply, consistency in self-portrayal of attitudes was found only among persons high in private and low in public self-consciousness.

The latter finding indicates once more that persons high in private self-consciousness have an accurate awareness of their beliefs. When such people were also relatively inattentive to their public self-aspects, their essays reflected this awareness quite clearly. As such, this finding supplements and extends related findings that persons high in private self-consciousness are more aware of their behavioral dispositions than are people low in private self-consciousness (Scheier et al., 1978; Turner, 1978). But these data also plainly indicate that awareness of the public self, in a context where verbal interaction with another is anticipated, is a potent moderator of the expression of those privately held beliefs. Even among subjects high in private self-consciousness, the cognizance of the more social aspects of the self (i.e., being also high in public self-consciousness) caused those opinions to be somewhat disregarded in the essays.

Private and Public Self-Awareness

All of the studies just described made use of individual differences in the disposition to focus on certain aspects of the self. As was suggested earlier, however, the public-private distinction may also be applicable to experimental manipulations. At least two research projects have been based on that supposition.

In one of these projects, Froming and Walker (Note 2, Experiment 2) set out to test the hypothesis that the presence of a mirror makes one selectively aware of the private self, and the presence of an audience makes one selectively aware of the public self. In order to do this, they selected subjects for their research who simultaneously satisfied two rather disparate criteria. First, they all expressed the belief that punishment was a relatively ineffective and inappropriate way to produce learning. Second, they also reported believing that most people held the opposite opinion (i.e., that punishment is both appropriate and effective). Several weeks after the opinion data were collected, subjects were induced to deliver shocks to an ostensible cosubject as punishments for incorrect answers in a supposed learning experiment.

For subjects in one condition, attention to the private self was increased by attaching a small mirror to the experimental apparatus. For subjects in another condition, attention to the public self was increased by the presence of two evaluative observers, who ostensibly were going to be rating the subjects on their effectiveness as teachers. A nonevaluative audience condition was also included in the study, comprised of "advanced students" who wanted to observe some psychological research. A control group was comprised of subjects who received no manipulation.

All subjects in this study had previously expressed personal opposition to the use of punishment in teaching. It was expected that the presence of a mirror would make them more cognizant of their private self-aspects, thus making that attitude more salient. The effect of such awareness was expected to be reduced aggression. The findings, which replicated earlier results obtained by Carver (1975), proved this to be exactly the case. On the other hand, the presence of an evaluative audience was expected to remind subjects of their nature as social objects. This, in turn, should have reminded them of the opinions that they believed most other people hold concerning the use of punishment in teaching. The result in this case should have been *increased* aggression, compared to the control group.

This prediction was also supported. Subjects in the nonevaluative audience condition did not differ in aggressiveness from the control group, however. This implies that the evaluative nature of the audience is an important cue in causing attention to shift to the public self.

Public and Private Self-Awareness and Dissonance Reduction

The Froming and Walker study is not the only experiment that bears on the question of whether self-awareness manipulations vary in the self-aspects to which they direct attention. We have also conducted research on this subject. This research had the broader goal of investigating the effects of self-directed attention on dissonance reduction in the induced-compliance paradigm (Festinger, 1957). Specifically, we were interested in determining whether directing attention to a particular cognitive element would—by rendering that element more central phenomenologically—make it more resistant to change.

In our initial study (Scheier & Carver, 1980, Experiment 1), we attempted to make cognitive elements salient by varying the *timing* of a self-awareness manipulation. Timing proved not to be important, however. In this experiment, the presence of a small mirror—whether during an attitude premeasure or during the counterattitudinal behavior and postmeasure—resulted in a decrease in attitude change.

This pattern of findings was somewhat surprising. Indeed, it apparently was inconsistent with the findings from conceptually similar research that had been conducted earlier. In one of these previous studies (Wicklund & Duval, 1971, Experiment 2), subjects wrote counterattitudinal essays, either with a television camera focused on their faces or with no camera. The presence of the camera caused subjects to report attitudes that agreed more with their essays—that is, it *increased* attitude change. In another study (Insko, Worchel, Songer, & Arnold, 1973), subjects defended a counterattitudinal position, under conditions of either high or low anticipated effort, in the presence or absence of a television camera. Once again, the camera enhanced attitude change among subjects who should theoretically have been experiencing the greatest degree of dissonance.

It seems nearly impossible to reconcile our data with these previous findings, until a relatively simple assumption is made. Once made, however, the results of the three studies become entirely consistent. The assumption is that the presence of a mirror enhances one's awareness of the private self, whereas the presence of a television camera enhances one's awareness of the public self. That is, in our study, mirror presence presumably caused subjects to be aware of their private self-aspects, thereby making their attitudes more salient. The result was that the attitudes became more resistant to change and attitude change diminished. The presence of a camera in the earlier studies presumably caused subjects to be more aware of their public self-aspects, thereby making their counterattitudinal *behaviors* more salient. The result was that attitude change was enhanced.

This reasoning did allow a parsimonious integration of the findings, but being post hoc it required additional verification. This was the purpose of the second study we conducted (Scheier & Carver, 1980, Experiment 2). Subjects participated in an induced-compliance paradigm in which they wrote counterattitudinal essays. Rather than vary the timing of the self-focusing manipulation, however, we varied the *nature* of the manipulation. Some subjects were exposed to a small mirror, others were exposed to a camera. On the basis of the previous findings, we expected the mirror to inhibit attitude change, and the camera to facilitate attitude change, compared to a no-manipulation control group.

We also undertook a more rigorous test of our underlying assumptions in this experiment. That is, if attending to a given cognitive element makes it more resistant to change, changes should occur in some *other* cognitive elements. More specifically, if the mirror causes enhanced awareness of one's initial attitudes, the result should not just be a decrease in attitude change but also a corresponding increase in the tendency to reduce dissonance via some other pathway (e.g., distorted recall of the counterattitudinal behavior). Thus, in this experiment we asked subjects to rate their behavior, as well as to indicate their attitudes.

Our predictions for this study, then, were the following. Mirror presence should cause distorted recall of the counterattitudinal behavior, but not attitude change. Camera presence should cause attitude change, but not distorted recall. In brief different types of self-awareness manipulations should cause dissonance to be reduced in two distinctly different ways. As can be seen in Table 3, the results of the study were entirely consistent with these hypotheses. Subjects exposed to a mirror tended to reduce dissonance by distorting their perceptions of their behavior, not by changing their attitudes. Subjects exposed to a camera tended to do the

TABLE 3   Mean ratings of final attitude and strength of essay (data from Scheier & Carver, 1980, Experiment 2).

Dependent measure		No choice control	Choice control	Choice mirror	Choice camera
Attitude [a] ratings	M	29.44	35.15	33.06	40.68
	s.d.	11.32	8.50	11.10	9.72
Strength [b] of essay	M	10.56	14.77	20.48	9.16
	s.d.	10.88	9.95	16.76	7.69

[a] The higher the number, the greater the dissonance reduction (i.e., the greater the assumed change in attitude in the direction of the counterattitudinal essay).
[b] The higher the number, the greater the dissonance reduction (i.e., the less strong the counterattitudinal essay was perceived to have been).

opposite. They changed their attitudes, but did not distort their behavior. Taken together, these findings provided strong additional evidence that mirrors and cameras tend to make people aware of very disparate aspects of self.

Public and Private Self-Consciousness and Dissonance Reduction

In order to further establish the parallel between manipulations of public and private self-awareness and the two dimensions of dispositional self-consciousness, we conducted one more study in this area (Scheier & Carver, 1980, Experiment 3). In this study we chose subject groups whose personality characteristics would lead them to have essentially the same psychological experiences as had been created by the experimental manipulations of the previous experiment. The camera manipulation would seem to be most comparable to the combination of high public self-consciousness and low private self-consciousness. The mirror manipulation would seem comparable to high private and low public self-consciousness.

There was some ambiguity about what combination of dispositions would be most similar to the no-manipulation control group, however. For this reason, predictions were tested by comparing the dissonance-arousal condition to a no-dissonance condition within each of the two combinations of dispositions just described. Dissonance reduction among high public-low private subjects was expected to occur via attitude change. Dissonance reduction among high private-low public subjects was expected to involve distorted recall of counterattitudinal behavior. The data provided support for both of these predictions.

We should note in passing that these two studies raise some interesting questions concerning dissonance theory and alternative interpretations of dissonance effects (see also Carver & Scheier, 1981). For example, the fact that a focus on the public self causes the greatest degree of attitude change may be viewed as implicit support for the impression-management interpretation of such effects (e.g., Tedeschi et al., 1971). On the other hand, the fact that awareness of the private self causes distorted recall of the counterattitudinal behavior seems hard to reconcile with such an interpretation. Perhaps it is a matter of different processes being evoked when different aspects of the self are taken as the object of attention. Though this possibility is intriguing, further discussion of it is beyond the scope of this chapter (see Carver & Scheier, 1981, however, for a more comprehensive treatment of this issue).[4]

NEW DIRECTIONS

Our discussion of research bearing on the public-private distinction has thus far emphasized two points. First, there are many situations in which *either* private, covert concerns *or* public, self-presentational concerns may guide behavior. Second, which of these actually occurs depends to a large degree on which aspect of the self is taken as the object of one's attention. A good deal of evidence has now accumulated to support both of these conclusions.

There is also another class of situations, however, in which behavioral phenomena are known to occur and for which the chain of mediation is not clear. That is, the behavior might stem from private egocentric motives; but it might just as plausibly stem from self-presentational motives. The existence of such cases suggests a potential new application for the Self-Consciousness Scale. Specifically, if the phenomenon involves private motives, it should be associated with private self-consciousness, but not with public self-consciousness. If the phenomenon is actually self-presentational in nature, it should be associated with public, rather than private self-consciousness. Use of the scale thus allows the gathering of evidence as to which of those mediational chains is involved in any given case. We would like to close this chapter by pointing to two places where such a research technique appears to be applicable. In one instance, the research has already been conducted. In the other, it has not.

The first case concerns one aspect of reference group behavior. Reference groups are groups to which we compare ourselves—to whom we wish to be similar (positive reference group) or dissimilar (negative reference group). Among the other functions that these groups serve, we use them to help determine our opinions. That is, we shift our opinions so that they are similar to the opinions held by positive reference groups and so that they differ from opinions held by negative reference groups (cf. Newcomb, 1950, 1958).

But is this a self-definitional process or is it a matter of self-portrayal? Recent research by Carver and Humphries (1981) provided some data on this question by investigating the use of a negative reference group by Cuban-Americans. The reference group, to which specific opinions were ascribed, was the Castro government in Cuba. The results of this study indicated that dispositional self-consciousness mediated subjects' responses to those opinions. More specifically, *public* self-consciousness was found to be correlated with a tendency to renounce the attitudes expressed by the disliked reference group. Private self-consciousness was unrelated to the effect. These findings suggest that the phenomenon was one of self-portrayal. This, in turn, raises questions about the meaning of reference group behavior more generally.

Our second example concerns the processes underlying the behavioral effects produced by deindividuation. Deindividuation has been described as a three-part construct, involving specific antecedent conditions, which lead to a psychological state, which in turn results in characteristic behaviors (cf. Diener, 1980). The question of present interest is precisely what constitutes the intervening state. Diener (1980) has suggested that group involvement (a deindividuating antecedent variable) results in a decrease in self-consciousness (see also Ickes, Layden, & Barnes, 1978) and that people thereupon stop regulating their behavior with regard to the standards that normally govern it. Evidence that deindividuating conditions actually do decrease self-attention has been obtained in two experimental settings (Diener, 1979; Prentice-Dunn & Rogers, 1980).

But does immersion in a group decrease awareness of *all* facets of self? Or does it differentially lower awareness of a *particular* self-aspect? Based on a variety of circumstantial evidence, we have suggested that the experience of deindividuation involves decreased awareness of the private self (see Carver & Scheier, 1981). Although this assertion has not yet been tested directly, the reasoning presented above suggests one way of approaching the problem—namely, by premeasuring subjects' levels of private and public self-consciousness and then relating those variables to the experiences and behaviors of deindividuation. Such an approach would appear to be an interesting direction for future research.

SUMMARY AND CONCLUSION

In this chapter we have attempted to indicate the potential importance of a simple dichotomy between two sets of self-aspects: the private self and the public self. Each can influence behavior, but only when taken as the object of one's attention. A review of recent studies in which this distinction was made appears to reveal considerable support for this position. We have also presented the argument that the instrument which measures the disposition to be self-conscious represents a useful research tool for gathering information about the underlying causes of yet-to-be understood phenomena.

We would like to close by noting one final contribution made by the research that we have summarized here. Specifically, these studies have utilized two very different approaches to gain information. Researchers in this area have used both experimental manipulations and individual differences to test predictions about the influences of the private and public components of self. There are two respects in which this converging approach is important. First, to the degree that comparable results are obtained from studies using such different methodologies, our faith in the validity of the underlying conceptualization is greatly strengthened.

The second respect in which we see this strategy as important is perhaps a bit more subtle than the first. But important it is nevertheless, even though it has relatively little to do with scientific inquiry per se. Put simply, the use of these two disparate techniques provides at least one concrete reminder of the benefits that can accrue when the methods of both social and personality psychology are simultaneously brought to bear on the same research problem. In our view, such a reminder is far from trivial, coming as it does at a time when the gulf and disenchantment between the two fields appear to be growing wider with each passing day.

NOTES

1. The third subscale comprising the Self-Consciousness Scale measures social anxiety. This scale differs from the private and public self-consciousness subscales in that it does *not* measure simply a tendency to focus on some aspect of the self. Instead, it measures a particular kind of *reaction* to being focused on the self, particularly the public self. Social anxiety presumably derives from public self-consciousness, in that social anxiety presumes an existence of focus on the public self. Yet awareness of the public self is not a sufficient condition for the development of social anxiety. There must also be a sense of apprehensiveness over being evaluated by the people in one's social contexts. Although social anxiety is clearly an important dimension in many behavioral settings (see Buss, 1980), our concerns in this chapter are more rooted in the consequences of being *aware* of aspects of the self than the consequences of being chronically uncomfortable in the presence of others. For this reason we will focus here on the private and public dimensions of self-consciousness.

2. We should acknowledge that on at least one occasion (Scheier & Carver, 1980, Experiment 3) we have allowed a similar confounding of these two dimensions to occur in our own research.

3. Some of the subjects in the study were also provided with specific information regarding the opinions held by the discussion partner. This manipulation proved not to have an impact on the study's findings. For this reason we will not mention it further here (for details see Scheier, 1980).

4. It is interesting, in this regard, that these theories have one similarity that is rarely recognized: both are consistency theories, though in different senses. Dissonance theory concerns intra-psychic consistency, impression-management theory concerns consistency of self-portrayal. It may be that this similarity warrants more careful scrutiny than it has received thus far.

REFERENCE NOTES

1. Santee, R. T. & Maslach, C. To agree or not to agree: Resistance and conformity as moderated by self-esteem, self-consciousness, and individuation. Unpublished manuscript. (Available from C. Maslach, Department of Psychology, University of California, Berkeley, CA 94720)

2. Froming, W. J. & Walker, G. R. Self-awareness and public versus private standards for behavior. Unpublished manuscript. (Available from W. J. Froming, Department of Psychology, University of Florida, Gainesville, FL 32611)

REFERENCES

Allport, G. W. *Pattern and growth in personality.* New York: Hold, Rinehart & Winston, 1961.

Apsler, R. Effects of embarrassment on behavior toward others. *Journal of Personality and Social Psychology,* 1975, *32,* 145-153.

Asch, S. E. Effects of group pressure upon the modification and distortion of judgments. In H. Guetzkow (ed.), *Group, leadership, and man.* Pittsburgh, Pa.: Carnegie Press, 1951.

Asch, S. E. Studies of independence and conformity: I. A minority of one against a unanimous majority. *Psychological Monographs,* 1956, *70,* 9 (Whole No. 416).

Blumer, H. *Symbolic interaction: Perspective and method.* Englewood Cliffs, N.J.: Prentice-Hall, 1969.

Bradley, G. W. Self-serving biases in the attribution process: A reexamination of the fact or fiction question. *Journal of Personality and Social Psychology,* 1978, *36,* 56-71.

Briggs, S. R., Cheek, J. M., & Buss, A. H. An analysis of the self-monitoring scale. *Journal of Personality and Social Psychology,* 1980, *38,* 679-686.

Buss, A. H. *Self-consciousness and social anxiety.* San Francisco: Freeman, 1980.

Carlsmith, J. M. & Gross, A. E. Some effects of guilt on compliance. *Journal of Personality and Social Psychology,* 1969, *11,* 240-244.

Carver, C. S. Physical aggression as a function of objective self-awareness and attitudes toward punishment. *Journal of Experimental Social Psychology,* 1975, *11,* 510-519.

Carver, C. S. Self-awareness, perception of threat, and the expression of reactance through attitude change. *Journal of Personality,* 1977, *45,* 501-512.

Carver, C. S. A cybernetic model of self-attention processes. *Journal of Personality and Social Psychology,* 1979, *37,* 1251-1281.

Carver, C. S. & Glass, D. C. The self-consciousness scale: A discriminant validity study. *Journal of Personality Assessment,* 1976, *40,* 169-172.

Carver, C. S. & Humphries, C. Havana daydreaming: A study of self-consciousness, and the negative reference group among Cuban-Americans. *Journal of Personality and Social Psychology,* 1981, *40,* 545-552.

Carver, C. S. & Scheier, M. F. Self-focusing effects of dispositional self-consciousness, mirror presence, and audience presence. *Journal of Personality and Social Psychology,* 1978, *36,* 324-332.

Carver, C. S. & Scheier, M. F. *Attention and self-regulation: A control-theory approach to human behavior.* New York: Springer-Verlag, 1981.

Carver, C. S. & Scheier, M. F. Self-consciousness and reactance. *Journal of Research in Personality,* 1981, *15,* 16-29.

Cialdini, R. B., Levy, A., Herman, C. P., Kozlowski, L. T., & Petty, R. E. Elastic shifts of opinion: Determinants of direction and durability. *Journal of Personality and Social Psychology,* 1976, *34,* 663-672.

Cooley, C. H. *Human nature and the social order.* New York: Scribners, 1902.

Crowne, D. P., & Marlowe, D. *The approval motive: Studies in evaluative dependence.* New York: Wiley, 1964.

Crutchfield, R. A. Conformity and character. *American Psychologist,* 1955, *10,* 191-198.

Davis, D. & Brock, T. C. Use of first person pronouns as a function of increased objective self-awareness and prior feedback. *Journal of Experimental Social Psychology,* 1975, *11,* 381-388.

Diener, E. Deindividuation, self-awareness, and disinhibition. *Journal of Personality and Social Psychology,* 1979, *37,* 1160-1171.

Diener, E. Deindividuation: The absence of self-awareness and self-regulation in group members. In P. B. Paulus (ed.), *The psychology of group influence.* Hillsdale, N.J.: Erlbaum, 1980.

Duval, S. & Wicklund, R. A. *A theory of objective self-awareness.* New York: Academic Press, 1972.

Fenigstein, A. Self-consciousness, self-attention, and social interaction. *Journal of Personality and Social Psychology,* 1979, *37,* 75-86.

Fenigstein, A., Scheier, M. F., & Buss, A. H. Public and private self-consciousness: Assessment and theory. *Journal of Consulting and Clinical Psychology,* 1975, *43,* 522-527.

Festinger, L. *A theory of cognitive dissonance.* Stanford, Calif.: Stanford University Press, 1957.

Freud, S. *A general introduction to psychoanalysis.* London: Bonji & Liveright, 1920.

Freud, S. *An outline of psychoanalysis.* New York: Norton, 1949.

Froming, W. J. & Carver, C. S. Divergent influences of private and public self-consciousness in a compliance paradigm. *Journal of Research in Personality,* 1981, *15,* 159-171.

Geller, V. & Shaver, P. Cognitive consequences of self-awareness. *Journal of Experimental Social Psychology,* 1976, *12,* 99-108.

Gerard, H. B. & Rotter, G. S. Time perspective, consistency of attitude, and social influence. *Journal of Abnormal and Social Psychology,* 1961, *62,* 565-572.

Goffman, E. *The presentation of self in everyday life.* Garden City, N.Y.: Doubleday, 1959.

Goffman, E. *Interaction ritual: Essays on face-to-face behavior.* Garden City, N.Y.: Doubleday, 1967.

Greenwald, A. G. Ego task analysis: An integration of research on ego-involvement and self-awareness. In A. Hastorf & A. Isen (eds.), *Cognitive social psychology.* New York: Elsevier North Holland, in press.

Hass, R. G. & Mann, R. W. Anticipatory belief change: Persuasion or impression management? *Journal of Personality and Social Psychology*, 1976, *34*, 105-111.

Ickes, W., Layden, M. A., & Barnes, R. D. Objective self-awareness and individuation: An empirical link. *Journal of Personality*, 1978, *46*, 146-161.

Insko, C. A., Worchel, S., Songer, E., & Arnold, S. E. Effort, objective self-awareness, choice, and dissonance. *Journal of Personality and Social Psychology*, 1973, *28*, 262-269.

Lecky, P. *Self-consistency: A theory of personality*. New York: Island Press, 1945.

Maslow, A. H. *Motivation and personality*. New York: Harper & Row, 1970.

Mead, G. H. *Mind, self, and society*. Chicago, Ill.: University of Chicago Press, 1934.

Miller, D. T. What constitutes a self-serving attributional bias? A reply to Bradley. *Journal of Personality and Social Psychology*, 1978, *36*, 1221-1223.

Miller, D. T. & Ross, M. Self-serving biases in the attribution of causality: Fact or fiction? *Psychological Bulletin*, 1975, *82*, 213-225.

Newcomb, T. M. *Social psychology*. New York: Dryden Press, 1950.

Newcomb, T. M. Attitude development as a function of reference groups: The Bennington study. In E. E. Maccoby, T. M. Newcomb, & E. L. Hartley (eds.), *Readings in social psychology*. New York: Holt, Rinehart & Winston, 1958.

Newtson, D. & Czerlinsky, T. Adjustments of attitude communications for contrasts by extreme audiences. *Journal of Personality and Social Psychology*, 1974, *30*, 829-837.

Prentice-Dunn, S. & Rogers, R. W. Effects of deindividuating situational cues and aggressive models on subjective deindividuation and aggression. *Journal of Personality and Social Psychology*, 1980, *39*, 104-113.

Rogers, C. R. Some observations on the organization of personality. *American Psychologist*, 1947, *2*, 358-368.

Scheier, M. F. Self-awareness, self-consciousness, and angry aggression. *Journal of Personality*, 1976, *44*, 627-644.

Scheier, M. F. Effects of public and private self-consciousness on the public expression of personal beliefs. *Journal of Personality and Social Psychology*, 1980, *39*, 514-521.

Scheier, M. F., Buss, A. H., & Buss, D. M. Self-consciousness, self-report of aggressiveness, and aggression. *Journal of Research in Personality*, 1978, *12*, 133-140.

Scheier, M. F. & Carver, C. S. Self-focused attention and the experience of emotion: Attraction, repulsion, elation, and depression. *Journal of Personality and Social Psychology*, 1977, *35*, 625-636.

Scheier, M. F. & Carver, C. S. Private and public self-attention, resistance to change, and dissonance reduction. *Journal of Personality and Social Psychology*, 1980, *39*, 390-405.

Scheier, M. F., Carver, C. S., & Gibbons, F. X. Self-directed attention, awareness of bodily states, and suggestibility. *Journal of Personality and Social Psychology*, 1979, *37*, 1576-1588.

Scheier, M. F., Fenigstein, A., & Buss, A. H. Self-awareness and physical aggression. *Journal of Experimental Social Psychology*, 1974, *10*, 264-273.

Schlenker, B. R. *Impression management: The self-concept, social identity, and interpersonal relations*. Monterey, Calif.: Brooks/Cole, 1980.

Shibutani, T. *Society and personality*. Englewood Cliffs, N.J.: Prentice-Hall, 1961.

Snyder, M. Self-monitoring of expressive behavior. *Journal of Personality and Social Psychology*, 1974, *30*, 526-537.

Snyder, M. Self-monitoring processes. In L. Berkowitz (ed.), *Advances in experimental social psychology* (Vol. 12). New York: Academic Press, 1979.

Tedeschi, J. T. (ed.). *Impression management theory and social psychological research*. New York: Academic Press, 1980.

Tedeschi, J. T., Schlenker, B. R., & Bonoma, T. V. Cognitive dissonance: Private ratiocination or public spectacle? *American Psychologist*, 1971, *26*, 685-695.

Turner, R. G. Consistency, self-consciousness, and the predictive validity of typical and maximal personality measures. *Journal of Research in Personality*, 1978, *12*, 117-132.

Turner, R. G., Scheier, M. F., Carver, C. S., & Ickes, W. Correlates of self-consciousness. *Journal of Personality Assessment*, 1978, *42*, 285-289.

Wallace, J. & Sadalla, E. Behavioral consequences of transgression: I. The effects of social recognition. *Journal of Experimental Research in Personality*, 1966, *1*, 187-194.

Watzlawick, P., Beavin, J. H., & Jackson, D. D. *Pragmatics of human communication: A study of interactional patterns, pathologies, and paradoxes.* New York: Norton, 1967.

Wicklund, R. A. The influence of self on human behavior. *American Scientist*, 1979, *67*, 187-193.

Wicklund, R. A. & Duval, S. Opinion change and performance facilitation as a result of objective self-awareness. *Journal of Experimental Social Psychology*, 1971, *7*, 319-342.

8

The Library Laboratory:
ARCHIVAL DATA IN PERSONALITY AND SOCIAL PSYCHOLOGY

DEAN KEITH SIMONTON

Dean Keith Simonton is Associate Professor at the University of California, Davis. His research focus in on the application of mathematical techniques to historical and biographical data in order to understand eminent creativity and leadership.

Personality psychology may be defined as the scientific study of individual differences, social psychology as the scientific study of individual behavior in a social context. These two definitions are substantive rather than methodological. Each discipline is delineated by the theoretical issues of phenomena to be discussed. The sole methodological component of these definitions is the insertion of the adjective *scientific,* but such a qualification is hardly restrictive. To be "scientific" means merely that the studies be dedicated to discovering general abstract principles or laws which can be subjected to objective empirical verification and replication via some systematic, quantitative technique. This conception of scientific may seem excessively broad, perhaps, but a more narrow definition would exclude far too much. We cannot restrict the term *scientific* to just those inquiries which are "experimental," for example, if by this descriptor we signify the active manipulation of independent variables. Virtually all of astronomy, astrophysics, meteorology, oceanography, geophysics, geology, epidemiology, taxonomy, paleontology, and economics—to cite a few conspicuous cases—would fail to qualify as sciences by such a narrow definition. These fields may feature systematic observations in which the scientist exerts some control over the collection and analysis of data, but no more than this. Therefore, it comes as no surprise that practically all sciences are defined by the substantive issues they address and not by the methodological approaches they employ. Yet de facto, personality and social psychology at times seem to include specific methodologies into their topic definitions. Personality research largely entails the administration of assessment devices to clinical or collegiate populations and social psychological research is dominated by the running of college students through laboratory experiments.

I would like to devote this review to discussing a methodology which is rare in personality and social psychology but which cannot be excluded as "unscientific" by any nonarbitrary criterion. That methodology usually passes by the name *archival*. Generally speaking, archival research means any investigation which draws data from archives, that is, from stored records of facts. Archival data may include such items as personal documents (e.g., letters and diaries), creative products (e.g., poems, paintings, musical compositions, and essays), biographies or autobiographies, and histories or governmental records—virtually any primary or secondary source deposited in a library or other data storage institution. Because archival research exploits data already collected by others for purposes often very different from the intentions of the researcher, this methodology constitutes a class of "unobtrusive measures" (Webb, Campbell, Schwartz, & Sechrest, 1966, chap. 3 and 4).

My plan is to spend most of this article reviewing some of the major examples of archival research in personality and social psychology. This review will focus on those archival studies which satisfy two fundamental prerequisites. First, I will examine only those investigations dedicated to unearthing general laws of human individual differences and social behavior. Nomothetic inquiries will thus be favored at the expense of more ideographic "case studies," thereby omitting psychohistorical and psychobiographical research (e.g., Erikson, 1958). Second, I will confine attention to archival studies which employ objective quantitative techniques. The data may come from the dusty shelves of the library, but the information must ultimately find, at least in principle, a home in the cleanly punched square holes of a computer data processing card. Therefore, qualitative studies making use of archives, no matter how meritorious in a nomothetic sense, will be ignored. A final restriction will be imposed, though in this case a far more arbitrary one: Cross-cultural research using ethnographic information, such as that found in the Human Relations Area Files, will not be reviewed. This omission is not due to any belief that such cross-cultural studies are not archival, for indeed they are whenever they utilize published ethnographic information. Nor is it a matter that cross-cultural research cannot make notable contributions to either personality of social psychology. On the contrary, the contributions are so numerous and so diverse as to defy review here (see, e.g., Levinson, 1977). Consequently, it is a space and not a taste which requires that this article confine its scope to just the nomothetic and quantitative use of content analytical, biographical, and transhistorical data.

EXAMPLES OF RESEARCH

Personality Psychology and Individual Differences

Personality psychologists have always been far more willing than social psychologists to utilize archival data. Probably this willingness stems from the intense fascination that personality theorists have for the extreme end-points of any dimension of individual differences. Most frequently this curiosity attaches to the pathological pole defined by clinical populations; yet the extremely creative, self-actualizing pole does receive attention in various studies of "genius" (Albert, 1980). For the most part, such excursions tend to be conducted by less well-known "marginal" researchers or by established researchers as one-shot affairs with no systematic pursuit. An instance of the latter is Cattell's (1963) attempt to apply the personality categories of his 16-Factor Inventory to eminent scientists (also see Cattel, 1953; Cattell & Adelson, 1951). Nonetheless, there are a few topics in personality psychology which have received sustained, focused, and notable treatment. These include intelligence and achieved eminence, creativity and productivity, conceptual or integrative complexity, and achievement or power motives.

Intelligence and achieved eminence. The scientific use of historical materials to test psychological hypotheses is now over a century old. The practice began with the now-classic book *Hereditary Genius* by Francis

Galton (1869). Galton sought to demonstrate that (1) there are tremendous individual differences in native intellectual ability, (2) these differences are subject more to genetic inheritance than to environmental nurturance, and (3) the intellectual differences would be outwardly reflected in the amount of eminence each individual achieves. To make his case, Galton examined eminent figures in a large range of activities, whether cultural or political, with the aim of showing that such persons are begotten by, or tend to beget, eminent families (also see Bramwell, 1948). The biologically and culturally prolific Bach family illustrates this point among artists, and the Darwin family makes the same point for scientists (the family including, in a twist of hidden self-flattery, Francis himself). Never mind that Galton's arguments have attracted considerable criticisms or that Galton can be said to be tainted with not a little of the then-fashionable Victorian racism and sexism. The fact remains that Galton's work posed both a theoretical and methodological challenge to subsequent researchers. Just why is it that eminent figures tend to display kinships surpassing chance expectations? Are there any flaws in the data collection procedures, such as sampling bias or failure to control for social advantage, which inadvertently tilt the evidence Galton's way?

Whatever the answer to these questions, Galton's work proved to be very influential, provoking two separate research traditions. On the one hand is the little-known "historiometric" investigation of Frederick Woods (1906) whose *Mental and Moral Heredity in Royalty* had two principal aims. First of all, Woods shared Galton's belief in the heritability of intellectual traits and so tried to prove the same basic proposition. But rather than dismiss royalty as Galton had done with a flash of democratic furor, Woods deliberately concentrated on this very group. Woods justified this switch by measuring intelligence directly rather than employing achieved eminence as a proxy indicator (for "achieved eminence" is a rather faulty gauge of intellect for those who are honored with a certain privileged status merely by birth). Second, Woods was also interested in morality, not only whether the virtue is governed by genetic laws but also whether morality and intelligence are strongly and positively correlated (cf. Kohlberg, 1969). Wood's response to both of these issues was affirmative. This work is every bit as impressive as Galton's, both in ambition and in execution, even though Woods is much less well-known. Woods himself was not a psychologist by trade, and the only psychologist to do a follow-up on Woods's efforts was the eminent Edward L. Thorndike (1936) who, however, published his successful replication study in a sociological journal. So this research tradition fell into neglect (except see Simonton, Note 1).

On the other hand, the second tradition continues to be active up to the present day. Its subject is achieved eminence rather than intelligence. This series of inquiries began with another eminent psychologist, James McKeen Cattell (1903), who scrutinized the transhistorical and cross-national distribution of eminent persons. Like Galton, some of Cattell's inferences are riddled with turn-of-the-century Anglo-Saxon prejudices. But Cattell did provide a forward impetus to research by his attempt to actually rank creators and leaders on the dimension of eminence. This methodological innovation was accomplished by measuring the amount of space devoted to each figure in standard reference works (cf. Farnsworth, 1969, chap. 16).

Cattell's eminence ranking was very effectively exploited by Catherine Cox (1926) in her book *The Early Mental Traits of Three Hundred Geniuses,* the second volume of Terman's (1926) ambitious *Genetic Studies of Genius.* Cox started by sampling the 301 highest ranked individuals on Cattell's list, subject to certain restrictions about historical period, field of endeavor, and data availability. Then after collecting massive amounts of biographical data on each sampled figure, she and her assistants calculated IQ scores for each—a truly painstaking enterprise to say the least—by estimating mental ages corresponding to certain precocious behaviors for which chronological ages were available. These scores, intrinsically interesting by themselves, were correlated with Cattell's rankings. Cox concluded that achieved eminence is positively correlated with IQ, even after partialing out data reliability. Since this conclusion has been replicated more recently (Walberg, Rasher, & Parkerson, 1980), it would seem that Galton was justified in using achieved eminence as an indirect index of intelligence. Unfortunately for Galton and Cox, however, multivariate analysis has proven that the correlation between eminence and intelligence is zero once birth year is controlled (Simonton, 1976a). This null result should not be taken to mean IQ is absolutely irrelevant to fame. After all, the estimated IQ scores for the 301 geniuses tend to be around three standard deviations above the mean. It is just that once you are looking at a sample of highly selected people, differences in intelligence have negligible consequences in comparison to other factors. A similar observation has been made about the relationship between intelligence and creativity, an association which all but vanishes once attention is confined to individuals who are bright, brilliant, or better (Hudson, 1966; NcNemar, 1964). To her credit, Cox (1926) does look into other personality variables which contribute to the attainment of eminence (also see White, 1931). She concludes that intellect must be supported by exceptional motivation and persistence of effort, a qualification which again is endorsed by research on contemporary subject pools (see, e.g., Albert, 1980; Stein, 1969).

Creativity and productivity. Clearly the study of creative productivity is closely allied with the study of intelligence and achieved eminence. Yet archival inquiries into creativity and productivity have pursued a rather different direction. Particularly conspicuous is the emphasis on nature over nature, that is, on environmental influences over genetic heritage. There thus have been a good many investigations into the early developmental experiences most central to the emergence of eminent creators, especially such personal factors as father absence (e.g., Martindale, 1972) or orphanhood (Albert, 1971; Eisenstadt, 1978), birth order or special family position (e.g., Albert, in press; Goertzel, Goertzel, & Goertzel, 1978), the quality of family relationships (Goertzel, Goertzel, & Goertzel, 1978; cf. Matossian & Schafer, 1977), formal education (e.g., Hudson, 1958; Simonton, 1976a), socioeconomic background (e.g., Goertzel, Goertzel, & Goertzel, 1978; Simonton, 1976a), and a great many more potential and demonstrated agents (see Goertzel, Goertzel, & Goertzel, 1978; Walberg, Rasher, & Parkerson, 1980). Some attention has also been recently given to the social, cultural, and political conditions which are more instrumental to the development of eminent creativity (Naroll, Benjamin, Fohl, Fried, Hildreth, & Schaefer, 1971; Schaefer, Babu, & Rao, 1977; Simonton, 1975b, 1976e, 1977b, 1978a). These studies have determined the causal effects of such variables as role model availability, intranational and international political violence, political fragmentation, geographic marginality, and the aesthetic, scientific, or philosophical Zeitgeist. As an example, the occurrence of extraordinary political instability—as gauged by coups d'etat, political assassinations, dynastic struggles, and the like—has an adverse impact on creativity some two decades later (Simonton, 1975b, 1976e). A picture is thus gradually emerging of the personal and social circumstances which favor the development of eminent individuals in various disciplines (Albert, 1980, Goertzel, Goertzel, & Goertzel, 1978; Gowan & Olson, 1980; Simonton, 1978a). Significantly, this picture is also generally corroborated by research on contemporary samples using more popular methodologies (see, e.g., Roe, 1952; Schaefer & Anastasi, 1968).

Besides the large body of literature on the developmental etiology of eminent creativity, there has grown an extensive archival literature on the relationship between age and creative productivity. This literature effectively began with Lehman's (1953) controversial *Age and Achievement* along with its critique by Dennis (1956a, 1956b, 1958; cf. Lehman, 1956, 1960), and the literature continues to the present day (e.g. Cole, 1979; Dennis, 1966; Lehman, 1966; Lyons, 1968; Simonton, 1975a, 1977a; Zusne, 1976). For the most part, this line of research is of more value to the developmental psychologist than to colleagues in personality or social psychology. There is one issue, nonetheless, which does have some interest for personality researchers, namely, the positive interrelationship among creative precociousness, productivity, and longevity (Albert, 1975). The most productive creators tend to begin their careers at exceptionally early ages, to produce at extraordinarily high rates, and to continue their careers late into life (Dennis, 1954a, 1954b; Simonton, 1977b; Zuckerman, 1977). Thus it is not true that productive precociousness is a harbinger of early "burn out"—for an early commencement to a career is probably the best single predictor of productivity, whether lifetime or rate per annum.

Closely connected to the preceding generalization is the well-established finding that individual differences in lifetime productivity tend to be highly skewed (Dennis, 1954c, 1955). To put this fact in concrete terms, the top 10% of the most productive individuals in any given field tend to make almost 50% of the total contributions, whereas the bottom 50% of the least productive are responsible for only about 15% of the total (Dennis, 1955). Among those who contribute anything at all—for the zero-producers comprise the largest group—the model number of contributions per individual is one, with a steep decline in frequency thereafter which approaches the zero point asymptotically. According to Lotka's (1926) law, the number of people who produce n publications is inversely proportional to n^2, or, according to Price's (1963, Ch. 2) law, half of all contributions are generated by the square root of the total number of contributors to the field (cf. Allison, Prices, Griffen, Moravcsik, & Stewart, 1976). Although Dennis (1954c) suggested that this skewed distribution may represent the upper tail of the normal distribution of human abilities, Simon (1954a, 1955) has shown this similarity to be only superficial and has therefore offered an alternative model which is more consistent with the sociological notion of "accumulative advantage" (Allison & Stewart, 1974; Price, 1976) or what Merton (1968) calls "Matthew's law." That is, the distribution may result not from any heterogeneity in abilities but rather from the selective and risky nature of publication coupled with the tendency for initial success to breed further success and first failure to breed further failure.

To be sure, some researchers are skeptical of productivity as an indicator of creativity (e.g., Rubin, 1978). Certainly a distinction must be made between quantity and quality. Yet the surprising thing is that quality tends to be a consequence of quantity—that the most productive individuals do tend to be judged by both contemporaries and posterity as the most creative or eminent as well (see, e.g., Albert, 1975; Dennis, 1954a; Simonton, 1977b, 1979a). For instance, using data published by Dennis (1954a) on scientists I have caluclated a phi coefficient of .46 between exhibiting above average total lifetime productivity and being honored with an entry in the *Encyclopedia Britannica* (Simonton, Note 2). Or taking psychology, there is a correlation of around .58 between individual productivity and the number of citations earned in the scientific literature (Rushton & Endler, 1979). Not only is the correlation between quantity and quality valid between individuals but also it holds within a single individual over time. That is, the number of major works per age period is highly correlated with the number of minor works produced concomitantly, and the proportion of major to total works stays constant with age (Simonton, 1977a). Hence, a constant-probability-of-success model has been proposed which holds for both cross-sectional and longitudinal data and which can be derived as a special case of Campbell's (1960) "blind-variation and selective-retention" model of creativity (see Simonton, 1977a; 1980d; cf. Dennis, 1954a, 1966). The individual creator may be little more than a "random" generator of idea combinations which then undergo a winnowing process in the hands of posterity.

Conceptual or integrative complexity. Peter Suedfeld and his students have launched a provocative research program concerning the single characteristic of conceptual complexity (Porter & Suedfeld, in press; Suedfeld & Rank, 1976; Suedfeld & Tetlock, 1977; Suedfeld, Tetlock, & Ramirez, 1977; Tetlock, 1979). Taking an established pencil-and-paper test as the point of departure (see Schroeder, Driver, & Suedfeld, 1967), Suedfeld devised a content analytical coding scheme which could be applied to letters, speeches, and other personal documents. The resulting measures have proven valuable in understanding a wide range of phenomena, including leadership, war, and creativity. Some of these contributions will be discussed later, so right now I wish merely to offer two illustrations which more specifically bear upon personality issues. Let us begin with an article by Suedfeld and Rank (1976) which attempted to determine whether the long-term success of revolutionary leaders could be predicted on the basis of a shift in cognitive style. The key hypothesis was that revolutionaries must display a simplistic single-mindedness of purpose in order to accomplish the overthrow of a government, but that revolutionaries who persist in such simple-mindedness will not long continue in power when the new revolutionary regime must face the hard realities of ruling a nation. After assessing the conceptual complexity revealed in letters, speeches, and other archival materials for 19 revolutionaries from five revolutions, Suedfeld and Rank found that those revolutionaries who managed to stay in power after the revolution did indeed exhibit a larger shift toward increased complexity in their thinking. In contrast, those revolutionaries who remained intransigent in their dogmatic inflexibility found themselves involuntarily ejected from the seats of their newly formed power.

The foregoing study raises the question of the longitudinal stability of conceptual complexity over time. Is it a stable individual difference variable or is it a transient cognitive strategy for coping with particular environmental conditions? Perhaps the successful revolutionaries who remained in power always were conceptually complex and just exploited ideological posing as a tactical measure, whereas the revolutionaries who failed to preserve their hard-won power positions may have been too conceptually simple by disposition to adopt complexity when the altered circumstances demanded. To address this question we need some longitudinal inquiry into conceptual complexity. And such a study was completed by Porter and Suedfeld (in press) using the personal correspondence of four eminent British novelists. They specifically examined how complexity is affected by personal stress, age, and social stress. Complexity was found to decrease with wartime and physical illness but to increase with civil unrest and age. These findings suggest that environmental conditions can influence the style of information processing adopted by an individual. It is for this reason that a distinction has been made between conceptual complexity as a stable personality attribute and integrative complexity as a flexible cognitive strategy for dealing with environmental tasks, even though these two variables are measured the same way (Suedfeld & Tetlock, 1977).

Achievement and power motive. Content analytical research has long been committed to assessing the individual attitudes, needs, values, drives, or dispositions reflected in personal documents such as letters, diaries, and speeches (see Holsti, 1969). Thus White (1951) introduced his "value analysis" over a quarter century ago, and Osgood (1959) has treated several schemes such as evaluation assertion anaylsis and contingency analysis. An important development in content analysis came with the introduction of computer systems, such as the General Inquirer programs of Philip Stone and his colleagues (Stone, Dunphy, Simth, & Ogilvie, 1966). To offer but one example, the General Inquirer has been applied to 20 presidential nomination acceptance speeches in order to see how political ideas and ideals alter over time and across the two major American political parties (Smith, Stone, & Glenn, 1966). But probably the most provocative research tradition is that which was at least partially inspired by Murray's (1938) *Explorations in Personality* and its methodological counterpart, the Thematic Apperception Test or TAT. This research has scrutinized two main needs or motives, namely, the need for achievement (n Ach) and the need for power (n Power). Archival studies of n Ach are primarily dedicated to showing that the achievement motive is ultimately responsible for economic growth and prosperity. The early efforts to make this case stand are summarized in McClelland's (1961) *The Achieving Society.* Maybe the most outstanding characteristic of this research is the impressive ingenuity exercised toward operationalizing the key variables of n Ach and economic prosperity. Achievement themes have been assessed in Greek vases, classical literature, and children's readers, and economic growth has been measured using vase distribution, coal imports, and patent indices—just to cite a few instances (see, e.g., Bradburn & Berlew, 1961; Cortes, 1960; DeCharms & Moeller, 1962). Although a few subsequent studies may have cast doubt on the basic proposition that individual n Ach is a causal agent of social economic well-being (e.g., Finison, 1976; Mazur & Rosa, 1977), the work of McClelland and his colleagues continues to represent a bold attempt to extend generalizations from contemporary populations back through history.

Archival research on n Power has tended quite naturally to look mostly at political leaders, especially at American presidents. The counterpart to McClelland's (1961) book may be said to be *The Power Motive* by Winter (1973). Winter applied objective coding schemes to presidential inaugural addresses in order to show hat those 20th century presidents who have the strongest need for power are more prone to enter the United States into war, to cause many cabinet changes, and to be the target of assassination attempts (Winter, 1973, Chap. 7). A strong power motive on the part of the nation's chief executive is also highly correlated with the president's rated "greatness" by American historians (Wendt & Light, 1976). Usually both n Ach and n Power are assessed with the ultimate goal of being able to forecast actual presidential performance in the White House (see, e.g., Donley & Winter, 1970). Naturally, precise predictions are far into the future, and the work on n Power tends to have a more exploratory "let's see what happens if . . ." character than holds for McClelland's (1961) work on n Ach. The aim remains a worthy one nonetheless.

Social and Political Psychology

As pointed out earlier, social psychologists are far less likely than personality psychologists to indulge in archival research. This fact is lamentable insofar as archival research may actually have more to offer social than personality psychology. Many individual and situational variables of significant relevance to the discipline are uniquely available in archival sources. This is not to say that archival research has not had its adherents. More recently William J. McGuire (1973, 1976) has advocated increased exploitation of such nontraditional methods, a recommendation which carries all the more weight given his impeccable credentials as researcher and editor. Thus with the aim of encouraging more social psychologists to engage in this type of research, let us review the five topics where archival studies have made permanent contributions, namely, leadership, attitudes and beliefs, aesthetics, aggression and violence, and the genius versus Zeitgeist question.

Leadership. In the previous section on individual differences we reviewed some studies directly bearing upon the subject of leadership. Thus Suedfeld and Rank (1976) attempted to employ conceptual complexity as a predictor of revolutionary success, Winter (1973) and Wendt and Light (1976) used both n Ach and n Power to predict presidential style, and Goertzel, Goertzel, and Goertzel (1978) and Simonton (1976a) have looked for early developmental experiences responsible for eminence as a leader. To these studies we may add more specialized studies devoted to the antecedents of charismatic (Cell, 1974), revolutionary (Rejai & Philips, 1979), and long-termed (Blondell, 1980) leaders. There also have been many attempts to measure leadership skills of historical figures, particularly of American presidents (e.g., Kynerd, 1971; Maranell, 1970; Simonton, Note 3). But I think that the most intriguing archival research may be the investigations into how patterns of interpersonal relationships and group dynamics affect the decision-making processes of national leaders. One fine example is Etheredge's (1978) demonstration that the foreign-policy recommendations of an American presidential adviser tend to be patterned after the individual's own orientation in interpersonal relationships (cf. Hermann, 1980). For instance, policy makers high in interpersonal dominance are more prone to propose the use of threat and coercion in foreign policy. Another illustration of this line of research is Tetlock's (1979) effort to apply a more quantitative test of the "group-think" phenomenon discussed by Janis (1972). Tetlock demonstrated that there is a tendency for highly cohesive groups of political decision decision makers to display a simple-mindedness that can lead to absurd decisions— such as the Bay of Pigs invasion under President Kennedy. Even though in a certain sense Tetlock's (1979) study is merely a "replication" of Janis's (1972), the fact that Tetlock employed quantitative methods using established content analytical instruments must represent a significant improvement. Along with Etheredge's (1978) study, moreover, Tetlock has shown how critically important policy decisions in the highest circles of government can be objectively monitored. The repercussion may be more efficacious policy formation in the future.

I have not by any means exhausted the literature on leadership. Many archival studies of attitude change, political violence, and the genius-Zeitgeist controversy are no less pertinent to the understanding of leader behavior, as will become evident below.

Attitudes and beliefs. The study of attitudes and attitude change is surely one of the best established research topics in social psychology. And as is typical of the discipline, such research tends to stress laboratory experiments, the spattering of field studies and opinion surveys notwithstanding. In contrast, archival data afford a unique opportunity to learn how beliefs develop and transform in the real world. One good example is a study by Sales (1972) which tried to show that the authoritarian personality is not so much a stable character trait as a transient adaptation to prevailing socioeconomic conditions. In particular, Sales found that authoritarian churches gained adherents during economic hard times whereas nonauthoritarian churches increase membership during economic prosperity. While Sales was looking at how adulthood attitudes adjust to environmental circumstances, I was intrigued with how religious and philosophical beliefs emerge in the first place (Simonton, 1976f; cf. Simonton, 1976c, 1978c). I discovered that youths who are exposed to certain political events—such as warfare, civil disturbances, and political fragmentation—tend to advocate a well-defined set of philosophical beliefs as adults. For instance, thinkers who grow up in times of civil disturbances are more likely to adopt extremist positions on almost all philosophical questions (cf. the "law of polarization" of Sorokin, 1962, pp. 487-488).

Of perhaps more practical value even if more provincial interest is the large amount of recent research on the determinants of presidential popularity and election success. Political scientists, naturally enough, have tended to take the lead in this field, beginning with Mueller's (1973) *War, Presidents and Public Opinion.* This book shows how presidential popularity from Truman to Johnson is affected by war, international crises, election or reelection, and economic downturns (also see Mueller, 1970). Although Mueller's contribution has received some deserved methodological criticisms by Kernell (1978) and others (e.g., Hibbs, 1974), we are still much closer to understanding how attitudes toward an American president alter according to the prevailing political conditions. To offer but one case in point, it is now established that the economy has an asymmetrical impact on the president's popularity: Though economic downturns damage a president's status in the polls, the president receives no boost when the economy improves (Kenski, 1977; Mueller, 1973). Since a president's popularity determines whether he is reelected (Sigelman, 1979), it is not surprising that similar variables emerge as predictors of the election success of not only an incumbent president, but incumbent congresspersons besides. For instance, Bloom and Price (1975) have demonstrated that the asymmetrical effect of the economy holds for congressional races, too. Moreover, a psychologist has recently entered this discussion by investigating the antecedents of success in presidential primaries (Grush, 1980). Almost 80% of the variance in voting outcomes for the 1976 Democratic Presidential Primaries could be accounted for by the candidates' expenditures, regional exposure, and prior primary outcomes.

Aesthetics. Since scientific aesthetics is primarily concerned with why some art objects are appreciated more than others, it would seem that archival data would have a conspicuous place in research. Certainly content analytical schemes would be applied to poems, paintings, or music compositions to unearth the attributes which distinguish successful from unsuccessful pieces—the masterwork from the esoterica. Yet, surprisingly, scientific aesthestics has also been dominated by the laboratory experiment (see, e.g., Berlyne, 1971). Rather than employ actual aesthetic objects, artificial stimuli are constructed in order to precisely manipulate the major dimensions thought to affect aesthetic likes and dislikes. Instead of measuring the actual aesthetic merit of a work in the community of art appreciators, these experiments are usually content to substitute the preferences of college students who volunteer for participation in laboratory studies, with or without any real enthusiasm for aesthetic activities. I am not by any means criticizing this new experimental aesthetics, for the movement represents a healthy advance over previous qualitative and speculative studies which constitute hardly more than psychological art criticism. Nonetheless, archival methods have progressed to the point that more objective and direct inquires can also be made into real-life aesthetic works. The first indication of this opportunity is the book *Romantic Progression* by Colin Martindale (1975). This work tied a theoretical model of literary creativity and experimental simulations of literary change (Martindale, 1973) with a most ambitious content analysis of English and French poetry.

More recently I have shown how computerized content analysis can be applied to over 15,000 melodies drawn from the classical repertoire (Simonton, 1980c, 1980d; cf. Brook, 1969; Paisley, 1964). I introduced a mutivariate design which allowed the simultaneous scrutiny of aesthetic attributes (e.g., fame, originality, form, and medium), developmental trends (linear and quadratic age), biographical factors (e.g., creative productivity and biographical stress), sociocultural context (e.g., musical Zeitgeist and contemporary competition), and numerous control variables (e.g., work size). This complex design revealed, among many other things, that melodic originality increases when a composer suffers severe stress due to extreme life changes (Simonton, 1980c), that a composer's creativity becomes increasingly free from the Zeitgeist with increased maturity (Simonton, 1980d), and that thematic fame as assessed by an archival citation measure is a curvilinear inverted-U function of melodic originality (Simonton, 1980d). This last finding enlarges the external validity of laboratory studies which indicate a similar curvilinear relationship between stimulus originality and aesthetic preference (Berlyne, 1971).

Aggression and violence. By the very nature of the data source, archival studies of human aggression tend to focus less on interpersonal violence and more on such mass violence as riot, revolution, and war (except see Bailey, 1980). Such research can be subdivided into two general classes. To begin with, some researchers have investigated the repercussions of political violence for individual behavior. We have already seen how I examined how warfare and civil disturbances shape the development of personal belief systems in the next generation of thinkers (Simonton, 1976f). I have also studied how certain varieties of political violence impede techno-scientific advance (Simonton, 1980b; cf. Simonton, 1975b, 1976b, 1976d, 1977a) and even how women's dress fashions are modified during times of international and intranational violence (Simonton, 1977d). Of greater practical value, perhaps, is the second line of research on the causal antecedents of political violence. Again it is not surprising that political scientists have tended to pioneer the archival study of warfare. The collection of articles in Russett's (1972) *Peace, War and Numbers* provides a fair idea of this recent and growing literature, much of which also appears in the *Journal of Conflict Resolution.* Nonetheless, these investigations have a distinct tendency to treat variables of little psychological interest, such as the degrees of polarization and rigidity of alliance systems. Even so, I can cite three areas of research where the etiology of violence is viewed in more psychological terms.

First of all, Suedfeld and his associates have quite successfully applied the construct of integrative complexity discussed previously to the problem of predicting whether an international crisis will result in an outbreak of warfare (Suedfeld & Tetlock, 1977; Suedfeld, Tetlock & Ramirez, 1977). They discovered that increases in the integrative complexity found in diplomatic exchanges tended to lower the chance of war, whereas decreases in complexity forebode the onset of violence. These studies open the very real possibility of monitoring communiqués of the opposing parties to an international crisis to obtain early warnings of pending war. Second, two historians, Matossian and Schafer (1977), have recently proposed a theory of political violence based on the causal interconnection between fertility, family relationships, and revolution. Rather than accept their theory on faith or on anecdotal or case study evidence, Matossian and Schafer subjected it to elaborate archival tests using demographic, political, and biographical data (cf. Davies, 1962). Third and last, I must mention the article by Baron and Ransberger (1978) which attempts to demonstrate the curvilinear relationship between ambient temperature and the probability of urban riot. Even though Carlsmith and Anderson (1979) have shown that the relation is actually linear, the fact remains that some notable experimental social psychologists have tired to see if laboratory studies can be generalized to the world of real human aggression.

Genius versus zeitgeist. One of the key theoretical issues in social psychology is the relative importance of individual and situation in the determination of social behaviors. Are certain persons more prone to obey authority, to be altruistic, or to emerge as leaders? Are there special environmental circumstances which tend to encourage or discourage the amount of obedience, altruism, or leadership displayed by any given person? This question is not necessarily one which demands an either/or response, but rather the issue concerns the comparative impact. When archival data are being exploited, this substantive problem can be naturally translated into more traditional, even if more romantic terms as the relative significance of the genius and the Zeitgeist in determining the course of history. Are a few "great" men and women responsible for the flow of larger human events? Or are even the greatest minds bound to the spirit of the times as replaceable pawns or even mere epiphenomena? This controversy has a long history, but the most outstanding statements of the opposing positions are probably to be found in, on the one hand, Thomas Carlyle's (1841) essay *On Heroes* which advocates the "great man" theory and, on the other hand, Leo Tolstoy's (1952/1865-1869) novel *War and Peace* which advocates the Zeitgeist theory. In more modern times, and within our own discipline, this debate has been profusely discussed in E. G. Boring's (1963) historical writings. Empirical research also has a long history. Frederick Woods (1913), who we have already mentioned as a successor to Galton, published a provocative book called the *Influence of Monarchs* in which he attempted to show that a nation's political, economic, social, and cultural well-being is dependent upon the quality of the leadership. After assessing ruler leadership and national condition for hundreds of monarchs in over a dozen European nations, Woods concluded that "Strong, mediocre, and weak monarchs are associated with strong, mediocre, and weak periods respectively" (1913: 246), with correlation somewhere between .60 and .70. I need not dwell on the methodological deficiencies of this study (see Wrightsman, 1977: 641-642). The crucial point is that Woods tried to exploit biographical and historical data in order to find out, by objective and quantitative means, if individuals can have a causal role in national events.

Since Woods, most archival research on this question has tended to be done by anthropologists or sociologists with the explicit aim of ushering evidence for a Zeitgeist interpretation of history. Within sociology, Pitirim Sorokin's (1937-1941) monumental *Social and Cultural Dynamics* may be cited as one case in point. Sociologists and historians of science have also employed the historical record to indicate how scientific knowledge is the product of certain sociocultural forces (e.g., Rainoff, 1929; Price, 1963; Sheldon, 1980). Within anthropology the seminal work is Kroeber's (1944) *Configurations of Culture Growth* which examines how individual creativity depends on a definite set of sociocultural conditions (also see Gray, 1958, 1961, 1966; Naroll, Benjamin, Fohl, Fried, Hildreth, & Schaefer, 1971). In a narrower vein, Kroeber's study of women's fashion fluctuations (Richardson & Kroeber, 1940) continues to inspire research as well (e.g., Robinson, 1975, 1976; cf. Simonton, 1977c). I have tired recently, as a personality-social psychologist, to reopen the genius-Zeitgeist question by launching a systematic program of gauging the relative explanatory assets of these two perspectives (Simonton, 1974 and following). This program specifically includes studies of philosophical creativity (Simonton, 1976c, 1976e, 1976f, 1978c), musical aesthetics (Simonton, 1977a, 1977b, 1980c, 1980d), scientific multiple discoveries (Simonton, 1978b, 1979a; cf. 1976d), and military leadership (Simonton, 1979b, 1980a). These investigations all examine the causal interplay between the individual creator or leader and the larger sociocultural system. And this research indicates the extreme relevance of both genius and Zeitgeist for our understanding of momentous human events.

I hardly need to admit that research on the genius-Zeitgeist question has still a long way to go before we can say anything conclusive about the interplay of genius and Zeitgeist in the flow of human events (see Simonton, Note 2). But this issue enjoys both theoretical and practical relevance and thus deserves more attention. And it is more reasonable to presume that archival studies will continue to dominate empirical investigations into this topic.

CONCLUSION

There is no scientific justification for rejecting the exploitation of archival data in personality and social psychology. Some researchers may doubt the reliability of such information, but this doubt is totally unfounded. The reliability coefficients calculated for content analytical, biographical, and historical data are the same league as those of more traditional methods, including survey questionnaires or interviews and personality or intellectual tests (see, e.g., Cox, 1926; Farnsworth, 1969; Kynerd, 1971; McClelland, 1961; Simonton, 1976a, 1976b, 1976e, 1977b, 1980c, 1980c, 1980d; Suefeld & Rank, 1976; Thorndike, 1936; Weitman, Shapiro, & Markoff, 1976; Winter, 1973). Nor is it fair to disparage the internal validity of archival investigations. To be sure, as any other correlational methodology, archival studies do not enjoy the security of causal inference featured by laboratory experiments. Nevertheless, the recent introduction of advanced multivariate statistics, structural equation modeling, and quasi-experimental designs has quite dramatically raised the inferential power of archival research (e.g., Simonton, 1975b, 1976f, 1977a, 1977b, 1978d). Indeed, since archival studies can often tap the timewise sequencing of events, whether longitudinal or transhistorical, archival analysis can frequently excel most other correlational methodologies in internal validity (see, e.g., Simonton, 1976f, 1978d). And we must not forget the causal inference is only half the story. Equally critical is external validity, that is, the ability to generalize to the real world. Here there can be no question whatsoever that archival data can complement if not surpass the laboratory experiment in the pursuit of many substantive issues. The library stores records of actual human behaviors of immense consequences—real aggressive acts such as riots or revolts, actual attitude change which determines the victor of presidential elections, world-renowned leaders and creators, established aesthetic masterworks, and decision-making processes which have altered the course of history. If the scientific worth of any method is gauged by the product of its external and internal validities, then the library can often be superior to the laboratory for the investigation of certain key topics in personality and social psychology.

Psychologists have traditionally looked to the natural sciences for models of methodological emulation. If Nobel prizes are granted to physicists, chemists, and biomedical researchers, and if these disciplines are exclusively devoted to experimental, laboratory techniques, then perhaps the prestige of our discipline can be heightened by imitating the work habits of these particular scientists. Yet physics, chemistry, and medicine or physiology may not provide the most suitable models for all substantive questions in the behavioral sciences. Indeed, the "queen of the sciences," astronomy, and the "dismal science," economics, may offer far more appropriate methodological guidelines for some areas of research. Both astronomy and economics depend quite heavily upon the methodological analysis of archival data, whether records of past systematic observations or governmental indicators of economic growth. Both disciplines emphasize the explanation and the prediction of events but not necessarily the control of such events. In fact, there is no assurance that any astronomical or economic theory, no matter how scientifically valid, can ever be put to practical use. The phenomena of the stars and of industry may be simply beyond the outer limits of human intentionality. At best, theories in these disciplines may help us prepare for future shocks through precise anticipation and bolster the spirit by removing the feeling of victimization by mysterious forces. Consequently, neither astronomy nor economics has evolved even a puny experimental literature. Yet the prestige of these two disciplines remains undiminished. Now Nobel prizes are awarded in economics, the only social science to be so honored. And many of these very prizes have been presented to persons who developed econometrics, a body of analytical tools which are almost ideal for the transhistorical analysis of archival data as well (see, e.g., Simonton, 1975b, 1977b). It is somewhat ironic that the only psychologist to win a Nobel prize did not do so in the medicine or physiology category but rather in economics. The recipient, Herbert A. Simon, has equally been in the forefront in the development of econometric methods and correlational causal inference (see, e.g., Simon, 1954b; Simon & Ando, 1961).

Hence, personality and social psychologists need not apologize to anyone about their use of archival data. Such unconventional researchers will be participating in the opening of the last frontier of scientific objectivity. Political scientists, sociologists, anthropologists, and even historians are all grasping the tremendous wealth of archival data available for the testing of nomothetic hypotheses about human behavior. The social sciences have advanced to the point that the discovery of the "laws of history" has become a realistic enterprise. And since the laws of history necessarily entail behavioral laws as a critical subset, psychologists cannot afford to miss the opportunity—if not shirk their scientific responsibility—to participate in this scientific revolution. To default on this commitment will ultimately mean that many of the most important substantive statements about human behavior will come from the mouths of social scientists outside our discipline. As a matter of pure duty, then, personality and social psychologists must be willing, whenever appropriate, to utilize the library as a scientific laboratory.

REFERENCES NOTES

1. Simonton, D. K. *Intergenerational transfer of individual differences in royalty: Genes, role-models, cohort effects, or sociocultural enertia?* Manuscript submitted for publication, 1980.
2. Simonton, D. K. *Zeitgeist, genius, chance, and history.* Manuscript submitted for publication, 1980.
3. Simonton, D. K. *Presidential greatness and performance: Can we predict leadership in the White House?* Manuscript submitted for publication, 1980.

REFERENCES

Adorno, T. W., Frenkel-Brunswik, E., Levinson, D. J., & Sanford, R. N. *The authoritarian personality.* New York: Harper and Row, 1950.

Albert, R. S. Cognitive development and parental loss among the gifted, the exceptionally gifted and the creative. *Psychological Reports,* 1971, *29,* 19-26.

Albert, R. S. Toward a behavioral definition of genius. *American Psychologist,* 1975, *30,* 140-151.

Albert, R. S. Genius. In R. H. Woody (ed.), *Encyclopedia of clinical assessment* (Vol. 2). San Francisco: Jossey-Bass, 1980.

Albert, R. S. Family positions and the attainment of eminence: A study of special family positions and special family experiences. *Gifted Child Quarterly,* in press.

Allison, P. D., Price, D., Griffith, B. C., Moravcsik, M. J., & Stewart, J. A. Lotka's law: A problem in its interpretation and application. *Social Studies of Science,* 1976, *6,* 269-276.

Allison, P. D. & Stewart, J. A. Productivity differences among scientists: Evidence for accumulative advantage. *American Sociological Review,* 1974, *39,* 596-606.

Bailey, W. C. A multivariate cross-sectional analysis of the deterrent effect of the death penalty. *Sociology and Social Research,* 1980, *64,* 183-207.

Baron, R. A. & Ransberger, V. M. Ambient temperature and the occurrence of collective violence: The "Long, Hot Summer" revisited. *Journal of Personality and Social Psychology,* 1978, *36,* 351-360.

Berlyne, D. E. *Aesthetics and psychobiology.* Englewood Cliffs, N.J.: Prentice-Hall, 1971.

Blondel, J. *World leaders.* Beverly Hills, Calif.: Sage, 1980.

Bloom, H. S. & Price, H. D. Voter response to short-run economic conditions: The asymmetric effect of prosperity and recession. *American Political Science Review,* 1975, *69,* 124 0-1254.

Boring, E. G. Introduction. In R. I. Watson & D. T. Campbell (eds.), *History, psychology, and science.* New York: Wiley, 1963.

Bradburn, N. M. & Berlew, D. E. Need for achievement and English economic growth. *Economic Development and Cultural Change,* 1961, *10,* 8-20.

Bramwell, B. S. Galton's "hereditary genius" and the three following generations since 1869. *Eugenics Review,* 1948, *39,* 146-153.

Brook, B. S. Style and content analysis in music: The simplified "Plaine and Easie Code." In G. Gerner, O. R. Holsti, K. Krippendorph, W. J. Paisley, & P. J. Stone (eds.), *The analysis of communication content.* New York: Wiley, 1969.

Campbell, D. T. Blind variation and selective retention in creative thought as in other knowledge processes. *Psychological Review,* 1960, *67,* 380-400.

Carlsmith, J. M. & Anderson, C. A. Ambient temperature and the occurrence of collective violence: A new analysis. *Journal of Personality and Social Psychology,* 1979, *37,* 337-344.

Carlyle, T. *On heroes, hero-worship, and the heroic.* London: Fraser, 1841.

Cattell, J. M. A statistical study of eminent men. *Popular Science Monthly,* 1903, *62,* 359-377.

Cattell, R. B. A quantitative analysis of the changes in culture patterns of Great Britain, 1837-1937, by p-technique. *Acta Psychologica,* 1953, *9,* 99-121.

Cattell, R. B. The personality and motivation of the researcher from measurements of contemporaries and from biography. In C. W. Taylor & F. Barron (eds.), *Scientific creativity.* New York: Wiley, 1963.

Cattell, R. B. & Adelson, M. The dimensions of social change in the U.S.A. as determined by p-technique. *Social Forces,* 1951, *30* 190-201.

Cell, C. P. Charismatic heads of state: The social context. *Behavior Science Research,* 1974, *9,* 255-305.

Cole, S. Age and scientific performance. *American Journal of Sociology,* 1979, *84,* 958-977.

Cortes, J. B. The achievement motive in the Spanish economy between the 13th and 18th centuries. *Economic Development and Cultural Change,* 1960, *9,* 144-163.

Cox, C. *The early mental traits of three hundred geniuses.* Stanford, Calif.: Stanford University Press, 1926.

Davies, J. C. Toward a theory of revolution. *American Sociological Review,* 1962, *27,* 5-19.

DeCharms, R. & Moeller, G. H. Values expressed in American children's readers: 1800-1950. *Journal of Abnormal and Social Psychology,* 1962, *64,* 136-142.

Dennis, W. Bibliographies of eminent scientists. *Scientific Monthly,* 1954, *79,* 180-193. (a)

Dennis, W. Predicting scientific productivity in later decades from records of earlier decades. *Journal of Gerontology,* 1954, *9,* 465-467. (b)

Dennis, W. Productivity among American psychologists. *American Psychologist,* 1954, *9,* 191-194 (c)

Dennis, W. Variations in productivity among creative workers. *Scientific Monthly,* 1955, *80,* 277-278.

Dennis, W. Age and achievement: A critique. *Journal of Gerontology,* 1956, *11* 331-333. (a)

Dennis, W. Age and productivity among scientists. *Science,* 1956, *123,* 724-725. (b)

Dennis, W. The age decrement in outstanding scientific contributions: Fact or artifact? *American Psychologist,* 1958, *13,* 457-460.

Dennis, W. Creative productivity between the ages of 20 and 80 years. *Journal of Gerontology,* 1966, *21,* 1-8.

Donley, R. W. & Winter, D. G. Measuring the motives of public officials at a distance: An exploratory study of American presidents. *Behavioral Science,* 1970, *15,* 227-236.

Eisenstadt, J. M. Parental loss and genius. *American Psychologist,* 1978, *33,* 211-223.

Erikson, E. H. *Young man Luther.* New York: Norton, 1958.

Etheredge, L. S. Personality effects on American foreign policy, 1898-1968: A test of interpersonal generalization theory. *American Political Science Review,* 1978, *78,* 434-451.

Farnsworth, P. R. *The social psychology of music.* Ames: Iowa State University Press, 1969.

Finison, L. J. The application of McClelland's national developmental model to recent data. *Journal of Social Psychology,* 1976, *98,* 55-59.

Galton, F. *Hereditary genius.* London: Macmillan, 1869.

Goertzel, M. G., Goertzel, V., & Goertzel, T. G. *Three hundred eminent personalities.* San Francisco: Jossey-Bass, 1978.

Gowan, J. C. & Olson, M. The society which maximizes creativity. *Journal of Creative Behavior,* 1980, *13,* 194-210.

Gray, C. E. An analysis of Graeco-Roman development: The epicyclical evolution of Graeco-Roman civilization. *American Anthropologist,* 1958, *60,* 13-31.

Gray, C. E. An epicyclical model for Western civilization. *American Anthropologist,* 1961, *63,* 1014-1037.

Gray, C. E. A measurement of creativity in Western civilization. *American Anthropologist,* 1966, *68,* 1384-1417.

Grush, J. E. Impact of candidate expenditures, regionality, and prior outcomes on the 1976 Democratic presidential primaries. *Journal of Personality and Social Psychology,* 1980, *38,* 337-347.

Hermann, M. G. Assessing the personalities of Soviet Politburo members. *Personality and Social Psychology Bulletin,* 1980, *6,* 332-352.

Hibbs, D. A. Problems of statistical estimation and causal inference in time-series regression models. In H. L. Costner (ed.), *Sociological methodology 1973-1974.* San Francisco: Jossey-Bass, 1974.

Holsti, O. R. *Content analysis for the social sciences and humanities.* Reading, Mass.: Addison-Wesley, 1969.

Hudson, L. Undergraduate academic record of Fellows of the Royal Society. *Nature,* 1958, *182,* 1326.

Hudson, L. *Contrary imaginations.* Baltimore: Penguin, 1966.

Janis, I. *Victims of groupthink.* Boston: Houghton Mifflin, 1972.

Kenski, H. C. The impact of economic conditions on presidential popularity. *Journal of Politics,* 1977, *39,* 764-773.

Kernell, S. Explaining presidential popularity: How ad hoc theorizing, misplaced emphasis, and insufficient care in measuring one's variables refuted common sense and led conventional wisdom down the path of anomalies. *American Political Science Review,* 1978, *72,* 506-522.

Kohlberg, L. Stage and sequence: The cognitive-developmental approach to socialization. In D. A. Goslin (ed.), *Handbook of socialization theory and research.* Skokie, Ill.: Rand McNally, 1969.

Kroeber, A. L. The superorganic. *American Anthropologist,* 1917, *19,* 163-214.

Kroeber, A. L. *Configurations of culture growth.* Berkeley: University of California Press, 1944.

Kynerd, T. An analysis of presidential greatness and "president rating." *Southern Quarterly,* 1971, *9,* 309-329.

Lehman, H. C. *Age and achievement.* Princeton, N. J.: Princeton University Press, 1953.

Lehman, H. C. The age of scheduled participants at the 1948 APA annual meeting. *American Psychologist,* 1953, *8,* 125-126.

Lehman, H. C. Reply to Dennis' critique of *Age and Achievement. Journal of Gerontology,* 1956, *11,* 333-337.

Lehman, H. C. The age decrement in outstanding scientific creativity. *American Psychologist,* 1960, *15,* 128-134.

Lehman, H. C. The psychologist's most creative years. *American Psychologist,* 1966, *21,* 363-369.

Levinson, D. What have we learned from cross-cultural surveys? *American Behavioral Scientist,* 1977, *20,* 757-792.

Lotka, A. J. The frequency distribution of scientific productivity. *Journal of the Washington Academy of Sciences,* 1926, *16,* 317-323.

Lyons, J. Chronological age, professional age, and eminence in psychology. *American Psychologist,* 1968, *23,* 373-374.

McClelland, D. C. *The achieving society.* New York: Van Nostrand, 1961.

McGuire, W. J. The yin and yang of progress in social psychology: Seven koan. *Journal of Personality and Social Psychology,* 1973, *26,* 446-456.

McGuire, W. J. Historical comparisons: Testing psychological hypotheses with cross-era data. *International Journal of Psychology,* 1976, *11,* 161-183.

McNemar, O. Lost: Our intelligence? Why? *American Psychologist,* 1964, *19,* 871-882.

Maranell, G. M. The evaluation of presidents: An extension of the Schlesinger polls. *Journal of American History,* 1970, *57,* 104-113.

Martindale, C. Father absence, psychopathology, and poetic eminence. *Psychological Reports,* 1972, *31,* 843-847.

Martindale, C. An experimental simulation of literary change. *Journal of Personality and Social Psychology,* 1973, *25,* 319-326.

Martindale, C. *Romantic progression.* Washington, D. C.: Hemisphere, 1975.

Matossian, M. K. & Schafer, W. D. Family, fertility, and political violence, 1700-1900. *Journal of Social History,* 1977, *11,* 137-178.

Mazur, A. & Rosa, E. An empirical test of McClelland's "achieving society" theory. *Social Forces,* 1977, *55,* 769-774.

Merton, R. K. Singletons and multiples of scientific discovery: A chapter in the sociology of science. *Preceedings of the American Philosophical Society,* 1961, *105,* 470-486.

Merton, R. K. The Matthew effect in science. *Science,* 1968, *159,* 56-63.

Mueller, J. E. Presidential popularity from Truman to Johnson. *American Political Science Review,* 1970, *64,* 18-34.

Mueller, J. E. *War, presidents and public opinion.* New York: Wiley, 1973.

Murray, H. A. *Explorations in personality.* New York: Oxford University Press, 1938.

Naroll, R., Benjamin, E. C., Fohl, F. K., Fried, M. J., Hildreth, R. E., & Schaefer, J. M. Creativity: A cross-historical pilot survey. *Journal of Cross-Cultural Psychology,* 1971, *2,* 181-188.

Ogburn, W. K. & Thomas, D. Are inventions inevitable? *Political Science Quarterly,* 1922, *37,* 83-93.

Osgood, C. E. The representational model and relevant research methods. In I. de Sola Pool (ed.), *Trends in content analysis.* Urbana: University of Illinois Press, 1959.

Paisley, W. J. Identifying the unknown communicator in painting, literature and music: The significance of minor encoding habits. *Journal of Communication,* 1964, *14,* 219-237.

Porter, C. A. & Suedfeld, P. Integrative complexity in the correspondence of literary figures: Effects of personal and societal stress. *Journal of Personality and Social Psychology,* in press.

Price, D. *Little science, big science.* New York: Columbia University Press, 1963.

Price, D. A general theory of bibliometric and other cumulative advantage processes. *Journal of the American Society for Information Science,* 1976, *27,* 292-306.

Rainoff, T. J. Wave-like fluctuations of creative productivity in the development of West-European physics in the eighteenth and nineteenth centuries. *Isis,* 1929, *12,* 287-319.

Rejai, M. & Philips, K. *Leaders of revolution.* Beverly Hills, Calif.: Sage, 1979.

Richardson, J. & Kroeber, A. L. Three centuries of women's dress fashions: A quantitative analysis. *Anthropological Records,* 1940, *5,* 111-150.

Robinson, D. E. Style changes: Cyclical, inexorable, and foreseeable. *Harvard Business Review,* 1975, *53,* 121-131.

Robinson, D. E. Fashions in shaving and trimming of the beard: The men of the *Illustrated London News,* 1842-1972. *American Journal of Sociology,* 1976, *81,* 1133-1141.

Roe, A. *The making of a scientist.* New York: Dodd, Mead, 1952.

Rubin, Z. On measuring productivity by the length of one's vita. *Personality and Social Psychology Bulletin,* 1978, *4,* 197-198.

Rushton, J. P. & Endler, N. S. Assessing impact (quality?) in psychology: The use of citation counts. *Personality and Social Psychology Bulletin,* 1979, *5,* 17-18.

Russett, B. M. (ed.). *Peace, war, and numbers.* Beverly Hills, Calif.: Sage, 1972.

Sales, S. Economic threat as a determinant of conversion rates in authoritarian and non-authoritarian churches. *Journal of Personality and Social Psychology,* 1972, *23,* 420-428.

Schaefer, C. E. & Anastasi, A. A biographical inventory for identifying creativity in adolescent boys. *Journal of Applied Psychology,* 1968, *58,* 42-48.

Schaefer, J. M., Babu, M. C., & Rao, N. S. *Sociopolitical causes of creativity in India 500 B.C. - 1800 A.D.: A regional time-lagged study.* Presented at the meeting of the International Studies Association, St. Louis, March 1977.

Schroder, H. M., Driver, M. J., & Suedfeld, P. *Human information processing.* New York: Holt, Rinehart & Winston, 1967.

Sheldon, J. C. A cybernetic theory of physical science professions: The causes of periodic normal and revolutionary science between 1000 and 1870 A. D. *Scientometrics,* 1980, *2,* 147-167.

Sigelman, L. Presidential popularity and presidential elections. *Public Opinion Quarterly,* 1979, *43,* 532-534.

Simon, H. A. Productivity among American psychologists: An explanation. *American Psychologist,* 1954, *9,* 804-805. (a)

Simon, H. A. Spurious correlations: A causal interpretation. *Journal of the American Statistical Association,* 1954, *49,* 467-479. (b)

Simon, H. A. On a class of skew distribution functions. *Biometrika,* 1955, *42,* 425-440.

Simon, H. A. & Ando, A. Aggregation of variables in dynamic systems. *Econometrica,* 1961, *29,* 111-138.

Simonton, D. K. *The social psychology of creativity: An archival data analysis.* Unpublished Ph.D. dissertation, Harvard University, 1974.

Simonton, D. K. Age and literary creativity: A cross-cultural and transhistorical survey. *Journal of Cross-Cultural Psychology,* 1975, *6,* 259-277. (a)

Simonton, D. K. Sociocultural context of individual creativity: A transhistorical time-series analysis. *Journal of Personality and Social Psychology,* 1975, *32,* 1119-1133. (b)

Simonton, D. K. Biographical determinants of achieved eminence: A multivariate approach to the Cox data. *Journal of Personality and Social Psychology,* 1976, *33,* 218-226. (a)

Simonton, D. K. The causal relation between war and scientific discovery: An exploratory cross-national analysis. *Journal of Cross-Cultural Psychology,* 1976, *7,* 133-144. (b)

Simonton, D. K. Does Sorokin's data support his theory? A study of generational fluctuations in philosophical beliefs? *Journal for the Scientific Study of Religion,* 1976, *15,* 187-198. (c)

Simonton, D. K. Interdisciplinary and military determinants of scientific productivity: A cross-lagged correlation analysis. *Journal of Vocational Behavior,* 1976, *9,* 53-63. (d)

Simonton, D. K. Philosophical eminence, beliefs, and zeitgeist: An individual-generational analysis. *Journal of Personality and Social Psychology,* 1976, *34,* 630-640. (e)

Simonton, D. K. The sociopolitical context of philosophical beliefs: A transhistorical causal analysis. *Social Forces,* 1976, *54,* 513-523. (f)

Simonton, D. K. Creative productivity, age, and stress: A biographical time-series analysis of 10 classical composers. *Journal of Personality and Social Psychology,* 1977, *35,* 791-804. (a)

Simonton, D. K. Eminence, creativity, and geographic marginality: A recursive structural equation model. *Journal of Personality and Social Psychology,* 1977, *35,* 805-816. (b)

Simonton, D. K. Women's fashions and war: A quantitative comment. *Social Behavior and Personality,* 1977, *5,* 285-288. (c)

Simonton, D. K. Independent discovery in science and technology: A closer look at the Poisson distribution. *Social Studies of Science,* 1978, *8,* 521-532. (b)

Simonton, D. K. Intergeneration stimulation, reaction, and polarization: A causal analysis of intellectual history. *Social Behavior and Personality,* 1978, *6,* 247-251. (c)

Simonton, D. K. Multiple discovery and invention: Zeitgeist, genius, or chance? *Journal of Personality and Social Psychology,* 1979, *37,* 1603-1616. (a)

Simonton, D. K. Was Napoleon a military genius? Score: Carlyle 1, Tolstoy 1. *Psychological Reports,* 1979, *44,* 21-22. (b)

Simonton, D. K. Land battles, generals, and armies: Individual and situational determinants of victory and casualties. *Journal of Personality and Social Psychology,* 1980, *38,* 110-119. (a)

Simonton, D. K. Techno-scientific activity and war: A yearly time-series analysis. 1500-1903 A. D. *Scientometrics,* 1980, *2,* 251-255. (b)

Simonton, D. K. Thematic fame and melodic originality: A multivariate computer-content analysis. *Journal of Personality,* 1980, *48,* 206-219. (c)

Simonton, D. K. Thematic fame, melodic originality, and musical Zeitgeist: A multivariate content analysis. *Journal of Personality and Social Psychology,* 1980, *39,* 972-983. (d)

Smith, M. S., Stone, P. J., & Glenn, E. N. A content analysis of twenty presidential nomination acceptance speeches. In P. J. Stone, D. C. Dunphy, M. S. Smith, & D. M. Ogilvie (eds.), *The general inquirer.* Cambridge: MIT Press, 1966.

Sorokin, P. A. *Society, culture, and personality.* New York: Cooper Square, 1962.

Stein, J. I. Creativity. In E. F. Borgatta & W. W. Lambert (eds.), *Handbook of personality theory and research.* Skokie, Ill.: Rand McNally, 1969.

Stone, P. J., Dunphy, D. C., Smith, M. S., & Ogilvie, D. M. (eds.), *The general inquirer.* Cambridge: MIT Press, 1966.

Suedfeld, P. & Rank, A. D. Revolutionary leaders: Long-term success as a computer-content analysis. *Journal of Personality,* 1976, *48,* 206-219. (c)

Suedfeld, P. & Tetlock, P. Integrative complexity of communications in international crises. *Journal of Conflict Resolution,* 1977, *21,* 169-184.

Suedfeld, P., Tetlock, P. E., & Ramirez, C. War, peace, and integrative complexity. *Journal of Conflict Resolution,* 1977, *21,* 427-442.

Terman, L. M. *Mental and physical traits of a thousand gifted children.* Stanford, Calif.: Stanford University Press, 1926.

Tetlock, P. E. Identifying victims of groupthink from public statements of decision makers. *Journal of Personality and Social Psychology,* 1979, *37,* 1314-1324.

Thorndike, E. L. The relation between intellect and morality in rulers. *American Journal of Sociology,* 1936, *42,* 321-334.

Tolstoy, L. *War and peace* (L. Maude & A. Maude, trans.). Chicago: Encyclopaedia Britannica, 1952. (Originally published 1865-1869).

Walberg, H. J., Rasher, S. P., & Parkerson, J. Childhood and eminence. *Journal of Creative Behavior,* 1980, *13,* 225-231.

Webb, E. J., Campbell, D. T., Schwartz, R. D., & Sechrest, L. *Unobtrusive measures.* Skokie, Ill.: Rand McNally, 1966.

Weitman, S., Shapiro, G., & Markoff, J. Statistical recycling of documentary information: Estimating regional variations in pre-censal population. *Social Forces,* 1976, *55,* 338-366.

Wendt, H. W. & Light, P. C. Measuring "greatness" in American presidents: Model case for international research on political leadership? *European Journal of Social Psychology,* 1976, *6,* 105-109.

White, R. K. The versatility of genius. *Journal of Social Psychology,* 1931, *2,* 460-489.

White, R. K. *Value-analysis.* Noth Holland, Ill.: Libertarian Press, 1951.

Winter, D. G. *The power motive.* New York: Free Press, 1973.

Woods, F. A. *Mental and moral heredity in royality.* New York: Holt, Rinehart & Winston, 1906.

Woods, F. A. *The influence of monarchs.* New York: Macmillan, 1913.

Wrightsman, L. S. *Social psychology.* Belmont, Calif.: Wadsworth, 1977.

Zuckerman, H. *Scientific elite.* New York: Macmillan, 1977.

Zusne, L. Age and achievement in psychology: The harmonic mean as a model. *American Psychologist,* 1976, *31,* 805-807.

9

Psychobiographical Methodology:
THE CASE OF WILLIAM JAMES

JAMES WILLIAM ANDERSON

James William Anderson is Visiting Lecturer in the Division of Psychology, Department of Psychiatry, Northwestern University Medical School in Chicago. He has written articles on the psychobiographical study of the James family, the political personality of Woodrow Wilson, and psychobiographical methodology.

No enterprise involving psychology—with the possible exception of brain-washing—receives as much criticism as psychobiography (see, e.g., Barzun, 1974; Coles, 1973; Crews, 1980; Himmelfarb, 1975; Stannard, 1980).[1] But those who champion psychobiography have to admit that the bulk of the criticism is richly deserved; studies in this area regularly transgress the standards of either psychology or history or of both those disciplines.

Before undertaking a psychobiographical study of William James's young adulthood (Anderson, 1980), I wrote a review of the methodological literature (Anderson, 1981). I described the central difficulties which, according to the literature, psychobiographers encounter, discussed the suggestions which scholars have made for minimizing these difficulties, and proposed a strategy for my investigation of James's life. But, of course, I discovered what experimental researchers have long known; it is far easier to design a strategy than to execute it.

This review is a reexamination of psychobiographical methodology in the light of what I learned since I began studying James. I will also suggest novel approaches which other researchers might adopt in their attempts to circumvent the more intransigent problems involved in psychobiographical writing.

RESEARCH AS THE FOUNDATION OF PSYCHOBIOGRAPHY

Psychologists who do quantitative research are aware that their conclusions can be no better than the data on which they are based. Discussions of psychobiographical methodology rarely focus on the research itself. (For exceptions, see Arzt, 1978; Elms, 1976; Greenstein, 1969; Manuel, 1971.) But research may be even more crucial in psychobiographical studies than in quantitative studies because of the subtlety of the interpretations which rest on this research.

Difficulties with psychobiographical research began with what is often cited as the first psychobiographical book, Freud's *Leonardo da Vinci and a Memory of His Childhood.* In the memory mentioned in the title, Leonardo related that when he was in his cradle a bird flew down and then used its tail to open his mouth and strike him against his lips. Freud organized the entire book around his interpretations of this memory—or fantasy, as he calls it. However, Freud made a critical error. He relied on German-language sources and did no research in primary materials. In his sources the Italian word *nibio* was mistranslated as vulture, while it actually means another type of bird, the kite (see Schapiro, 1956). Freud's misidentification of the bird undermined his intricate interpretations.

For example, one of his chief conclusions was that Leonardo had spent the formative first years of his life with his mother but with no father. Other scholars had determined that Leonardo's birth was illegitimate and that by the age of five he had been taken into his father's household, but there was no indication when his reunification with his father took place: shortly after his birth, shortly before he reached the age of five, or some time in between.

The ancient Egyptians, according to Freud, believed that all vultures were female and that they were impregnated by the wind. But, Freud acknowledged, it might seem unlikely that Leonardo would have been familiar with this belief since hieroglyphics were not deciphered until centuries after his death. However, Freud discovered that the Church

Fathers frequently quoted the Egyptian idea about vulture conception because it offered support for the plausibility of the Virgin Birth. Hence he offered his reconstruction. Leonardo had once read about this belief in the Church Fathers or in a book of natural history. "At that point a memory sprang to his mind, which was transformed" into the fantasy about the vulture. The fantasy signified that "he also had been such a vulture-child—he had had a mother, but no father."

The importance of the fantasy, according to Freud, is that it seems to tell us that Leonardo "spent the critical first years of his life not by the side of his father and stepmother, but with his poor, forsaken, real mother, so that he had time to feel the absence of his father." Freud observed, "This seems a slender and yet a somewhat daring conclusion to have emerged from our psycho-analytic efforts" (1910: 90-91). He then went on to describe the far-reaching consequences for Leonardo of living during his first three to five years with only his mother. But, of course, Freud's intricate speculations collapse because the bird was not a vulture. Psychological interpretations often rest on minute details; knowing the exact word or phrasing or the context of a quotation can make all the difference.

Although in the earlier article I briefly mentioned the advantages of primary research, once I became involved in psychobiographical work myself I learned first-hand about the stark differences between the historical figure as portrayed in secondary accounts and that same person as he is revealed in the primary materials.

What has been called James's "spiritual crisis" was the focus of my study. For six years while in his 20s (1867-1872), he was depressed and at times suicidal. He had difficulty working and frequently complained of his lack of willpower. He also suffered from a number of psychologically based symptoms, such as eye trouble, back pain, and insomnia.

Perry, a philosophy professor at Harvard who had studied under James, developed the interpretation of James's spiritual crisis which has dominated James scholarship. Psychological approaches were alien to Perry. His only attempt to use psychology in understanding James was to label him as "neurasthenic" (Perry, 1935: I, 322). James himself at times talked about suffering from neurasthenia.[2] But the term, popular during the second half of the nineteenth century, had become obsolete by 1910, a full 25 years before Perry published his work. And it explains little. Neurasthenia simply means "nerve weakness," and it was used to cover virtually all nonpsychotic psychological problems other than hysteria and hypochondria (see Chatel and Peele, 1970-1971). Not surprisingly, Perry emphasizes a philosophical, instead of a psychological, explanation of James's difficulties. "The spiritual crisis was the ebbing of the will to live, for lack of a philosophy to live by," he wrote. And he added that James "experienced a personal crisis that could be relieved only by a *philosophical* insight" (Perry, 1935: I, 322-323).

Even this brief summary is sufficient to indicate that a psychobiographer would be in danger if he attempted to base a study of James on Perry's biographical treatment of him. But Perry also exercised considerable control over the published sources. His two-volume study of James includes hundreds of James's letters as well as diary extracts and other materials. But Perry systematically edited the documents in such a way that they support his portrait of James. Probably he was not consciously attempting to give a misimpression. But, because of his emphasis on philosophy, comments which seem psychologically relevant to us appeared extraneous to him; so he often omitted them.[3]

What matters is the cumulative effect of hundreds of deletions, but one specific example will illustrate the nature of Perry's editorial work. One of James's most dramatic diary entries concerns his decision to abandon his desire to become a philosopher. (Later, of course, James reversed this decision.) He wrote that his "strongest moral and intellectual craving [was] for some stable reality to lean upon" but a philosopher forfeits such stability because his responsibility is "every day to be ready to criticize afresh and call in question the grounds of his faith of the day before." The crucial sentence, as quoted by Perry, reads: "I fear the constant sense of instability generated by this attitude would be more than the voluntary faith I can keep going is sufficient to neutralize" (Perry, 1935: I, 343). But Perry omitted the second half of the sentence. James actually continued: "—and that dream-conception, 'maya,' the abyss of horrors, would 'spite of everything grasp my imagination and imperil my reason.'"[4] Perry's deletion takes the reader's attention away from James's fear of losing his psychological stability, falling into an "abyss of horrors," and becoming bereft of reason, and it serves to stress James's concern with the philosophical issue of "voluntary faith."

Perry's work on James demonstrates that not only are secondary sources unreliable but even published letters and diary extracts may be misleading. The only safe alternative is to work directly in the primary materials.

Most scholars who did not do research in the primary materials have accepted Perry's interpretation of James's spiritual crisis. For example, Fancher (1979), using published sources, wrote a 21-page account of James's life and repeated Perry's interpretation. In his book-length study of Freud, by contrast, Fancher (1973) provided a number of perceptive original insights into the development of Freud's work.

The suggestion is that psychobiographical portraits which rest on secondary sources—and whose authors have not immersed themselves in the data—are bound to be inadequate. One of the most respected psychobiographies is the George and George (1956) study of Woodrow Wilson. When I first read it, I found their depiction of Wilson's personality to be persuasive on the whole. But Arthur S. Link, a Wilson specialist, told me that Wilson scholars have never taken the book seriously. The Georges largely wrote the book from secondary sources and made virtually no use of the Wilson papers, which were available in the Library of Congress. When I studied the papers in depth I discovered that the data contradicted the Georges' portrait of Wilson (see Weinstein, Anderson, and Link, 1978).

Hjelle and Ziegler provide another example of psychobiography based on secondary sources. In a recent textbook they note that a personality theorist's "basic assumptions about human nature reflect [his] *own personality structure*," and therefore they provide biographical sketches of each theorist to help the reader "understand *him or her* as a person" (1981: 443). But these short sketches are filled with errors which a scholar who had immersed himself in the data on the theorists' lives would have avoided. For example, they overlook the identity-related issues involved in Erik H. Erikson's name change. In their account, his father's name was Erikson, and his mother was remarried to a Dr. Homburger when he was three. They continue, "Later, in signing his first psychoanalytic articles, Erikson used his stepfather's surname as his own, although he chose to be known by his original name when he became a naturalized American citizen in 1939" (1981: 113-114). In fact, Erikson's father was not named Erikson, and his mother's maiden name was not Erikson either. Apparently he grew up, from an early age, with the name Erik Homburger. In choosing the name Erikson he was making a statement—that he was not Dr. Homburger's son, and not the son of his "mythical" father, but his own son: Erikson. As an ambivalent expression of "gratitude" to his stepfather, he demoted the name Homburger to the status of a middle name and retained just the initial "H" in his name when it was printed on the title pages of his books.[5]

The chief point I have been making is that extensive research is the *sine qua non* of psychobiography. However, a biographer must not become so involved in ascertaining the facts as to forget that *psychological* reality is what matters most.

For example, biographers have gone to heroic lengths to determine whether Adolf Hitler had a Jewish grandfather. There is suggestive—but not definitive—evidence that his grandmother had worked as a servant in a Jewish household, had become pregnant by her employer, and had subsequently given birth to Hitler's father. However, as Waite (1977) points out, the important question is not whether Hitler's grandfather was Jewish but whether Hitler suspected that he was. And, in fact, there is ample evidence that Hitler did have such a suspicion. He ranted that the Aryan race would suffer "blood poisoning" because of the Jews living in its midst, and, apparently feeling his own blood was tainted, he regularly applied leeches to himself and directed his physician to remove blood with a syringe. He deprecated Jews for supposedly having bodily odors and "offensive" noses, and he also had phobic concerns about his own bodily odors and his large nose. He promulgated a law that Jews could not employ young, Gentile household servants, and more than once he inexplicably flew into a rage when Catholic household servants were mentioned. Eventually, he directed the Gestapo to conduct a private investigation of his genealogy, presumably in the hope that his fear would finally be put to rest. Only the conclusion that Hitler was afraid he had Jewish blood explains his strange behavior. But what should be emphasized here is that the historical truth of whether or not he had a Jewish grandfather is secondary; it was his *suspicion* that played such a central role in the development of his rabid anti-Semitism. If he had known about his ancestry with certainty, the consequences would have been radically different. There is ample evidence that Hitler, from an early age, felt worthless and degraded. His suspicion of being part Jewish assisted him in developing a defense against these feelings. He projected the darkest side of his self-image onto Jews; he said in a sense: I am not ugly, unlikable, and depraved—Jews are. The parts of himself which he detested he identified with his suspected Jewish blood and then tried to externalize them. His whole career announced that he could not be Jewish because he was the greatest Jew-hater in history. There are many reasons for Hitler's anti-Semitism, but it probably would not have reached such a virulent intensity without his suspicion that he was part Jewish himself.

A psychobiographer, despite his immersion in the data, must remember that his chief purpose is to reconstruct the inner world of his subject.

THE PSYCHOBIOGRAPHER'S RELATIONSHIP WITH
HIS OR HER BIOGRAPHICAL SUBJECT

As the literature on psychobiographical methodology recognizes, one of the most perilous pitfalls in the field is the tendency to denigrate or idealize the biographical subject (Donald, 1972; Erikson, 1968; George and George, 1973).

Recently I attended a symposium at which a historian presented a psychobiographical paper on one of history's most admired martyrs. Her paper revolved around her reassessment of his act of martyrdom. She argued that in giving his life for his beliefs he was also damaging his wife and children who were left by his death with little money and with no father and husband. Perhaps, she went on, his martyrdom represented his way of punishing or sadistically injuring his family. In the ensuing discussion she revealed that when her own parents had gotten divorced, her father had moved to another part of the country, and his absence had felt to her like a painful abandonment. No doubt the martyr's family suffered. But the psychobiographer failed to weigh their suffering against the benefits which accrued to the thousands of people who shared his beliefs. Her personal experience kept her from taking a balanced view toward her subject.

In the anecdote, denigration may have been involved. But my experience in working on James's life showed me that the issue is more complicated than simple denigration or idealization. I found that I developed an intense relationship through my years of involvement with his life. At times I idealized him and enjoyed the status of being connected to so exalted a figure. At other times I found fault with him in order to convince myself momentarily that I was smarter or saner or friendlier than he. Occasionally, I dreamt about him, and, as my wife will attest, I mentioned him in social conversations with intolerable frequency. In many intricate ways my basic myths about myself, my conflicts, and my preoccupations became intermixed with my understanding of his life.

Loewenberg (1980) observed recently that the biographer's emotional reactions may help the reader identify the subject's central conflicts. For example, he noted that Deutscher (1959), while describing Leon Trotsky's struggle with Josef Stalin, becomes angry with his subject, Trotsky. Presumably Deutscher identified with Trotsky but did not share his wariness over assuming power, and therefore Deutscher felt angry with him for acting in a seemingly inexplicable way.

Based on my own experience, I am convinced that every psychobiographer will have complicated and intense personal reactions to his subject. Merely satisfying himself that his view is not based exclusively on either idealization or denigration is not enough. The first step is to admit openly—to himself at least—that he is emotionally involved. What follows then is the hard work of constantly examining and reexamining his relationship with his subject. He can attempt to determine the extent to which his reactions stem from his own concerns and conflicts and the extent to which they offer insights into his subject's personality. If he can disentangle his feelings, he then can use them as an important tool in his investigation of the figure whom he is studying. If the scholar who studied the martyr had been aware of the sources of her resentment toward him, she could have avoided her one-sided, exaggerated condemnation of him. At the same time, with such self-awareness, she might have been able to use her personal reaction constructively. For example, her emotional response might have alerted her to the possibility—overlooked by other scholars—that the martyr's familial relationships were worth investigating. Similarly, Deutscher, instead of simply becoming angry at Trotsky and leaving it to perceptive readers such as Loewenberg to divine the source of his anger, could have focused more deliberately on the conflicts which underlay Trotsky's discomfort with power.

But in working on James I have seen how difficult it is to get in touch with all of one's personal feelings about a subject. There are further steps which psychobiographers potentially could take.

Perhaps it should be standard practice for each psychobiographer to include an appendix describing his feelings about his subject, his biases, and the way in which he decided to write about that particular person. Freud did something like that in his introduction to the psychobiography of Wilson on which he collaborated with Bullitt. Freud made the "confession that the figure of the American President . . . was from the beginning unsympathetic to me, and that this aversion increased in the course of years the more I learned about him and the more severely we suffered from the consequences of his intrusion into our destiny." He claimed that his "antipathy" gave way to "pity" once he began studying Wilson. But his description of his pity makes it clear that, however his emotions may have changed, his hostility to Wilson did not abate. He noted that the feeling of pity becomes overwhelming when one compares Wilson's weakness to "the greatness of the task which he had taken upon himself" (Freud and Bullitt, 1967: xi; xiii). Freud's attempt to come to grips with his feelings about Wilson did not prevent him from contributing to a distorted, denigrating examination of the American President. But at least, since Freud discussed his feelings, the reader has the opportunity to take them into account when assessing the biography.

An interview with an author can help make similar information available. For example, I questioned Edel (1953-1972), the author of a five-volume, psychologically informed biography of Henry James, regarding his feelings about the novelist. Before the interview Allen (1967), who wrote the standard biography of William James, commented to me that Edel's own family constellation had led him into an identification with Henry James. Allen noted that Edel, an English professor, was 15 months younger than his brother, a philosophy professor, just as Henry, the man of letters, was 15 months younger than William, the philosopher. As a result, Allen explained, Edel tended always to favor Henry's perspectives over William's. This rumor—and similar ones—circulate among scholars of the James family, but no one had ever directly asked Edel about it, not even Allen, who had been Edel's colleague for years in New York University's Department of English. When I brought up the subject with Edel I learned that the story was incorrect; actually Edel was the elder not the younger brother. In a number of ways his role was more like William's than Henry's. Like William, he was more "gregarious" and less bookish and he "bossed" his brother "around a great deal." One direct consequence of his familial situation, Edel added, was that it led him to ask "what effect Henry James had on William" and to include a chapter in the second volume which focused on William. In other ways, however, Edel's role was similar to Henry's. His brother, like William, was the better student, and Edel felt like a younger brother when his brother was tutoring him (Anderson, 1979: 21). In short, the facts are considerably more complicated than the rumors. That is the advantage of such interviews: They give us access to rich material pertaining to the relationship between author and subject.

Another possibility would entail the psychobiographer asking others, particularly individuals who are intimately acquainted with his personality and scholars who specialize in the study of the same figure, to read the manuscript and to comment specifically on his relationship with his subject. Individuals who know the psychobiographer well would be able to recognize where his personal preoccupations might be coloring his interpretations, while readers who specialize in the study of the same subject would be able to point to areas where he might be providing a distorted picture of the subject.

Two scholars have carried this approach a step further. Pletsch, a historian writing a psychobiography of Friedrich Nietzsche, and Moraitis, a psychoanalyst with an interest in psychohistory, collaborated on an exploration into the process of writing a biography. Pletsch did not merely ask Moraitis to comment on his work; they met systematically for 12 sessions, and both of them wrote about their work together (Moraitis, 1979; Pletsch, 1977). As an example of the process they used, they differed on a particular interpretation and sought to understand the reason for their disagreement. They found that it was related to "two distinct transference reactions toward the material" and that their views "represented partial insights about Nietzsche that could complement each other rather than being antithetical" (Moraitis and Pletsch, 1979: 73). Once the transference reactions were identified and analyzed, they concluded, it was possible to use them in developing a more comprehensive understanding of the subject.

PSYCHOBIOGRAPHY AS CROSS-CULTURAL RESEARCH

Psychobiography is a form of cross-cultural research; the subject, unless he is a contemporary, lived in a culture significantly different from our present-day culture. (For other discussions of this issue, see Fischer, 1970; Elms, 1976; LeVine, 1975).

Often a behavior of the subject will not have had the same meaning in the subject's era as it does in our era. Yet psychobiographers often make interpretations on the basis of 20th-century values and standards. For example, the Georges focused on several well-known facts about Wilson's childhood: He did not learn the alphabet until he was 9 and did not read with facility until 11, and he entered school at the age of 10 but did poorly at first. They concluded that "perhaps ... failing–refusing–to learn was the one way in which the boy dared to express his resentment against his father" (1956: 7). The Georges assumed that Wilson's slowness in learning to read was the sort of behavior which might have served as an expression of resentment. But they brought with them, to this interpretation, today's emphasis on learning to read punctually at the age of 6. Wilson's behavior would have appeared far less deviant in the mid-19th century. Furthermore, the period from ages 3 1/2 to 8 1/2 in his childhood coincided with the Civil War. In Augusta, Georgia, where he lived, the schools were in a chaotic condition, and Wilson, along with many other children, did not begin attending school until well after Appomattox. During Wilson's childhood, tardiness in developing a facility for reading was not an apt vehicle for venting hostility toward a scholarly father as it would be during our era.

The work of another historian illustrates a more thoughtful approach to the interpretation of a psychobiographical subject's behavior. Studying an early 19th-century diary, Ranlett noticed that the diarist, a school teacher named Cynthia Everett, stressed the benefits of beating her students whenever they needed discipline. But Ranlett realized that her subject was not necessarily brutal just because 20th-century standards condemn corporal punishment; such punishment was common while Everett was a teacher. The challenge was to determine whether or not Everett's use of force was excessive according to early 19th-century mores. Ranlett discovered that eventually Everett was dismissed for her abuse of corporal punishment. At this point—but not sooner—Ranlett (n.d.) was justified in concluding that her subject had a sadistic tendency for which psychological explanations could be sought. (For a similar incident in anthropological research, see Parsons, 1969.)

If it is important with behaviors to consider the cultural context, it is even more crucial with ideas, since they gain their meaning from their relationship to larger currents of thought. For example, in studying James's personality I noticed that more than once he described himself as suffering from "nervous weakness" (Perry, 1935: I, 346). I recognized this phrase as a potentially revealing indication of his image of himself and his understanding of his psychological difficulties. But in order to uncover what the idea meant to him I had to examine it in relation to the complex of attitudes toward mental illness which he adopted from his culture.

During the second half of the 19th century there was wide agreement that a "hereditary taint" was implicated in all forms of mental illness. James accepted this belief. In an early review he referred approvingly to the contention of a leading psychiatrist, Henry Maudsley, that "the heredi-

tary element holds the first place in the production of insanity." No doubt
one of the reasons James was so hesitant to get married—he finally was
married at the age of 36—was that he feared passing on the taint to his
children.[6] In the same review he noted that "right breeding" was "one of
the most important means" of averting mental illness (James, 1974: 43).
During his long and tumultuous courtship with Alice Gibbens, the woman
he eventually married, he wrote her that "the marriage of unhealthy
persons" was a crime against natural law.[7]

Defining his condition as basically inherited and physiological deflected
his attention from psychological factors. In addition, medical experts
specifically warned against introspection (Feinstein, in press). James took
their warnings to heart; for example, he wrote his brother Henry that he
welcomed a job teaching physiology because it offered "a diversion from
the introspective studies which had bred a sort of philosophical hypochondria in me of late."[8] In looking at James's experience, we can see obvious
psychological issues, such as his conflicts about his choice of vocation and
his struggle to achieve autonomy. But it was unlikely that James would see
these issues because his culture did not provide ready ways to conceptualize them.

In the view of the period, an individual's inherited nervous weakness
was part of his lower self, the savage, uncivilized residue from his evolutionary ancestors, and if he surrendered to his lower self, he would be
condemned to a life of invalidism and insanity. But his higher faculties—his
capacity for volition and virtue—could do battle against his nervous weakness (Fullinwider, 1975). Accepting this view, James pictured himself as
fighting a constant war, but he complained that his lack of strength made
"inward virtue" all the more difficult. "Constant reflection, inhibition,
resolution, whipping up of courage, adopting of privation, everything
volitional in short," he wrote, "tax unbearingly an already overtaxed
nervous system; and invalids who let everything 'slump' have much to be
said in their favor."[9]

In short, James held various views which were associated with his image
of himself as suffering from nervous weakness; he believed that he had a
hereditary defect, that he should not get married, that introspection was
dangerous, and that he would become an invalid if he relaxed in his
constant battle against his inner tendencies. This pattern is understandable
only when considered in cultural context. (For a sensitive reconstruction
of the view James's sister, Alice, had of her "nervous" problems, see
Strouse, 1980.)

All of an individual's behaviors and ideas are deeply embedded in the historical period in which he lives. The psychobiographer's interpretations are likely to be mistaken if he is not careful to determine what his material would have meant from his subject's point of view. As I noted in the earlier article, the psychobiographer's chief defense against this danger is to immerse himself in his subject's era so that he will be able to understand the subject's experience much as the subject himself would have understood it. I would also like to propose some additional strategies which the psychobiographer might adopt.

A specific strategy for dealing with cross-cultural differences would involve three steps. First, the psychobiographer would make an explicit effort to reconstruct the subject's way of seeing his experience. My remarks on James's understanding of his nervous weakness and its connotations illustrate the first step. Second, he would try to determine precisely where the subject's understanding—even in the subject's own opinion—was inadequate. For example, James acknowledged that he could not fathom why his symptoms came and went as they did. To him it was all "a dark business."[10] The psychobiographer may regard James's confusion as an invitation to attempt to provide the missing interpretation. And that leads to the third step: The psychobiographer, building on his subject's own way of conceptualizing his experience, would attempt to make sense of what was inexplicable to his subject. For example, one might explore the way tensions within James's family were related to the vicissitudes of his symptoms. Using such a strategy, the psychobiographer not only shows his respect for his subject's viewpoint but also takes advantage of psychological perspectives which can deepen our understanding of his subject's experience.

There is another, more novel, strategy which the psychobiographer sensitive to cross-cultural difficulties could employ: He would search for living individuals who largely share his subject's cultural values and then he would conduct a series of interviews with them. Sometimes an archeologist specializing in the Late Stone Age will study an existing stone-age culture. For example, he might investigate the ways these living people use stone tools which look much the same as the artifacts of an extinct culture (Gould, 1980). Similarly, a scholar interested in James could find individuals from a certain kind of eastern, New England background and explore their attitudes toward, for example, nervous weakness.[11] He could ask them what they thought of introspection and, if they had their hesitancies about it, why. A psychobiographer studying the Kennedy family could familiarize himself with the values and beliefs of Irish-Americans, and someone studying Douglas MacArthur might concentrate on learning about people who grew up in military surroundings. Of course, the parallels between the subject's views and those of the living people would not be exact, but still the psychobiographer would have the opportunity to attain valuable insights on many topics.

USE OF PSYCHOLOGICAL THEORY

In the earlier article I discussed some of the difficulties in applying psychological theory to biography (also see Arzt, 1978; George, 1971; Glad, 1973), and I specifically commented that psychodynamic theory seemed to be the most appropriate perspective for such work since it gives promise of supplying answers to the kinds of questions which biographers find most vexing.

In recent years there has been increased awareness of the possibilities for using other types of psychological theory in historical work (Gilmore, 1979). Horn (1980a, 1980b) applies family-systems theory to the Black-wells and shows that it illuminates many elusive problems, such as the tendency toward invalidism in the family. Crosby (1979) has considered the use of social-psychological concepts, such as attribution theory, in biography. Hoffer (1979) and Wernik (1979) both make use of cognitive psychology in their psychohistorical work. Craik (1977) has pioneered in the application of trait psychology to historical studies. There can be no doubt that all of these approaches contribute to our understanding of the individual in his or her complexity.

Nonetheless, in my study of James I found not only that psycho-dynamic theory was valuable but also that specific, recently developed psychoanalytic approaches seemed to clarify material whose meaning was particularly elusive. Object-relations theory—both the British approach of Winnicott (1958, 1965, 1971) and Guntrip (1961, 1969, 1971) and the American version of Kernberg (1975, 1976, 1980)—helped me understand James's relationships. It provided perspectives useful in analyzing the expectations which he brought to his friendships and romances and which underlay his tendency toward isolation. (Cf. Mazlish's, 1978, and Demos's, 1980, emphasis on transference.) Mahler's (1968, 1979; Mahler, Pines, and Bergman, 1975) separation-individuation theory offered a way of concept-ualizing James's early experiences and assessing their impact on his later personality. Finally, Kohut's (1971, 1977, 1978) psychology of the self seemed particularly well-suited to the exploration of issues that were central in James's life. Two other psychobiographers—Strozier (1981) in his work on Abraham Lincoln and Bongiorno (1980) in his work on Wilson—have also made use of the psychology of the self. Strozier (1978) and Demos (1980) have discussed the applicability of Kohut's work to historical studies.

To give an example of my use of Kohut's approach, I will focus on a central issue in my study of James's life and discuss how the psychology of the self contributed to my investigation of that issue. One question which any scholar of James's young adulthood must answer is why this individual—who later became one of our most influential and productive scholars—went through a period of six years in which he was so disabled. As noted before, Perry's explanation emphasizes James's difficulty in finding a philosophical meaning of life. The chief psychological interpretation, developed by Strout (1968) and Feinstein (1977), explores his conflicts with his father over his choice of vocation. Certainly these issues played a role in James's difficulties, but they do not account for the severity of his suffering. He did not merely ruminate over the meaning of life; for six years he was often unable to motivate himself to accomplish even the simplest of tasks. He was not just mildly depressed; he periodically had to struggle to avoid killing himself.

Kohut's emphasis on the self draws attention to James's fear of fragmentation. During James's spiritual crisis his underlying concern was with his fragile self. At one point he actually experienced what Kohut calls fragmentation of the self. He was suddenly enveloped "as if it came out of the darkness" by "a horrible fear of my own existence." He later recalled that "it was as if something hitherto solid within my breast gave way entirely, and I became a mass of quivering fear." He quickly regained his equilibrium, but, afterward, he noted, "I awoke morning after morning with a horrible dread at the pit of my stomach, and with a sense of the insecurity of life that I never knew before" (James, 1936: 157-158). Three or four years later he was still terrified that his self would shatter again. He confided in his diary that he had a need "for some stable reality to lean upon" (Perry, 1935: I, 343).

Even in the latter years of his life, after his most serious symptoms had long since abated, James remained uneasy about his underlying susceptibility to fragmentation. After reading Pierre Janet's pioneering work on dissociative states, James suspected that he himself had a "soul" that was "disintegrated" (1920: I, 347). Some 38 years after the fragmentation experience, he underwent an experience that was nearly as terrifying. He awoke one night in the middle of a dream, and while he was thinking about it he became "suddenly confused by the contents of two other dreams that shuffled themselves abruptly in between the parts of the first dream." He feared that he was suffering from "an invasion" of multiple personality. "Decidedly I was losing hold of my 'self' and making acquaintance with a quality of mental distress that I had never known before," he concluded. He could find no way to brace himself against his anxiety. "In this experience," he commented, "all was diffusion from a centre, and a foothold swept away, the brace itself disintegrating all the faster as one needed its support more direly" (James, 1910: 207-208).

James's despondency over his failure to find a philosophical meaning of life and his conflicts with his father over the question of vocation were both real, but neither can be fully understood without reference to his fragile self. According to Kohut, an individual who lacks a cohesive self will also be without a deeply anchored set of values. It was only when James's inability to find meaning in the outer world was combined with his unreliable inner values that he felt so lost. Similarly, a well-developed self provides the only foundation on which an individual can establish true independence. James's troubles with his dependency on his father make sense only when we realize that, with his difficulties in the sphere of the self, he had no alternative to his reliance on his father.

Using Kohut's psychology of the self also draws our attention to other topics which we can predict, given James's self-pathology, will have mattered in his life. A person such as James can be expected to have failed to receive empathic care from his parents, particularly his mother, in early life; so Kohut's theory leads us to examine his relationship with his mother (Anderson, 1979). In addition, such a person would be expected to have had troubles in the area of idealization; James's father was so inconsistent and idiosyncratic that he undermined his children's attempts to idealize him. Kohut's approach also has consequences for understanding the improvement in James's condition—a topic which I shall consider later in this review.

In short, Kohut's psychology of the self has all the characteristics of a powerful theory. It explains material that is otherwise inexplicable, draws together issues that had seemed disparate, and suggests additional topics which are worth exploring. In my experience the approaches of Mahler, Kernberg, Winnicott, and Guntrip provided similar benefits, and I also recommend their use in psychobiographical work.

ANALYZING AN ABSENT SUBJECT

Some critics argue that psychobiography is futile from the start. They concede that a psychotherapist, in the course of many sessions, has an opportunity to uncover his patient's inner world. But in psychobiography the subject is absent; the psychobiographer has to assemble his portrait from written materials, and he is never able to question his subject directly (Barzun, 1974; Stannard, 1980). (For responses to this criticism, see Gedo, 1972; George and George, 1964; Wolfenstein, 1972; Wyatt, 1963; Zonis, 1977.) Certainly these critics have a point. Freud, if he had been able to talk to Leonardo, would not have gone careening off in the wrong direction. He would have asked Leonardo whether he was familiar with myths about vultures. And Leonardo would have answered, "But the bird wasn't a vulture; it was a kite!"

Nonetheless, as I noted in the earlier article, the psychobiographer actually has certain advantages compared to the psychotherapist. What follows is a description of three advantages from which I benefited in my work on James.

First, as Mazlish has pointed out (1978), the psychobiographer is able to draw on the testimony of other people who knew his subject, while a psychotherapist rarely has a chance to talk to those who are acquainted with his patient. The accounts of James's contemporaries heavily influenced my understanding of him. In particular, what they wrote about him occasionally clashed with what he said about himself. These disparities forced me to find explanations that could reconcile them, and they also taught me that I could not always accept James's self-descriptions.

Second, when a psychobiographer studies someone like James who was an author, he can search the author's body of written work for self-revealing information; the psychotherapist has no comparable source. We know about James's (1936) experience of fragmentation only because he included a vivid description of it in *The Varieties of Religious Experience;* in that work he disguised the passage's source by noting that an anonymous Frenchman had sent it to him, but he later admitted that he had written it himself. In his early works he often dealt with topics which we can now recognize as reflecting his own experience. For example, in "Is Life Worth Living?" he dealt with a struggle over suicidal impulses much like the one he had undergone (James, 1897), and in *The Principles of Psychology* he (1890) analyzed "abulia," the lack of willpower from which he had suffered. Even in his later philosophical works he often indulged in personal asides. There is evidence that he developed the tendency of systematically directing his attention away from his weaknesses as a defense against depression. "Must my thoughts dwell night and day on my personal sins and blemishes because I truly have them?" he asked in one philosophical work, "or may I sink and ignore them in order to be a decent social unit, and not a mass of morbid melancholy and apology?" (James, 1967: 441).

Third, James was a talented artist, and many of his sketches have survived. A subject's drawings are invaluable to a psychobiographer because they literally depict his idiosyncratic way of viewing the world. He drew a particularly striking sketch in 1865 while participating in a natural history expedition in Brazil (see Figure 1). Despite his original hopes, he found the journey tedious and anything but glamorous. Another member of the expedition was a burly young man named Simon Dexter; he seemed rather intimidating to the frail James. In the sketch James portrayed a muscular, nearly naked, godlike figure and labelled it "Dexter." The godlike figure is holding in his hand a tiny, supplicating figure labelled "James." The description accompanying the sketch reads: "Colossal statues of Messrs. James & Dexter erected by the city of Boston 1866."[12] The sketch expresses James's coexisting feelings of inferiority and grandiosity. On some level he probably thought of himself as being small, impotent, and even cowardly, as he appears to be in the sketch. But at the same time he was not merely portraying himself in life, but rather he drew a statue of himself which the city of Boston was to erect, and he described, not just the statue of Dexter, but both of the statues as "colossal." In addition, the sketch expresses his ability to use humor to foster a friendship. He probably drew the sketch for Dexter; if it were just for himself he would not have labelled it. Through the sketch he transformed his feeling of inferiority into a vehicle for amusing Dexter and becoming closer to him. In his later psychological and philosophical works he showed this same ability to transform his inner concerns into creative products.

One of the gravest disadvantages a psychobiographer faces is that he has to deal with a finite body of information. By contrast, throughout the

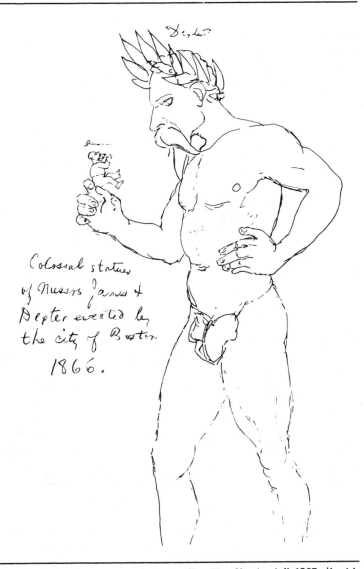

Colossal statues
of Messrs James &
Dexter erected by
the city of Boston
1866.

Figure 1. Sketch by William James from his "Brazilian Notebook," 1865. (I wish to thank Alexander R. James. By permission of the Houghton Library, Harvard University.)

time a psychotherapist works with a patient the information about the patient's experience is continually growing. A psychotherapist often makes hypotheses and then watches to see whether subsequent data confirm or contradict the hypotheses.

Without planning it, I had a similar experience of making a crucial generalization at one stage in my work and gaining access at a later stage to information which bore on the generalization. One of the central hypotheses in the first draft of my study of James was based on scanty evidence. The issue was why James's condition improved so substantially. Just a year before his death he commented that he had borne "neurasthenic fatigue" throughout his life.[13] But there is no question that James in his 40s and afterward was dramatically different from James in his 20s. In later adulthood he no longer suffered from prolonged depression, the temptation to commit suicide, or a chronic inability to work. Other scholars have suggested that his development of his philosophy (Perry, 1935) or his finding of a vocation (Feinstein, 1977) was the therapeutic factor. But my understanding of his underlying difficulties with a fragile self persuaded me that only a factor capable of drastically strengthening his self could have led to the major change he experienced. In the first draft I suggested that his relationship with his wife was what was decisive. But the corroborating evidence consisted of nothing more than a handful of stray comments, such as his son's observation that his marriage worked "an abiding transformation in James's health and spirits" (James, 1920: I, 192).

After completing the first draft I noticed a manuscript I had previously overlooked. The manuscript included excerpts from a series of otherwise unavailable letters in which James wrote his wife about the changes he had undergone in the 10 years that had passed since their wedding. He began one letter by recalling how he had appeared to be "a man morally utterly diseased" at the time of their courtship. "Your unswerving trust . . . ," he went on, "has wrought . . . my transformation into the normal man and husband you have now." He concluded, "As God made me, as I then made myself, so have you remade me." In another letter he reflected on the "intimate character of the change" that had taken place in him. "I'm strong and sound," he wrote, "and that poor diseased boy whom you raised up from the dust no longer exists." He concluded, "I am born again through and through, your child as well as husband."[14] In this instance, then, I found unexpected support, from the testimony of the subject himself, for a hypothesis.

Quantitative researchers have employed the "split-half" approach: They divide their data in half, develop their hypotheses by examining one half, and then test the hypotheses statistically against the other half. A psycho-biographer could employ a similar strategy deliberately—rather than for-tuitiously, as was my experience in the anecdote just described. He would split his material into two parts. For example, he might start with the published material and examine, only after he has framed his basic hypoth-eses, the unpublished material. Or, if the material were housed in several archives, he could conduct research at some of them, then form his hypotheses, and then look to see whether his research in the remaining archives confirms or contradicts the hypotheses.

Most psychobiographers would accept that studying a subject in person is preferable to working with written remains, but no one actually knows how much of a disadvantage it is to analyze an "absent" subject. There is a straightforward, but time-consuming, study which would shed light on this question. Three groups of investigators would do research on the same subject (or perhaps several subjects would be appropriate). The first group would have access only to written records; it would be necessary to select a subject who could provide a substantial body of letters and other documents. The second group would intensively study the subject through interviews and psychological tests. Each group would then write a portrait of the subject's personality. Finally, the third group, which would have access to all the information as well as both portraits, would address itself to the central question of the study: What were the advantages and disadvantages of the two approaches? Did the two groups arrive at similar conclusions, or did the researchers who used written records miss the flesh-and-blood person? Or perhaps these researchers found evidence about important issues overlooked by the other researchers?

CONCLUSION: WHAT DOES PSYCHOBIOGRAPHY CONTRIBUTE?

I have saved the first question for last. Before becoming involved in psychobiography, a scholar must ask himself: What is the value of this approach? What does it contribute?

It seems to me that if psychology has anything to say about people—their complexities and their accustomed patterns and their motiva-tions—then biography is an area to which that understanding should be applied. There is a great deal of interest in the lives of historical, literary, and artistic figures; if psychologists can help us make sense of the lives of these figures, then they have the responsibility to do so.

But one limitation in the field is that so few psychologists have participated. Psychologists would seem to have certain advantages compared, for example, to historians and psychiatrists. Psychologists are likelier than historians to have a thorough grounding in psychological theory, and psychologists, more often than psychiatrists, are involved in academic departments and have easy access to historians, political scientists, and literary specialists. The Board of Editors of the leading psychohistorical journal, *The Psychohistory Review,* reflects the involvement in the field of the various disciplines. The board consists of eight historians, seven psychiatrists, three political scientists, two members of English departments, one sociologist, and no psychologists.

Psychobiography also may serve as a way of disseminating the findings of psychology. Many laymen who would never look at a book of psychological theory read biographies and find them all the more fascinating when they are psychologically informed.

In addition, psychobiography offers possibilities for contributing to our understanding of personality. Certain historical figures are marvelously articulate about their experience (Demos, 1980). William James was a master at describing his own behavior. Authors such as D. H. Lawrence, Leo Tolstoy, and Virginia Woolf had rare and penetrating insights into the intricacies of their lives. Psychobiography makes this unique evidence available to the field of personality.

There are several topics which are particularly appropriate for psychobiographical research. One of these topics is leadership. Especially if one wants to learn more about the "great man" or woman, one has little choice but to choose a historical figure. Erikson (1958, 1969), in his psychobiographical work, offered new perspectives on the roles of Martin Luther and Mohandas Gandhi and the way in which these dynamic leaders interacted with their followers. Another of these topics is creativity. One of the shortcomings of laboratory research into creativity is that it is often doubtful whether the subjects designated as being particularly creative actually are so (Maddi, 1965). But it is possible to choose a psychobiographical subject who is widely acknowledged to have been a creative genius. In my work on James I focused on the interplay between his personality and his creative work. Mitzman's (1969) study of Max Weber and Manuel's (1968) study of Isaac Newton are just two other examples of psychobiographies which make contributions to our understanding of creativity.

As I have noted throughout this review, there are many pitfalls to psychobiography. But, if it can shed light on some of the most elusive issues which psychologists face, then all of the demands which it makes on its practitioners are justified.

NOTES

1. Psychobiography, as used in this review, may be defined as the study, using psychological perspectives, of a historical, literary, or artistic figure.

2. Letter, William James to George H. Howison, July 17, 1895, in Perry, 1935: II, 207; letter, William James to Henry P. Bowditch, July 1, 1909 (The James Papers, Houghton Library, Harvard University, hereinafter referred to as James Papers). I wish to thank Mr. and Mrs. Alexander James and the Houghton Library for permission to quote from The James Papers.

3. William James's son Henry James (1920) edited the other of the two chief published sources of primary materials. Coincidentally, this work also frequently omits references to his psychological struggles. Probably Henry James took this editorial approach because he was embarrassed by the extent of his father's psychological suffering.

4. Diary of William James, April 10, 1973 (James Papers). "Maya" refers to the Hindu belief that what we usually think of as the real world is actually an illusion.

5. On Erikson's early life and his name change, see Berman (1975a, 1975b), Coles (1970: 13; 82), Erikson (1970: 742-744), and Roazen (1976).

6. When his second son was a sophomore at Harvard, he warned him against participating in crew. "The strain of mere length of endurance and the dead pull of mental excitement," he wrote, were too dangerous "for a fellow of your inheritance and temperament." Letter, William James to William James, Jr., Sept. 21, 1900 (James Papers).

7. Letter, William James to Alice Howe Gibbens, June 13, 1876 (James Papers).

8. Letter, William James to Henry James, Jr., Aug. 24, 1872 (James Papers).

9. Letter, William James to Kate E. Havens, Dec. 25, 1876 (James Papers).

10. Letters, William James to Henry James, Jr., July 10, 1868, Oct. 2, 1869, Dec. 5, 1869, Dec. 27, 1869 (James Papers).

11. In a conversation Robert A. LeVine, a specialist in culture and personality, suggested this strategy.

12. The sketch is from James's "Brazilian Notebook" (James Papers).

13. Letter, William James to Henry P. Bowditch, July 1, 1909 (James Papers).

14. Letters, William James to Alice Howe James, March 4, 1888, and March 10, 1888, quoted in H. James (1938: 43; 45).

REFERENCES

Allen, G. W. *William James: A biography.* New York: Viking Press, 1967.

Anderson, J. W. An interview with Leon Edel on the James family. *Psychohistory Review,* 1979, *8,* nos. 1-2, 15-22. (a)

Anderson, J. W. In search of Mary James. *Psychohistory Review,* 1979, *8,* nos. 1-2, 63-70. (b)

Anderson, J. W. *William James's depressive period (1867-1872) and the origins of his creativity: A psychobiographical study.* Ph.D. dissertation, University of Chicago, 1980.

Anderson, J. W. The methodology of psychological · biography. *Journal of Interdisciplinary History,* 1981, *11,* 455-475.

Arzt, D. Psychohistory and its discontents. *Biography,* 1978, *1,* no. 3, 1-36.

Barzun, J. *Clio and the doctors: Psycho-history, quanto-history and history.* Chicago: University of Chicago Press, 1974.

Berman, M. *Review of life history and the historical moment* by Erik H. Erikson. *New York Times Book Review,* 1975a, March 30: 1-2, 22.

Berman, M. Reply. *New York Times Book Review,* 1975b, May 4: 57-58.

Bongiorno, J. A. Woodrow Wilson revisited: The prepolitical years. Unpublished, 1980.

Chatel, J. C. and Peele, R. The concept of neurasthenia. *International Journal of Psychiatry,* 1970-1971, *9,* 36-49.

Coles, R. *Erik H. Erikson: The growth of his work.* Boston: Atlantic Monthly Press, 1970.

Coles, R. Shrinking history. *New York Times Book Review,* 1973, Feb. 22: 15-21 and March 8: 25-29.

Craik, K. H. Assessing historical figures: The uses of observer-based personality descriptions. *Historical Methods Newsletter,* 1977, *10,* no. 2, 66-76.

Crews, F. Analysis terminable. *Commentary,* 1980, July, 25-34.

Crosby, F. Evaluating psychohistorical explanations. *Psychohistory Review,* 1979, *7,* no. 4, 6-16.

Demos, J. Comments at summer seminar, sponsored by the National Endowment for the Humanities, on "Theory and Practice in Psychohistory," 1980. (a)

Demos, J. Remarks at symposium on Reflections on Self Psychology, Boston, Oct. 31 to Nov. 2, 1980. (b)

Deutscher, I. *The prophet unarmed: Trotsky, 1921-1929.* New York: Oxford University Press, 1959.

Donald, D. Between history and psychology: Reflections on psychobiography. Presented at the meeting of the American Psychiatric Association, 1972.

Edel, L. *The life of Henry James* (5 vols). Philadelphia: J. B. Lippincott, 1953-1972.

Elms, A. C. *Personality in politics.* New York: Harcourt Brace Jovanovich, 1976.

Erikson, E. H. *Young man Luther: A study in psychoanalysis and history.* New York: Norton, 1958.

Erikson, E. H. *Gandhi's truth: On the origins of militant nonviolence.* New York: Norton, 1969.

Erikson, E. H. Autobiographic notes on the identity crisis. *Daedalus,* 1970, *99,* 730-759.

Erikson, E. H. On the nature of psycho-historical evidence: In search of Gandhi. In F. I. Greenstein and M. Lerner (eds.), *A source book for the study of personality and politics.* Chicago: Markham, 1971.

Fancher, R. E. *Psychoanalytic psychology: The development of Freud's thought.* New York: Norton, 1973.

Fancher, R. E. *Pioneers of psychology.* New York: Norton, 1979.

Feinstein, H. H. *Fathers and sons: Work and the inner world of William James.* Ph.D. dissertation, Cornell University, 1977.

Feinstein, H. M. Charles Renouvier and the "crisis" of William James: A revisionist view. *Psychohistory Review* (in press).

Fischer, D. H. *Historians' fallacies: Toward a logic of historical thought.* New York: Harper & Row, 1970.

Freud, S. Leonardo da Vinci and a memory of his childhood. In J. Strachey (ed.), *The standard edition of the complete psychological works of Sigmund Freud* (Vol. 11). London: Hogarth Press, 1957.

Freud, S. and Bullitt, W. C. *Thomas Woodrow Wilson: A psychological study.* Boston: Houghton Mifflin, 1967.

Fullinwider, S. P. William James's "spiritual crisis." *Historian,* 1975, *8,* 39-57.

Gedo, J. E. The methodology of psychoanalytic biography. *Journal of the American Psychoanalytic Association,* 1972, *20,* 638-649.

George, A. Some uses of dynamic psychology in political biography: case materials of Woodrow Wilson. In F. I. Greenstein and M. Lerner (eds.), *A source book for the study of personality and politics.* Chicago: Markham, 1971.

George, A. and George, J. *Woodrow Wilson and Colonel House: A personality study.* New York: Day, 1956.

George, A. and George, J. Preface to the Dover Edition. In *Woodrow Wilson and Colonel House.* New York: Dover, 1964.

George, A. and George, J. Psycho-McCarthyism. *Psychology Today,* 1973, June, 94-98.

Gilmore, W. Paths recently crossed: Alternatives to psychoanalytic psychohistory. *Psychohistory Review,* 1979, *7,* no. 3, 43-49; no. 4: 26-42; *8,* no. 3: 55-60.

Glad, B. Contributions of psychobiography. In J. N. Knutson (ed.), *Handbook of political psychology.* San Francisco: Jossey-Bass, 1973.

Gould, R. A. *Living archeology.* Cambridge, England: Cambridge University Press, 1980.

Greenstein, F. I. *Personality and politics: Problems of evidence, inference and conceptualization.* Chicago: Markham, 1969.

Guntrip, H. *Personality structure and human interaction.* New York: International Universities Press, 1961.

Guntrip, H. *Schizoid phenomena, object relations and the self.* New York: International Universities Press, 1969.

Guntrip, H. *Psychoanalytic theory, therapy, and the self.* New York: Basic Books, 1971.

Himmelfarb, G. The "new history." *Commentary*, 1975, Jan., 73-78.

Hoffer, H. Is psychohistory really history? *Psychohistory Review*, 1979, 7, no. 3, 13-21.

Horn, M. The effect of family life on women's role choices: The case of the Blackwell women. Unpublished, 1980. (a)

Horn, M. Family processes. Unpublished, 1980. (b)

Hjelle, L. A. & Ziegler, D. J. *Personality theories: Basic assumptions, research, and applications.* New York: McGraw-Hill, 1981.

James, H. [the son of William James] (ed.). *The letters of William James* (2 vols). Boston: Atlantic Monthly Press, 1920.

James, H. [the son of William James] *Alice Howe Gibbens.* Unpublished manuscript, The Papers of William James, Houghton Library, Harvard University, 1938.

James, W. Recent works on mental hygiene. *Nation*, 1874, July 16: 43.

James, W. *The principles of psychology* (2 vols). New York: Holt, Rinehart & Winston, 1890.

James, W. Is life worth living? In *The will to believe and other essays in popular philosophy.* New York: Longmans, Green & Co., 1897.

James, W. *The varieties of religious experience.* New York: Modern Library, 1936.

James, W. Pragmatism's conception of truth. In J. J. McDermott (ed.), *The writings of William James: A comprehensive edition.* New York: Modern Library, 1967.

James, W. A suggestion about mysticism. In G. W. Allen (ed.), *William James reader.* Boston: Houghton Mifflin, 1910.

Kernberg, O. *Borderline conditions and pathological narcissism.* New York: Jason Aronson, 1975.

Kernberg, O. *Object relations theory and clinical psychoanalysis.* New York: Jason Aronson, 1976.

Kernberg, O. *Internal world and external reality: Object relations theory applied.* New York: Jason Aronson, 1980.

Kohut, H. *The analysis of the self.* New York: International Universities Press, 1971.

Kohut, H. *The restoration of the self.* New York: International Universities Press, 1977.

Kohut, H. *The search for the self: Selected writings of Heinz Kohut, 1950-1978* (2 vols). New York: International Universities Press, 1978.

LeVine, R. A. Discussion. *Annual of Psychoanalysis*, 1975, 3, 383-385.

Loewenberg, P. Remarks at conference on Psychohistorical Meanings of Leadership, Chicago, June 6-8, 1980.

Maddi, S. R. Motivational aspects of creativity. *Journal of Personality*, 1965, 33, 330-347.

Mahler, M. *On human symbiosis and the vicissitudes of individuation.* New York: International Universities Press, 1968.

Mahler, M. S. *The selected papers of Margaret S. Mahler* (2 vols). New York: Jason Aronson, 1979.

Mahler, M. S., Pine, F., & Bergman, A. *The psychological birth of the human infant.* New York: Basic Books, 1975.

Manuel, F. *A portrait of Isaac Newton.* Cambridge, Mass.: Harvard University Press, 1968.

Manuel, F. Use and abuse of psychology in history. *Daedalus,* 1971, *100,* 187-213.

Mazlish, B. Psychoanalytic theory and history: Groups and events. *Annual of Psychoanalysis,* 1978, *6,* 41-64.

Mitzman, A. *The iron cage: An historical interpretation of Max Weber.* New York: Alfred A. Knopf, 1969.

Moraitis, G. A psychoanalyst's journey into a historian's world: An experiment in collaboration. *Annual of Psychoanalysis,* 1979, *7,* 287-320.

Moraitis, G. & Pletsch, C. Psychoanalytic contributions to method in biography. *Psychohistory Review,* 1979, *8,* nos. 1-2, 72-74.

Parsons, A. Expressive symbolism in witchcraft and delusion: A comparative study. In R. A. LeVine (ed.), *Culture and personality: Contemporary readings.* Chicago: Aldine, 1969.

Perry, R. B. *The thought and character of William James* (2 vols). Boston: Little, Brown, 1935.

Pletsch, C. *A psychoanalytic study of Friedrich Nietzsche.* Ph.D. dissertation, University of Chicago, 1977.

Ranlett, J. Work-in-progress on the diary of Cynthia Everett. n.d.

Roazen, P. *Erik H. Erikson: The power and limits of a vision.* New York: Free Press, 1976.

Schapiro, M. Leonardo and Freud: An art historical study. *Journal of the History of Ideas,* 1956, *17,* 147-178.

Stannard, D. E. *Shrinking history: On Freud and the failure of psychohistory.* New York: Oxford University Press, 1980.

Strouse, J. *Alice James: A biography.* Boston: Houghton Mifflin, 1980.

Strout, C. William James and the twice-born sick soul. *Daedalus,* 1968, *47,* 1062-1082.

Strozier, C. B. Heinz Kohut and the historical imagination. *Psychohistory Review,* 1978, *7,* no. 2, 36-39.

Strozier, C. Work-in-progress on Abraham Lincoln. 1981.

Waite, R.G.L. *The psychopathic god: Adolf Hitler.* New York: Basic Books, 1977.

Weinstein, E. A., Anderson, J. W., & Link, A. S. Woodrow Wilson's political personality: A reappraisal. *Political Science Quarterly,* 1978, *93,* 585-598.

Wernik, U. Cognitive dissonance theory, religious reality and extreme interactionism. *Psychohistory Review,* 1979, *7,* no. 3, 22-28.

Winnicott, D. W. *Collected papers: Through paediatrics to psycho-analysis.* New York: Basic Books, 1958.

Winnicott, D. W. *The maturational processes and the facilitating environment.* New York: International Universities Press, 1965.

Winnicott, D. W. *Playing and reality.* New York: Basic Books, 1971.

Wolfenstein, E. V. Some technical aspects of applied psychoanalysis. *Psychoanalytic Study of Society,* 1972, *5,* 175-184.

Wyatt, F. The reconstruction of the individual and of the collective past. In R. W. White (ed.), *The study of lives.* Englewood Cliffs, N.J.: Prentice-Hall, 1963.

Zonis, M. Meaning and method in psychohistory. *Journal of Psychohistory,* 1977, *4,* 389-400.

10

Mental Health Policy as a Research Site for Social Psychology

CHARLES A. KIESLER

Charles A. Kiesler is Bingham Professor and Department Head at Carnegie-Mellon University. His books include *Attitude Change: A Critical Analysis of Theoretical Approaches* (with B. E. Collins and N. Miller), *Conformity* (with S. Kiesler), and the *Psychology of Commitment,* and an edited collection, *Psychology and National Health Insurance: A Sourcebook* (with N. Cummings and G. VandenBos). He is presently writing a book on the development of research issues in national mental health policy.

The purpose of this chapter is threefold: one, to introduce people to the social psychological aspects of policy research, in general, and mental health policy, in particular; two, to interest people in the mental health policy area, because so little is known about this fascinating field and so much research is needed; and three, to encourage the use of social psychological principles and training in addressing social problems. Because both the level and style of research in this area differ from the typical experience of social psychologists, the approach can add a methodological arrow even for those with limited interest in mental health policy.

This chapter describes less *the* problems of mental health policy research than *some* problems which should particularly interest social psychologists. Three types of problems are discussed which are underemphasized in social psychological research. One problem is how the *social systems and structures* affect the potential viability of policy alternatives, in part how the total setting and the parameters of the problem affect the specific details of everyday life. A second type of problem is the effect of *longer term interactions,* such as work, marriage, and institutionalization. Yet a third problem concerns *total institutions,* in a sense the logically extreme test of hypotheses about social control and influence. Consequently we discuss aspects of mental institutionalization, including the decision structure to institutionalize, other factors which affect whether one is institutionalized, and the effects of institutionalization.

WHY STUDY MENTAL HEALTH POLICY?

There are several reasons why mental health policy research might intrigue social psychologists. It involves millions of people. For example, almost two million people are placed in mental institutions every year in the United States.[1] Yet, we do not have a deep understanding of why some people are institutionalized and not others, the specific and long-term outcomes of such institutionalization, and the cost/benefit and efficacy of various treatment alternatives. Those two million are perceived to be the most serious cases. The best estimate of who needs general mental health care at a particular time is 15% of the population. High level officials in the National Institute of Mental Health (Regier, Goldberg, and Taube, 1978) and the President's Commission on Mental Health (Mechanic, 1978) have each arrived at that estimate using somewhat different methods. That 15% figure translates to 30 million to 40 million people in need of mental health services, only a small minority of whom now receive services from mental health professionals (Regier and Goldberg, 1976). Who are these people? What is wrong with them? What sorts of lives are they leading? How important are these problems? Are there techniques of behavior and attitude change that can be applied to 30 million or 40 million people? Which methods of prevention might work best? This is a fascinating set of questions.

If one is interested in groups or organizations, the mental health policy field is replete with them for study, ranging from formal, funded organizations, such as community mental health centers, to informal groups such as Alcoholics Anonymous. Some are highly organized nationally while others are more regionally independent and lack organization from group to group.

The study of mental health policy embodies important aspects of life as dependent measures. There are data on employment and absenteeism, data related to the conditions under which one is sent to a total institution and how long one remains there (often years), issues that affect marriage and its success, child-rearing practices, and money earned over a lifetime. These are each critical aspects of life; and mental health policy research is one avenue to examine systematically social psychological variables affecting such significant outcomes.

We know much more about human behavior and social systems than is reflected in current national mental health policies, which raises significant issues of knowledge use and diffusion. Resistance to new information, ineffective use of knowledge and systems for developing new knowledge, and critical views of mental health policy research can all be documented. The pragmatic aspects of politics affect mental health policy as well. Mental health priorities are first on the cutting block with conservative administrations. They continue to be not understood well by the average voter and suffer often when put before the public.

It is not necessary to be a clinical psychologist or a psychiatrist to be an effective investigator in mental health policy. Indeed, many policy questions are sociological or social psychological, and it could help on some policy problems not to be captured by a professional perspective. Of course, most general mental health research has been conducted by mental health professionals. Although much of that research is excellent, an array of policy-oriented substantive questions remains that are not specifically professional in nature. This article emphasizes the latter set of questions.

There is a great difference—one neither well-understood nor often discussed—between research in mental health and research in mental health *policy*. To lay the groundwork for the rest of this chapter, it will help to consider what policy research is and what it is not, to discuss current national mental health policy, both de facto and de jure, and then to identify substantive problems in the area that should interest social psychologists.

WHAT IS POLICY RESEARCH?

Policy research and analysis is often used to mean the logical or mathematical assessment of the alternatives in almost any decision. Although still not well-known by psychologists, policy analysis flourishes in sociology, political science, and particularly economics, and some universities even offer advanced degrees in the "policy sciences." There is a solid mathematical and statistical base for the analysis of decision structures for considering alternative policies (e.g., Stokey and Zeckhouser, 1978).

It may be helpful to distinguish, albeit briefly and arbitrarily, among policy analysis, policy research, evaluation research, applied research, and problem-oriented research. Although the categories overlap in practice, forcing arbitrary distinctions among them can sharpen discussion of policy research.

Policy analysis is a technique of estimating the desirability of a particular decision alternative (often including as a parameter the biases of the decision maker) or of assessing the relative efficacy of decision alternatives.

Policy research is the other half of that coin: to determine what is known about policy alternatives and investigate aspects of the decision structures which are not well-known. The two approaches can lead in different directions. For example, if we assume the primary national problem in mental health is to treat 30 million or 40 million people who need care, then a policy analysis would focus on techniques that can be applied to 30 million or 40 million people. As a result, one might propose seriously that drug treatment is the only logical treatment to use in mental health. As a one-time solution to potential decision alternatives in this field, such a recommendation might not be implausible (and indeed has been implicitly accepted by a number of high level officials). Policy research would go farther with this question, analyzing more deeply what we know about human behavior and its potential for change. Policy research would learn more about the problems people have and services needed, emphasize the comparative effectiveness of different treatment modalities including cost/benefit analysis and efficacy analysis, assess the potential usefulness of less popular alternatives, and investigate techniques of prevention. In effect, policy analysis assesses decision alternatives at any one time whereas policy research is a way of accumulating more knowledge about policy alternatives.

The focus of policy research is different from evaluation research. The latter encompasses specific methodological techniques of assessing the efficacy of a project or program. One could easily understand evaluating the effectiveness of a project such as Headstart. Even if the project were not a complete success, policy analysis might still lead one to recommend its continuation because of a lack of compelling alternatives. Policy research, by contrast, might investigate alternative methods of accomplishing the same goals.

Problem-oriented research differs from the preceding approaches. It seeks to investigate the totality of a specific, carefully defined problem, such as developmental differences between sexes. Doing so could involve diverse disciplines and investigatory techniques. Techniques could include survey sampling, quasi-experimental techniques, secondary analysis of existing data bases, and participant observation. Such an ambitious undertaking could involve the disciplines of psychology, psychiatry, sociology, anthropology, and even economics. In problem-oriented research the problem is carefully described: It can be studied by any relevant discipline and a variety of scientific techniques.

I bring up applied research last because discussion of the other types of research points to the inherent ambiguity in that term. *All* of the above are often applied, if applied research is taken to mean the application of basic scientific knowledge to real-world problems.

The basic theme of this chapter is policy research. However, we drift occasionally into policy analysis and problem-oriented research and frequently call for specific evaluation studies. The terminology is somewhat arbitrary and does not play a critical role in the discussion to follow except in the following sense. We wish to direct attention to policy issues and stimulate thought about what is and what is not known about mental health and human behavior, in ways that can help to assess current national policies and to propose new ones. The approach is from the top down: What are our policies? What do they imply? Do they fit with what we know about human behavior? What else do we know that might usefully be applied?

WHAT IS OUR NATIONAL MENTAL HEALTH POLICY?

Mental health policy is defined as the "de facto or de jure aggregate of laws, practices, social structures, or actions occurring within our society, the intent of which is improved mental health of individuals or groups. The study of such policy includes the descriptive parameters of the aggregate, the comparative assessment of particular techniques, the evaluation of the system and its subparts, human resources available and needed, cost-benefit analysis of practices or actions, and the cause and effect relationships of one set of policies, such as mental health, to others, such as welfare and health, as well as the study of institutions or groups seeking to affect such policy" (Kiesler, 1980a: 1066). The terms *de jure* and *de facto* are used because discussions of school desegregation have accustomed us to them. De jure refers to the system defined by legal or legislative means. De facto policy is that implicit in the national system whether intended or not. This difference is important for mental health policy, since the de facto and the de jure mental health policies are often at odds.

Our de jure national policy is determined partly by the U.S. Congress and partly by the federal Executive branch through the Department of Health and Human Services. The Health and Human Services Secretary is responsible for, in decreasing order, the Assistant Secretary for Health; the Alcohol, Drug Abuse, and Mental Health Administration (ADAMHA); and the National Institute of Mental Health (NIMH). NIMH makes recommendations on mental health policy and implements policy once adopted. The de jure national policy has two main thrusts. First, since 1963 we have built a network of 600 community mental health centers, to bring mental health services within the geographical and financial reach of every American citizen. The federal government now provides about 20% of the total support for these centers with about 60% provided by the state, county, and city governments, and 20% through fee-for-service. The second cornerstone of our de jure national mental health policy is deinstitutionalization: shortening the stay of patients in mental hospitals. Fuchs (1974) estimates that the average stay in a mental hospital has been cut from 8 months 20 years ago to 2 months today (NIMH says the average stay is much shorter). Controversy about the effectiveness of deinstitutionalization has focused on the public's lack of acceptance of deinstitutionalized patients into neighborhoods and the lack of other facilities and service providers to meet the needs of deinstitutionalized patients. De jure national mental health policy is primarily deinstitutionalization and out-patient care through community mental health centers.[2]

The de facto policy includes other federal programs, such as Medicare and Medicaid, which unintentionally have a powerful effect on mental health practices. Were the effect intentional, we would regard them as part of the de jure policy. Although the national policy emphasizes out-patient care, 70% of the national mental health dollar is spent for inpatient care, for which the largest single provider of funds is Medicaid. Indeed, Medicaid is the largest single mental health program in the country, providing over $4 billion per year for mental health services compared to $500 million of federal money to support the 600 community mental health centers.

Part of the structural press for hospitalizing patients through the Medicare and Medicaid programs comes through a lack of easily available alternatives for patient and attending therapist. A therapist might, for example, think that a patient would benefit more from outpatient care than inpatient care. However, the patient personally might not be able to afford either one. So the question is really what insurance programs are available in order to pay for the care. In the Medicare and Medicaid programs, outpatient care is unintentionally discouraged by requiring the patient to share substantially in the cost of therapy. Conversely, the cost of inpatient care is totally borne by the insurance program. Given those pragmatic alternatives, the only viable option for a specific patient may be a mental institution.

This is a good example of a total social system unintentionally offering incentives which produce undesired outcomes. Ironically, one major section of the Department of Health and Human Services strives to keep people out of mental institutions by advocating and funding outpatient care, whereas the other section (Human Services) unintentionally implements programs that puts people in hospitals as quickly as the other policy gets them out.

Private-office psychiatrists and clinical psychologists also treat a large number of people. Individual patients pay for some of the services, but insurance plans probably cover most of the bill. However, psychiatrists and psychologists are not the principle agents of treatment in mental health. Nonpsychiatric physicians see more mental health patients than do psychiatrists and clinical psychologists combined. In part that reflects the stigma of mental health problems and a lack of knowledge about recognizing them. The American Medical Association estimates that approximately 50% of the cases handled by a general medical practitioner do not represent physical problems but are largely psychological in nature. Others (e.g., Cummings, 1979) have estimated the percentage to be as high as 70%. Indeed, NIMH estimates that the average nonpsychiatric physician sees more "mental patients" (52) in a year than does the average psychiatrist (48; cf. National Institute of Mental Health, 1976). In addition to system incentives for institutionalization of mental patients, a majority of outpatient care is provided by people who are inappropriately trained.[3]

There are many other services related to mental health. Some are federally funded and to some extent organized nationally. The most formally organized has been called the Community Support System: formal mechanisms to help bridge private and public systems of care in such areas as justice, health, and social services, and, most specific to our purposes here, to lessen the impact of deinstitutionalizing patients. Social psychologists should be interested in the large number of volunteer groups whose primary purpose is related to mental health. For example, the President's Commission on Mental Health estimates that there are over 500,000 self-help groups in the United States. Alcoholics Anonymous alone has over 750,000 members worldwide, and the National Association for Retarded Citizens has more than 130,000 members spread across 1,300 local units. The impact of these volunteer groups must be substantial, although it has not been researched extensively.

THE IMPACT OF MENTAL HEALTH SERVICES: THEORETICAL AND EMPIRICAL ISSUES

As one issue with policy implications, consider the differences in outcome results when mental health services are added to organized systems of care and those regarding the effectiveness of psychotherapy. The effectiveness of psychotherapy has been a bone of some contention in psychology for decades. Recent reviews suggest that psychotherapy is effective, although not overwhelmingly so. For example, Smith and Glass (1978) reviewed 375 studies involving 50,000 people, in which people who sought psychotherapy were either randomly assigned to treatment or to a untreated control group. For each study Smith and Glass calculated an effect size based on mean differences observed corrected for the measure's variance. Thus, whatever measures a particular study used—for example, self-esteem, employment, ratings by others, and the like—observed group differences could be reported in terms of standardized units. Summing across all therapy studies Smith and Glass calculated that the average client had an outcome equal to about the 75th percentile of the untreated controls. Given the number of people and studies involved, we can conclude confidently that psychotherapy does have a positive effect. On the other hand, the effect is not very large. The change from the 50th to the 75th percentile following psychotherapy is still only about two-thirds of a standard deviation. What exactly is the level of mental health experienced by the 75th percentile of untreated patients?

These effects are much less substantial than those found in studies of mental health services in organized systems of care. The most dramatic of the latter data have been reported for Kaiser-Permanente Health Plan in California (Cummings and Follette, 1976). Cummings and Follette report that one hour of psychotherapy within the Kaiser-Permanente Plan resulted in a 50% reduction in medical charges for the following five years and a 50% reduction in absenteeism for the same period of time. Eight hours of psychotherapy led to 70% reductions in both variables over the five-year period. These dramatic effects conflict with the smaller effects obtained in isolated tests of psychotherapy.

The savings in medical costs, typically referred to as the offset in medical utilization, have recently begun to receive national attention. Jones and Vischi (1979) reviewed 13 studies and found in 12 of them savings in medical costs following mental health intervention to range from 5% to 85% with a median savings of 20%.[4] Since total medical costs in the United States run between $200 billion and $300 billion per year and mental health costs one tenth of that, the potential of mental health services to produce savings in medical costs is substantial. The effect on absenteeism could be equally important for other national priorities. Absenteeism affects national productivity and has other direct and indirect costs as well.

The effects of psychotherapy in different treatment settings provide a neat methodological example of potential differences between policy research and experimental research. In this case, the best experimental evidence taken from studies of the treatment (psychotherapy) in isolation shows a positive but fairly small effect. Typically, anything that shows a small effect in the laboratory studied under the most controlled conditions will have an even smaller effect when studied in the field with less control over experimental conditions. The data on psychotherapy are just the opposite. When we add psychotherapy to an existing organized system of care we observe some rather dramatic effects on both medical utilization and absenteeism. So, there is a small effect under laboratory conditions and large effect under field conditions. Why? Well, no one really knows, but let me suggest some possible reasons.

Differences in patient populations provide one possible explanation for these discrepancies. The Cummings and Follette sample averaged 38 years old and were disproportionately blue colloar (63%). The Smith and Glass studies report an average age of 22 and were probably disproportionately college students.[5] College students are more likely to have developed attributes conducive to personal change and coping. Thus the untreated college student controls are more likely to undergo positive change and thus reduce the comparative size of treatment effects than are noncollege students (see Bandura, 1969).

Differences in measurement are another possible explanation. The studies reported by Smith and Glass typically used categories of improvement and measures of psychological variables such as anxiety and self-esteem. Measures of behavioral functioning usually yield larger differences than ratings of improvement (Bandura, Note 1). The lack of comparability of the criteria makes it difficult to gauge the relative strengths of treatment effects.

Another difference involves the immediate prior experiences of clients in the two arrays of studies. For example, one is struck by the dramatic impact of the Kaiser-Permanente Studies of a single hour of psychotherapy. Keep in mind that the single hour is self-selected: The patient decides not to return after that hour (instead of the therapist deciding that the treatment is completed). How is it possible that a single hour of treatment has such a dramatic effect? One possibility relates to the state of mind of these patients. Judging from medical utilization rates, these patients have already gone through a series of medical treatments which were unsuccessful. They might well be very worried that something is seriously wrong with them either physically or mentally. Perhaps a single hour of reassurance that they are not seriously ill might have a dramatic effect on their perception of the problem and of what a physical health system can and cannot do. In this view the psychotherapist sees the patient at the peak crisis moment—the time of greatest worry, as it were—and can capitalize on a time period having the potential for great change.[6] However, this view is different than mental health treatment causing reduced medical utilization. Instead, the patients have only been using medical services both incorrectly and substantially. In that sense, reduced medical utilization following therapy would depend on prior misuse of the medical system.

The self-presentation aspects of physicians' behavior are part of the problem in misusing medical services. Mechanic says:

> Because the outcomes of illness and disability are often uncertain, physicians are frequently vague and evasive in response to questions. They dislike to relay what appears to be bad news, often delaying the process through which patients can realistically come to terms with their conditions. Patients, dissatisfied with ambiguity, may continue their search for information through other patients and other physicians. They tend to obtain a great deal of conflicting information with no one to sort and explain it to them. Patients tend to think of their own reactions to events as relatively unique.

When they join self-help groups, they are often surprised and relieved to learn how typical their internal feelings and social experiences are [1980: 109].

Yet another difference is related to the perception of the care given in a psychotherapeutic setting and barriers to such care. For example, participants in the Kaiser-Permanente Plan have a medical check-up upon entering the plan (Cummings, Note 2). One station on this complicated check-up is mental health services. Perhaps the juxtaposition of a mental health check-up with a physical health check-up is implicitly an endorsement of mental health services by the organization. If so, the stigma of mental health services might be lessened; the clients are more aware of services available and who delivers them; and the services might seem more routine and ordinary to the participant. These perceptions enhance services delivered and lower the barriers to mental health care. The participants should then use the services more rationally and make more intelligent decisions about their usefulness. If so, patients might take vague problems to the general practitioner and the specific behavioral problems to the mental health unit. In the former case, only after a series of medical tests and consequent failures would the person be referred to the mental health unit. That would artificially inflate the medical utilization rate—patients who had overused the medical services for purposes that were not medical. This notion also leads to the conclusion that mental health services ultimately get patients who have been misusing the medical system and should have been in mental health to begin with. It suggests a lack of proper referral from the medical system and, further, that under certain circumstances mental health services might increase medical utilization.

The differences between the experimental studies and the less controlled outcome studies in organized systems of care provide a potential example of the differences between experimental and policy research. The more pragmatically oriented studies indicate that the treatment does work and therefore can be considered as a plausible policy alternative in national mental health policy. On the other hand, we are not sure why those effects occur and have no deep scientific and theoretical understanding of the process producing the effects. Both points of view are essentially correct. In that apparent paradox lies a good deal of intellectual excitement that a study of mental health policy can produce.

The fact that therapeutic services delivered within the Kaiser-Permanente Plan had an effect on absenteeism raises other interesting possibilities. In studies of the impact of psychological services one should be looking for outcomes which are easily observed, which the paying public values, and which relate to other social goals. The notion that such services can affect absenteeism raises other questions for data gathering in the future. To be useful, psychotherapeutic services should produce outcomes valued by society. One would suggest that medical utilization is one such outcome, and obviously absenteeism is another. Other possibilities for study would include productivity (at least in certain work environments), school drop-outs, use of alcohol and drugs, and holding a productive job (in the sense of not being a financial burden to society).

Mental health services must have outcomes that are not only beneficial but also cost beneficial. A specific alternative policy must compete in the marketplace for public attention and public funds. If mental health services are to compete in the policy arena, then the outcomes of such services should be both valued and easily understood. The public should be interested in promoting and funding services which affect absenteeism, medical utilization, drug use, and the like. I note parenthetically that what the public will or will not accept in terms of potential mental health policy is itself an empirical question which has not received adequate study. Survey research of how the public sees mental health services (there has been a little of that) and which potential outcomes of mental health services it values most would be very useful. To do a cost-benefit analysis of mental health services, one has to develop estimates of the possible benefits: The perceived value of the general public of various possible outcomes could be an integral part of this approach. In any event, a cost-benefit analysis of psychotherapy is not a simple matter (see a recent report by the Office of Technology Assessment: Saxe, 1980).

POLICY ALTERNATIVES AS A FUNCTION OF PROVIDERS AVAILABLE

An analysis of national mental health policy as a function of the number of potential service providers available also provides an interesting example in policy study (Kiesler, 1980a, 1980b). We assume that mental health services are delivered by people with particular kinds of training, that there is only a certain number of these people in the country, and that one can calculate how many hours of potential service are available therefore to the national for potential service delivery. One can view the service providers and hours available for service delivery as a national resource and examine both de facto and de jure national mental health policy accordingly. To do so in the case of the United States provides a good example of a national policy doomed to fail.

In the United States, there are about 25,000 psychiatrists and about 25,000 licensed psychologists. Many of them are in administrative positions (such as heads of psychology departments and the staff of the National Institute of Mental Health) and all have some responsibilities other than simply delivering mental health services to clients. They need to keep up with the professional literature and development of new techniques; they spend time consulting with school systems and so forth. If we assume that 45,000 of these people are available to deliver services and that they could each deliver as much as 30 hours per week of services, this would add up to a potential service pool as a national resource of approximately 67 million hours of mental health services for the country. (I have suggested elsewhere—Kiesler, 1980a—that psychiatrists and psychologists now deliver somewhere between 35 million and 40 million hours of service per year.)

The notion is to compare hours available with the potential national need for them. We can estimate need for mental health services in several ways. As previously noted, between 50% and 70% of visits to general practitioners are for problems largely psychological in nature. If so, the need for psychological services might involve as many as 100 million people per year. Alternative estimates suggest approximately 15% of the population are in need of mental health services, which would amount to 30 million to 40 million people (Mechanic, 1978; Regier, Goldberg, & Taube, 1978).

You can see the contrast between service need, roughly 30 million to 40 million people a year, and the providers available, 67 million service hours. Thus if 35 million people need service we have a national potential of providing each of them *two hours* a year from either a psychiatrist or a licensed psychologist. If we encouraged three times a week psychotherapy, then all of the psychiatrists and psychologists together could only treat about 400,000 people in all—less than 2% of the need. Clearly a national policy cannot encourage the traditional form of care (or traditional provider) as the treatment of choice. It is simply logically impossible to do. Obviously policy research is needed regarding alternative forms of care and prevention that could easily be implemented at a national level, as well as various ways of extending the service capacity of psychiatrists and psychologists (through use of paraprofessionals and the like).

We also cannot encourage hospitalization as a treatment of choice. If we guess that one person in five who needed mental health services had problems serious enough to be hospitalized, that would amount to 7 million people. Assuming that we have the hospital beds to implement this policy, which unfortunately we probably do, and assuming the cost of an average of $300 per day (Bureau of the Census, 1978), the actual cost of hospitalizing somewhat over 7 million people for mental health reasons is over $2 billion a day. Further assuming an average hospital stay of 26 days (which is ADAMHA's estimate for state and county mental hospitals: Vischi et al., 1980), the total cost of that national policy would be over $50 billion per year. Note that even if the ratio of people needing to be hospitalized compared to the total needing mental health services is only 1 in 10, the annual cost is still over $25 billion per year. Both of these numbers are logically silly and politically impossible. Consequently, it would seem that we should be actively discouraging national policies which encourage hospitalization directly or indirectly. In fact that is not the case. Quite the opposite is true.

Medicare and Medicaid unintentionally encourage hospitalization for a substantial segment of our population. While needing treatment, hospitalization in a mental institution may be the only affordable alternative open to Medicaid and Medicare participants. Ironically, it is also the treatment alternative most costly to society as a whole. This is a good example of individuals solving a problem in the most rational way, whereas the aggregate of such people produces a system of treatment that is most costly and an implicit policy which cannot logically handle the aggregate of problems. Further, one should question whether hospitalization in a mental institution is cost beneficial or even efficacious. It is this question, the effects of institutionalization, that we raise in the next section.

SOCIAL PSYCHOLOGICAL ISSUES IN THE INSTITUTIONALIZATION OF MENTAL PATIENTS

The Overall Picture

As we have described, the national policy in mental health is deinstitutionalization of mental patients from hospitals and the development of a national organized system of outpatient care. Also as we have described, the institutionalization of mental patients continues to thrive as a national practice in spite of this policy planning. Today, there are approximately 1.8 million episodes of hospitalization of mental patients annually in the United States (the number of people hospitalized is somewhat less, since some people are rehospitalized after initial discharge thus counting for more than one episode in the national statistics). NIMH estimates that each episode lasts about 20 days, although the average stay depends considerably on the type of hospital. This estimate from NIMH is probably on the low side, since Fuchs (1974) estimates from statistics provided by the American Hospital Association that the average stay is more on the order of two months. The cost of hospitalizing these patients is substantial. Again we do not have firm national statistics on this issue, but the Bureau of the Census (1978) has provided a recent estimate of institutionalized patients and their costs.

Costs vary substantially as a function of the size of the hospital ranging from somewhat under $300 per day in the smaller hospital to over $800 in some of the larger hospitals. If we multiply $300 per day times 20 days times 1.8 million episodes, we can see that the total direct national cost of institutionalization of mental patients is approximately $11 billion per year. If Fuchs's estimate of average length of stay is accurate, then the cost is doubled or tripled.

National officials in Washington take some justifiable pride in the development of a system of outpatient care in the United States over the last 15 to 20 years. Indeed, the proportion of total mental health episodes nationally that are handled on an outpatient basis has gone from 23% in 1955 to 77% in 1975. In terms of frequency, in 1955 it was estimated nationally that there were 380,000 outpatient clinical episodes. In 1975, the number of outpatient clinical episodes nationally was estimated to be 4.6 million, a 12-fold increase in 20 years. Somewhat obscured in this comparison is that the number of institutionalized patients has also continued to increase. In the period 1955 to 1975 there was a 38% increase in the number of inpatient episodes, a rate that exceeds the population increase over the same period of time. In that sense, even controlling for population increase, we are institutionalizing more patients now than ever before.

Why Institutionalize? Partly, this is due to the fact that institutionalization has been a professional treatment of choice for over 150 years in psychiatry. Indeed, the American Psychiatric Association was originally begun by a group of superintendents of state and county mental hospitals. Partly, this statistic is due also to the overdeveloped analogy of mental health with medicine, that is, that the most serious cases—physical or mental—should go to a "hospital." Politicians and insurance executives intuitively accept that and have been supportive in developing funds for hospitalization of mental patients.[7] We agree that hospitalizing serious mental cases has face validity, even to the very best trained professionals. This acceptance of the face validity of institutionalization has helped produce the environmental press in the overall system.

The same bias exists typically in private insurance programs as well. In my own university, the overall insurance program provides all of the costs of going to a general MD for any physical problem, and all of the costs for going to a mental hospital for up to 120 days. However, it has provided only 50% of the costs for going to a psychotherapist. To the extent that psychotherapy and other services are preventative, lowering the probability of a patient needing to be hospitalized in a mental institution, their potential for doing so is undercut by incentives for hospitalization. For example, one would find difficulty getting the most effective treatment for alcoholism under such a program. It has been found that alcoholism treatment in hospitals is less effective (and certainly less cost effective) than various methods of treatment outside of a hospital (Vischi et al., 1980). In our insurance program, however, it is much less costly to the patient to receive his or her treatment in a hospital. Unless the patient is aware of the complex data existing on this issue (and most would not be), the overall structure of the situation leads the patient to choose the less effective care. Similar sorts of structural biases exist in the general treatment of mental patients.

In the discussion to follow, we will emphasize the processes leading to the institutionalization of a mental patient, as well as those leading to alternative modes of care and their joint effect on issues of national policy. I emphasize again that my intent is not to second guess professional clinical judgment of individual cases. I am not a clinical psychologist and do not imply that I can in any sense tell whether an individual patient should be hospitalized or not. However, we will look at the overall effectiveness of the system of hospitalizing patients; we will discuss the nonclinical aspects of the professional decision to institutionalize someone; and we will look at the outcomes of various forms of alternative treatment.

The Efficacy and Cost of Mental Institutionalization

There are five requirements for a reasonable scientific test of the effectiveness of mental institutionalization: one, the random assignment of patients to mental institutions versus other modes of care; two, the involvement of multiple institutions so that findings could not be attributed to a specific staff or set of physical facilities; three, equally enthusiastic staff in both programs to rule out a "Hawthorne Effect" which would limit the generality of the study; four, representative types of patients so that results could be generalized to the whole array of patients now hospitalized; and five, following up using clinical, objective, and behavioral measures looking at long-term outcomes of treatment.

Of course no such study exists. However, recently I was able to approximate such a study using existing data bases. Struck by a statement in the Fact Book from ADAMHA that no decent study existed with random assignment of patients to an institution of some alternative mode of care, I began to scour the literature to see whether in fact that was true. With the help of *Psychological Abstracts,* knowledgeable friends, and cross-checking references in articles that came close to a true experimental study, I was ultimately able to discover 10 studies with a true experimental design and random assignment of patients to a mental institution or an alternative mode of care. Although none of these studies is an ideal test of the effectiveness of institutionalization, in aggregate they provide clear evidence on this issue (see Kiesler, 1981, for a more complete description).

In essence, each of the studies was designed to test the effectiveness of some pet alternative mode of care. For example, in each study the hospitalized group is referred to as the "control" group. However, one can look at the studies as a whole, regrouping them such that the hospitalized group in each case is considered to be the experimental group and the alternative mode of care as a well-conceived comparison group. In intent, this approach is a meta-analysis of the 10 studies with a hospitalized group represented in every study, and across the 10 studies a very heterogeneous alternative comparison group. In some of the studies, patients were excluded from randomization, because they were either "too sick" in the minds of the professionals to take a chance on alternative nonhospital care or "too well" to need hospitalization at all. In the most extreme example, 78% of the patients were excluded prior to randomization, in some others no patients were excluded. In some studies the experiment was limited to particular kinds of patients: Three studies included only schizophrenics.

Looking across the 10 studies, the data are striking. In no case were the outcomes of institutionalization more positive than the alternative models of care. Further, the alternative care was more effective regarding such variables as psychiatric evaluation, probability of subsequent employment, independent living arrangements, and staying in school. The cost of alternative care never exceeded that of institutionalization, and typically was decidedly less expensive. Furthermore, across the 10 studies there was clear evidence of a process of self-perpetuation of hospitalization. That is, people who were randomly assigned to a mental institution were more likely after being discharged to be subsequently readmitted to a mental institution than were people in the alternative mode of care ever to be institutionalized.

The impact of the data is clear. It suggests a shift in national policy of institutionalization, as well as a strong emphasis on further policy-oriented research and some attention to basic scientific questions in mental health. It is not entirely clear why such an effect would be produced. As Goffman (1961) has suggested, there seems to be something in the process of institutionalization which undercuts effective treatment. For example, in one of the studies (Herz, Endicott, Spitzer, and Mesnikoff, 1971) daycare treatment was compared with regular inpatient treatment. This study is unique because the patients received exactly the same professional treatment. The daycare patients showed up at the mental hospital at 9:00 in the morning and left at 5:00 in the afternoon. The hospitalized patients stayed overnight. The daycare patients were treated on the same ward as the inpatients, received the same treatments, and even were mixed in with the same group therapy. Thus, during the day all patients received the active forms of treatment, and all were intermixed in the treatment process. In spite of the fact that the hospitalized patients spent an average of 139 days in the hospital, 50% of them were ultimately readmitted, whereas only 30% of the daycare patients were ever admitted to a mental hospital. There were substantial differences between the two sets of patients after four weeks, which were found to be less after two years (at least for those who were discharged).

Several researchers in this area (e.g., Fairweather, 1964) have emphasized the need for the development of a sense of competence and responsibility for one's life in psychotic patients. It may be that the total care environment in a mental institution undercuts the development of these feelings. If so, such well-studied social psychological variables as perceived responsibility for behavior and attribution of causality for one's behavior could pay important roles in the effectiveness of treatment of mental patients. One is reminded of, for example, the finding of Davison and Valins (1969) that drug-induced changes tend not to persist since the person attributes such changes, even the positive ones, to external causes.

This is a good example of how some basic research in social psychology could be meaningfully fitted to significant applied social problems.

Other Variables

There is also an interesting set of questions related to the decision to institutionalize a specific patient. As Fuchs (1974) has noted, physicians decide to hospitalize patients for a number of reasons. The hospital atmosphere gives the attending physician more control over the patients' treatment and regimen. Grouping patients under the same roof allows more efficient treatment of a number of patients and requires less total professional time in treating each. Further, the reimbursement to the physician is often easier to handle under hospitalized conditions than under nonhospitalized conditions. Others (e.g., Fink, Longabough, and Stout, 1970) have also noted the pressures from hospital administrators to fill beds, a problem that is becoming more significant with other political pressures to deinstitutionalize patients.

Family members often have focal roles in the decision to hospitalize a patient, putting their own form of pressure on the physician to separate the family member from the rest of the family. Indeed, physicians often feel that the patient's problems are sufficiently related to interaction with the family that treatment would proceed better with separation from the family. There is no question that physicians in general tend to feel that treatment of severe mental patients in hospitals results in better care than any alternative mode of treatment.

Several authors of the 10 studies (e.g. Fink et al., 1970) described negative reactions of the professional staff to the random assignment of patients to any alternative mode of care. The physicians sometimes felt so strongly that the alternative mode of care was a less efficacious mode of treatment that they thought it was unethical to allow such a study to go on. Even when results showed that the alternative mode of care was more effective than hospitalization, resentment and concern did not cease.

It seems clear that the process of professional judgment in deciding to hospitalize a mental patient involves much more complex psychological variables than only professional expertise. This process itself would be fascinating to study. One review, for example, reports family pressure on the physician is the most important determinant of the decision to institutionalize (Lorei and Gurel, 1973). That a family gives up a member and decides implicitly to remove him or her from normal society is an interesting topic for study. The epidemiological data on institutionalization regarding social class, race, and sex might provide some understanding of the family's decision process. The decision to institutionalize probably depends on availability of insurance, whether the family member is working, whether there are related problems which others feel might affect the development of children (e.g., alcoholism), as well as issues of predictability and control. The need of the individual family members to predict and control their environment may be dramatically undercut by the psychoticlike behavior of the family member. All of these are interesting psychological questions.

Yet another fertile field of inquiry is the investigation of the system under which hospital administrators exert pressure to fill hospital beds. A study using the method of participant observation by someone who was knowledgeable about the processes of social influence and decision making would be intriguing.

The study of total institutions in general has implications for mental institutions in particular. In mental institutions, as in the military, prisons, and small private schools, a counterculture develops to resist the press of total institutional involvement and impact (McEwen, 1980). This apparently ubiquitous and natural reaction would undercut whatever helping orientation the mental hospital might have. The implications of the similarity of the mental hospital to other total institutions have not been well-developed.

CONCLUSION

We have only scratched the surface of issues in mental health policy that might interest social psychologists. Mental health policy study is a field only on the verge of beginning, with great need of deft methodological and conceptual hands. It is both a field site for testing social psychological theory and an area of great national importance that should provide new levels of theory and data about human behavior.

As I have said elsewhere,

Psychologists are often reluctant to apply their laboratory-based theories and data to large scale social problems. That reluctance is well justified. The chasm between laboratory results and public policy is typically too wide. But bridge building requires a careful assessment of the terrain on both sides of the gap: a careful assessment of research findings is obvious to us; less obvious is the need for extensive analysis of the policy problem and related descriptive data. The bridges between the two perspectives must often rest on new levels of theory and new data bases [Kiesler, 1981: 1080].

NOTES

1. The statistics include those patients resident at the beginning of the year plus all inpatient admissions during the year (cf. Vischi, Jones, Shank, and Lima, 1980).

2. One important aspect of the national decision to deinstitutionalize patients is that the program did not originate with mental health professions. The priority in this program depended on class action lawsuits regarding commitment procedures and the right to the least restrictive therapeutic setting (cf. Rubin, 1978). Indeed, partly because of the imposition from the courts, many mental health professionals have opposed this social movement, resulting, in part, in a lack of professional involvement and dedication toward needed care and facilities following deinstitutionalization.

3. This does not mean the professional groups compete for patients. The three groups together provide only a minority of services estimated to be needed (cf. Vischi et al., 1980).

4. The 13th study tracked a new neighborhood health center in a medically underserved area and found an increase in medical utilization following mental health intervention.

5. The investigators of therapy outcome have worked typically in a university. It is also easier to study the effects of therapy in that setting with easy access to materials, tests, computers, and the like.

6. Cummings and Follette (1976) did an eight-year follow-up of 85 patients who had undergone one to eight sessions of psychotherapy under the Kaiser Plan: 84 recalled the problem and 83 felt they were now getting along well with regard to the problem. However, almost 90% felt they had worked the problem out on their own and that the therapy was of little benefit to them.

7. The support of insurance companies for the most expensive and least effective therapeutic technique may seem irrational. One can only assume that they feel that everyone would take advantage of a psychotherapy benefit if it were available. Copayments and the like are barriers to financial charges against the system in this view. Data do not support this view, however (cf. Dorken, 1977).

REFERENCE NOTES

1. Bandura, A. Personal communication, 1981.
2. Cummings, N. Personal communication, 1981.

REFERENCES

Bureau of the Census. *1976 survey of institutionalized persons: A study of persons receiving long-term care.* Washington, D.C.: Department of Commerce, Series, P-23, No. 69, 1978.

Cummings, N. A. The anatomy of psychotherapy under national health insurance. *American Psychologist,* 1977, *32,* 711-718.

Cummings, N. A. & Follette, W. T. Brief psychotherapy and medical utilization. In H. Dorken et al. (eds.), *The professional psychologist today.* San Francisco: Jossey-Bass, 1976.

Davison, G. C. & Valins, S. Maintenance of self-attributed and drug-attributed behavior change. *Journal of Personality and Social Psychology,* 1969, *11,* 25-33.

Dorken, H. CHAMPUS ten state claim experience for mental disorder: Fiscal year 1975. *American Psychologist,* 1977, *32,* 697-710.

Eysenck, H. F. The effects of psychotherapy: An evaluation. *Journal of Consulting Psychology,* 1952, *16,* 319.

Fairweather, G. W. *Social psychology in treating mental illness.* New York: Wiley, 1964.

Fink, E. B., Longabough, R., and Stout, R. The paradoxical underutilization of partial hospitalization. *American Journal of Psychiatry,* 1976, *135*: 713-716.

Fuchs, V. R. *Who shall live? Health, economics and social choice.* New York: Basic Books, 1974.

Goffman, E. *Asylums: Essays on the social situation of mental patients and other inmates.* Garden City, N.Y.: Doubleday, 1961.

Herz, M., Endicott, J., Spitzer, R., & Mesnicoff, A. Day versus inpatient hospitalization: A controlled study. *American Journal of Psychiatry,* 1971, *127,* 1371-1380.

Jones, K. and Vischi, T. Impact of alcohol, drug abuse, and mental health treatment on medical care utilization: Review of the research literature. *Medical Care* (supplement, 1979, *17,* 12).

Kiesler, C. A. Mental health policy as a field of inquiry for psychology. *American Psychologist,* 1980, *35,* 1066-1080. (a)

Kiesler, C. A. Psychology and public policy. In L. Bickman (ed.), *Applied social psychology annual* (Vol. 1). Beverly Hills, Calif.: Sage, 1980. (b)

Kiesler, C. A. On being insane in sane places: Non-institutionalization as potential public policy for mental patients, 1981. (unpublished)

Lorei, T. W. and Gurel, L. Demographic characteristics as predictors of posthospital employment and readmission. *Journal of Consulting and Clinical Psychology,* 1973, *40,* 426-430.

McEwen, C. A. Continuities in the study of total and nontotal institutions. *Annual Review of Sociology,* 1980, 143-185.

Mechanic, D. (coordinator) Report of the task panel on the nature and scope of the problem: President's Commission on Mental Health (Vol. 2). Washington, D.C.: Government Printing Office, 1978.

Mechanic, D. *Mental health and social policy.* Englewood Cliffs, N.J.: Prentice-Hall, 1980.

National Institute of Mental Health *The financing, utilization, and quality of mental health care in the United States.* Rockville, Md.: Author, 1976. (draft)

Regier, D. A., Goldberg, I. D., and Taube, C. A. The de facto U. S. mental health services system: A public health perspective. *Archives of General Psychiatry,* 1978, *35,* 685-693.

Rubin, J. *Economics, mental health, and the law.* Lexington, Mass.: D.C. Heath, 1978.

Saxe, L. *The efficacy and cost-effectiveness of psychotherapy.* Office of Technology Assessment, U.S. Congress (GPO stock #052-003-00783-5), 1980.

Smith, M. L. & Glass, G. V Meta-analysis of psychotherapy outcome studies. *American Psychologist,* 1977, *32,* 752-760.

Stokey, E. and Zeckhauser, R. *A primer for policy analysis.* New York: Norton, 1978.

Vischi, T. R., Jones, K. R., Shank, E. L., & Lima, L. H. *The alcohol, drug abuse, and mental health national data book.* Washington, D.C.: Department of Health, Education and Welfare, 1980.